Best Hikes Near
Milwaukee

HELP US KEEP THIS GUIDE UP TO DATE

Every effort has been made by the author and editors to make this guide as accurate and useful as possible. However, many things can change after a guide is published—trails are rerouted, regulations change, techniques evolve, facilities come under new management, and so forth.

We would appreciate hearing from you concerning your experiences with this guide and how you feel it could be improved and kept up to date. While we may not be able to respond to all comments and suggestions, we'll take them to heart, and we'll also make certain to share them with the author. Please send your comments and suggestions to the following address:

Globe Pequot
Reader Response/Editorial Department
246 Goose Lane
Guilford, CT 06437

Or you may e-mail us at: editorial@falcon.com

Thanks for your input, and happy trails!

Best Hikes Near
Milwaukee

KEVIN REVOLINSKI

FALCONGUIDES

GUILFORD, CONNECTICUT
HELENA, MONTANA

In honor of Raymond Zillmer and the Ice Age Trail Alliance, and all
those who have contributed to the preservation and enjoyment of
Wisconsin's glacial heritage.

An imprint of Rowman & Littlefield
Falcon, FalconGuides, and Outfit Your Mind are registered trademarks of Rowman & Littlefield.

Distributed by NATIONAL BOOK NETWORK

Copyright © 2015 by Rowman & Littlefield

"Geocaching Capital of the Midwest" on p. 103 is a registered trademark of West Bend, Wisconsin.

Photos by author unless otherwise noted.

Maps: Alena Pearce © Rowman & Littlefield

British Library Cataloguing-in-Publication Information Available

Library of Congress Cataloging-in-Publication Data
Revolinski, Kevin.
  Best hikes near Milwaukee / Kevin Revolinski.
    pages cm
  Includes bibliographical references.
  ISBN 978-1-4930-0035-7 (pbk. : alk. paper) — ISBN 978-1-4930-1476-7 (electronic)
  1. Hiking—Wisconsin—Milwaukee—Guidebooks. 2. Trails—Wisconsin—Milwaukee—Guidebooks.
  I. Title.
GV199.42.W6R49 2015
796.5109775'95—dc23
                                                                              2015011328

∞™ The paper used in this publication meets the minimum requirements of American National Standard for Information Sciences—Permanence of Paper for Printed Library Materials, ANSI/NISO Z39.48-1992.

The author and Rowman & Littlefield assume no liability for accidents happening to, or injuries sustained by, readers who engage in the activities described in this book.

Contents

Acknowledgments viii
Introduction 1
How to Use This Guide 18
Map Legend 20
Trail Finder. 21

Milwaukee Metro

1. Milwaukee Rotary Centennial Arboretum Trails 26
2. Three Bridges Park with Mitchell Park Trails 31
3. Retzer Nature Center Trails 36
4. Muskego Park Trails 40

North of Milwaukee

5. Lion's Den Gorge Nature Preserve Trails. 45
6. Harrington Beach State Park Trails 49
7. Kohler-Andrae State Park—Dunes Cordwalk 53
8. Kettle Moraine State Forest—Northern Unit: Greenbush Hiking Trails . . 57
9. Kettle Moraine State Forest—Northern Unit: Parnell Tower Hiking Trail 62
10. Kettle Moraine State Forest—Northern Unit: Butler Lake Hiking Trail . . . 67
11. Kettle Moraine State Forest—Northern Unit: Summit Trail 72
12. Kettle Moraine State Forest—Northern Unit: Zillmer Hiking Trails 77
13. Kettle Moraine State Forest—Northern Unit: Tamarack Circle
    Hiking Trail 82
14. Kettle Moraine State Forest—Northern Unit: New Fane Hiking Trails . . . 87
15. Horicon National Wildlife Refuge Trails. 91
16. Horicon Marsh State Wildlife Area Trails. 96
17. Glacial Blue Hills Recreation Area with Ice Age Trail. 101
18. Ice Age National Scenic Trail: Cedar Lakes Segment 106
19. Kettle Moraine State Forest—Pike Lake Unit Trails. 111
20. Ice Age National Scenic Trail: Holy Hill Segment. 116
21. Ice Age National Scenic Trail: Monches Segment 120

West of Milwaukee

22. Nashotah Park Green Trail 125
23. Aztalan State Park Trails 129
24. CamRock County Park—Area 2 Trails 134
25. Kettle Moraine State Forest—Lapham Peak Unit: Meadow Trail 138
26. Kettle Moraine State Forest—Lapham Peak Unit: Kame Terrace Trail . . 143
27. Kettle Moraine State Forest—Southern Unit: Scuppernong Trails 147

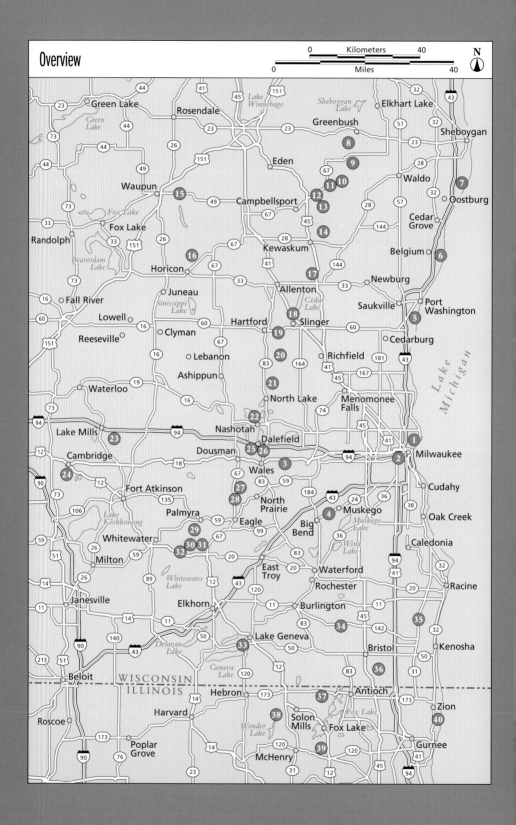

28. Kettle Moraine State Forest—Southern Unit: Scuppernong
Springs Nature Trail 151
29. Ice Age National Scenic Trail and Bald Bluff Nature Trail 155
30. Kettle Moraine State Forest—Southern Unit: John Muir Trails 160
31. Kettle Moraine State Forest—Southern Unit: Nordic Ski Trails 165
32. Ice Age National Scenic Trail: Whitewater Lake Segment 170

South of Milwaukee
33. Geneva Lake Shorepath 176
34. Richard Bong State Recreation Area Trails 182
35. Petrifying Springs County Park Trail 186
36. Bristol Woods County Park Trails 190
37. Chain O'Lakes State Park Trails 195
38. Glacial Park Trails 200
39. Volo Bog State Natural Area Trails 204
40. Adeline Jay Geo-Karis Illinois Beach State Park Trails 209

Honorable Mentions
A. Kettle Moraine State Forest—Northern Unit 214
B. Kettle Moraine State Forest—Southern Unit 215
C. Bender Park Trails 215
D. Emma Carlin Trails 216
E. Moraine Hills State Park Trails 216
F. Glacial Drumlin State Trail 217
G. Riveredge Nature Center Trails 217

Glossary 218
Clubs and Trail Groups 220
Further Reading 221
About the Author 223

Acknowledgments

I remain a big fan of Eric Sherman and all the people at the Ice Age Trail Alliance, and of the trail that gives them their name and purpose. Get out there and support it! A hearty thanks to the various park managers and personnel who helped me keep this accurate and suggested better routes than the ones I had in mind.

Once again I am forever grateful to the Friends' Hotel Network, especially Erica Chiarkas (who also hiked!); Veronica and Alexandra; Robert and Susan Wilson; Rob, Amber, and Graeham Bundy; and Mark Dimeo. A big thanks for an Ice Age Trail drop-off (not to mention a great Turkish dinner!) goes out to Tom and Bezmi Kranick, who are always supportive of whatever I am working on. And for efforts above and beyond the call of duty, I express my deepest gratitude to my wife, Preamtip, my steadfast trooper who cries, "Damn the mosquitoes, full speed ahead!" I'd be lost in the woods without her patience, assistance, and good humor.

Introduction

When you think Milwaukee, the first thing you think of is . . . well, beer. And I might be foolish to think hiking would be up there near the top of the list, but it should be. This major metropolitan area spreads out from its perch on the shores of Lake Michigan, and within about a 60-mile radius is some of the finest hiking in the land. The fact that such a major metro area still has access to so much wilderness can be credited to two major influences.

The first is the ice age. The last major advance of ice, from 85,000 to 11,000 years ago, is referred to as the Wisconsin Glacial Episode. During that time massive sheets of ice more than a mile thick in places invaded from Canada and altered the landscape drastically, bringing us such wonders as the Great Lakes, Wisconsin's many lakes, Horicon Marsh, and the amazing geological formations such as those found in the Kettle Moraine area.

The second is a long history of Wisconsinites and organizations that were and still are passionate about preserving the beauty of our fair state and getting people outdoors to appreciate it: Gaylord Nelson, Aldo Leopold, Sigurd Olson, John Muir, John Nolen. Governor and US Senator Robert "Fighting Bob" La Follette fought lumber barons to preserve the forests. Raymond Zillmer dreamed of a hiking trail accessible to everyone that would showcase the beauty of the

Scenic overlook of Lake Michigan.

Kettle Moraine and more; today, thanks to him and the many who took up the torch after his death, we have the Ice Age National Scenic Trail, a world-class thru-hike trail over 600 miles long on its goal to break 1,000. Fond du Lac native William Mauthe, head of the Wisconsin Conservation Commission, the precursor to the Department of Natural Resources, led the efforts to acquire much of the land that makes up the Kettle Moraine State Forest today. And, of course, Increase Lapham, who was Wisconsin's first scientist and the founder of the state's conservation movement. Projects such as the Urban Ecology Center right here in Milwaukee move forward with that ecological vision.

The terrain is incredibly diverse—from the rising dunes along Lake Michigan to the 32,000 acres of Horicon Marsh—including patches of rolling prairie full of wildflowers, wetlands, woodlands, bogs and fens, rivers and creeks, oak savanna and pine plantation. Milwaukee has green space right down through the city's river valleys and straight on out to Kettle Moraine State Forest. This book will show you how to get there.

The All-Stars of Milwaukee's Natural Wonders

Lake Michigan

The Great Lakes are inland seas for Wisconsinites, and rightly so: Many a ship has been lost in them, and Lake Michigan storms can produce waves in excess of 20 feet in height. In summer one can count on some relief as it is "cooler by the lake." Hikes along Lake Michigan are a must, and within this volume they range as far north as Kohler-Andrae State Park and as far south as Illinois Beach State Park. Both parks offer treks through the sand dunes and access to fine beaches. While Harrington Beach is level to the water, Lion's Den Gorge offers lake access and high cliffs for great overlooks.

Kettle Moraine

The Laurentide Ice Sheet reached its farthest point south during its last advance 20,000 years ago, extending through much of the hiking area here. Two major lobes of the creeping ice—the Green Bay and the Lake Michigan Lobes—came crushing together in a line running more or less northeast to southwest, and when they retreated, their combined glacial sediment—rock, sand, even large boulders—was left behind in a long moraine, an *interlobate* moraine. Large chunks of ice remained trapped in many places along this moraine, and when those last chunks finally melted, the piles of glacial deposits sunk in on themselves, forming all sorts of depressions, or "kettle moraines," along this one long geological feature. Some of the larger ones became lakes (such as Geneva and Pike Lakes), and others are small depressions among ridges (see many of the hikes within the forest dedicated to the glacial phenomenon: Kettle Moraine State Forest).

Greenbush Kettle, a kettle moraine.

The state forest is divided into five units. The Northern Unit and Southern Unit, which contribute excellent hikes in the North of Milwaukee and West of Milwaukee sections of this book, and in three smaller stand-alone units, two of which are also described here: Lapham Peak and Pike Lake Units.

Ice Age National Scenic Trail

The beginnings of this phenomenal rustic hiking trail trace back to the early conservation efforts in the Kettle Moraine and a trail that developed in those protected lands. Milwaukee attorney Raymond Zillmer, a passionate force in that conservation effort, dreamed of a longer trail. It didn't come to fruition in his lifetime, and to be fair, even now it's not complete. For now there are over 600 miles of mostly volunteer-built trail along what will someday be a 1,200-mile trail within Wisconsin's borders. The path, marked by yellow blazes on trees and posts, roughly follows the line where the last glaciers stopped—and where many of the most impressive geological formations appear. While many segments of the trail are point-to-point, some of them work well as out-and-back hikes, while others have alternate parallel trails, marked with white blazes, which make hiking loops possible. Several of those Ice Age Trail hikes can be found in the North and West Milwaukee sections of this book. Thru-hiking is an option, and hikers can camp in designated rustic camping zones or in simple shelters such as those found along

The Ice Age National Scenic Trail is rustic but marked well with trailhead signs and yellow blazes on posts and trees.

the 31 miles of Ice Age Trail in the Northern Unit of Kettle Moraine State Forest. All the units of the state forest contain major portions of this national scenic trail, and all of those segments are within about an hour's drive of Milwaukee.

Horicon Marsh

The 32,000-acre marsh, another leftover from the retreat of the last ice sheet, is preserved in both state and national refuges, each offering hiking and some excellent bird watching. The abundant wetlands are a mecca for migrating birds and the people who love them.

For the Kids: Wisconsin Junior Explorer Program

Many of Wisconsin's state parks participate in the Junior Rangers/Wisconsin Explorers Program, an environmental education activity program for children and their parents. Activity booklets for Junior Rangers (grades K–3) or Wisconsin Explorers (grades 4 and up) are available at most state park offices. When at least half of the activities in the booklet are completed, the child is awarded a patch and certificate available either from the park office or by mail. State parks also offer collectible cards for flora and fauna.

Weather

Weather is a funny thing in Wisconsin, or maybe not so funny, depending on who you ask. A surprise 50-degree F day in January can send everyone outside without their jackets. A sudden front moving in on a summer day can drop the temperature 20 degrees, and out come the jackets. Having a good idea about the immediate forecast is a good idea, and weather apps on smartphones can be helpful. Any place in close proximity to Lake Michigan can expect a temperature a bit lower by a few degrees.

Expect spring to start any time from March to May. Temperatures often get above freezing in March and stay there by April. Fifties, 60s, and even 70s can be expected in April and May. Mosquitoes start coming out later in May, or if you're lucky, June. Some deep woods or marshy areas might have a bumper crop of them, while the next county over isn't so bad.

Summer temperatures can range from 60s and 70s in June up to 80s and 90s in July and August. But don't be surprised by 85 one day and 65 the next day—or even a couple of hours later. Mosquitoes and summer go hand in hand, I'm afraid, as do ticks. Watch for thunderstorms or the occasional windstorm or tornado.

Fall brings amazing colors starting in late September and hanging on through mid-October or perhaps even past Halloween if we're lucky. Some 70s and 80s heat can linger through September, but generally temperatures are mild and the mosquitoes have gone for the year. Nights are chilly.

Winter means snow. This does not, however, mean the end of the hiking season. Most trails are still open in the winter, and snowshoe enthusiasts are happy. However, watch for trails that are closed to hikers when cross-country skiing is possible. Groomed trails as a rule prohibit hiking.

Flora and Fauna

Southeastern Wisconsin has abundant hardwood forest with sugar maples, oaks, hickory, basswood, black walnut, as well as various evergreens, cedars, tamaracks, apple trees, and so much more. Fall colors are expected just about everywhere, and the state tourism board keeps track of the change, county by county, on their Fall Color Report at www.travelwisconsin.com/fall-color-report. Wildflowers are abundant, and you'd be hard-pressed to find a state or even a county park that hasn't done at least a bit of prairie restoration and has brought back the native species. Starting with pasque flowers popping through the melting snow in March, the land here runs rich in nature's floral arrangements.

The wild berries—raspberries, black caps, blackberries—are common in many of the parks, and you are allowed to pick them. That goes for wild mushrooms as well, of which there are at least thirty varieties of edibles—just be sure you know how to identify them properly.

Wildlife is a veritable open-air zoo. Deer are everywhere, and at some point in summer you will see one with a fawn if you spend any amount of time out in

A blue heron along the lagoon path at Mitchell Park.

the woods and prairies. Raccoons, rabbits, various squirrels and chipmunks, possums, groundhogs, beavers, muskrats, crazy numbers of turkeys, turtles—snapping and others—coyotes, and rarer critters such as river otters or mink are just some you might see. Bird species number several hundred, but count on blue herons, sandhill cranes, assorted woodpeckers, and birds of prey including owls, hawks, and eagles. Wisconsin occupies a sweet spot for bird migration with good stopping points, the Great Lakes and Horicon Marsh being two. You won't find poisonous snakes in this corner of the state. Field guides are a good idea if you're curious about what you're seeing.

Wilderness Restrictions/Regulations

Always stay on the trails in state and county forests. Portions of the Ice Age Trail may skirt along easements or property lines. Your permission to hike there is a privilege not a right. Respect park and trail boundaries. Removal of plants from state natural areas is prohibited, with the notable exception of foraging for edibles. You *are* allowed to pick wild berries and mushrooms, for example, but only for personal consumption. In other words, you are not allowed to gather wild mushrooms to sell at the next farmers market.

Most state parks in Wisconsin require a vehicle fee. These can be paid daily at park offices or entrance stations, or in the absence of either, at self-pay tubes. An annual vehicle sticker is a good investment if you plan to spend more than three or four days in a state park in a calendar year. These can also be purchased at park offices and are good for all Wisconsin state parks.

Getting Around

Area Codes
The Milwaukee area code is 414. Surrounding Milwaukee are the suburbs with 262, areas to the north with 920, and farther west toward Madison with 608. The northern Illinois area code in this book is 815.

Roads
For current information on Milwaukee road conditions, weather, and closures, call 511 for the Wisconsin Department of Transportation's automated service or go online at www.511wi.gov. Construction is a season in Wisconsin. Check the Department of Transportation's website as well at www.dot.wisconsin.gov/travel/Milwaukee.

By Air
General Mitchell International Airport (MKE) is 5 miles south of downtown Milwaukee. The website is www.mitchellairport.com. To book reservations online, check out your favorite airline's website or search one of the following travel sites for the best price: www.cheaptickets.com, www.expedia.com, www.cheapoair.com, www.previewtravel.com, www.orbitz.com, www.priceline.com, http://travel.yahoo.com, www.travelocity.com, or www.trip.com—just to name a few.

By Rail
Milwaukee is served by AMTRAK. Schedules and pricing are at www.amtrak.com or by calling (800) 872-7245.

By Bus
Milwaukee County Transit System serves the greater metropolitan area; call (414) 344-6711 or visit their website at www.ridemcts.com, or even try Google maps directions and click on the mass transit icon. Megabus connects Milwaukee to long-range intercity routes; call (877) 462-6342 or visit http://us.megabus.com. Greyhound serves many towns in the region; call (800) 231-2222 or visit www.greyhound.com for more information. Badger Coaches operates between Milwaukee and Madison; call (877) 292-8259 or visit www.badgerbus.com. Van Galder Bus Company and CoachUSA also run buses to and from downtown Chicago and Chicago O'Hare Airport (ORD) as well as the Twin Cities in Minnesota; call (800) 747-0994 or visit www.coachusa.com.

Visitor Information

For general information on Wisconsin, visit the website of the Wisconsin Department of Tourism at www.travelwisconsin.com, or call (800) 432-8747. For information on visiting Milwaukee, see Visit Milwaukee at www.visitmilwaukee.org, or call (800) 554-1448.

Trail Etiquette

Leave no trace. Always leave an area just like you found it—if not better than you found it. Avoid camping in fragile prairies and along the banks of streams and lakes. Use a camp stove versus building a wood fire. Pack up all your trash and extra food. Bury human waste at least 100 feet from water sources under 6 to 8 inches of topsoil. Don't bathe with soap in a lake or stream—use prepackaged moistened towels to wipe off sweat and dirt, or bathe in the water without soap.

Stay on the trail. Straying from a designated trail may seem innocent, but it can cause damage to sensitive areas—damage that may take years to recover, if it can recover at all. Even simple shortcuts can be destructive. So, please, stay on the trail. Several of the hikes in this book pass through state natural areas where rare species of plants might be at risk if you venture off the path. Unauthorized trails can also lead to erosion problems, washing out surprisingly large areas along the approved trails as well.

With the abundance of private lands as are common along the Ice Age National Scenic Trail, this is also important. Many landowners have granted easements so that we may hike a continuous trail across Wisconsin. Bad behavior may result in them withdrawing that permission. It has happened before, and whole segments have been rerouted or lost until an alternative was found.

Leave no weeds. Invasive plants are a big issue in Wisconsin, and the Department of Natural Resources and a slew of volunteers work hard each year to stem the tide of unwanted plants such as buckthorn and garlic mustard, just to name a couple. Help them out by regularly cleaning your boots and hiking poles. Also brush your dog to remove any weed seeds before heading off into a new area. Some trails offer boot scrubbers at the trailheads; use them.

Keep your dog under control. You can buy a flexi-lead that allows your dog to go exploring along the trail, while allowing you the ability to reel him in should another hiker approach or should he decide to chase a rabbit. Always obey leash laws, and be sure to bury your dog's waste or pack it out in resealable plastic bags. A good rule of thumb is to assume that your dog will travel twice as far as you will on the trail. If you plan on doing a 5-mile hike, be sure your dog is in shape for a 10-mile hike.

Respect other trail users. Know whether you're on a multiuse trail, and assume the appropriate precautions. Note that you're not likely to hear a mountain biker coming, so be prepared and know ahead of time whether you share the trail with them. Cyclists should always yield to hikers, but that's little comfort to the hiker. On designated mountain biking trails, there is often a one-way rule for the bikers. Hike contrary to it so you can see them coming. When you approach horses on the trail, always step quietly off the trail, preferably on the downhill side, and let them pass. Do not duck into the woods and hide from them; no one likes a startled horse. If you have your dog with you, be sure it remains under control.

Preparedness

Take the necessary time to plan your trip. Whether going on a short day hike or an extended backpack trip, always prepare for the worst.

Water. Even in frigid conditions, you need at least two quarts of water a day to function efficiently. Add heat and taxing terrain and you can bump that figure up to one gallon. That's simply a base to work from—your metabolism and your level of conditioning can raise or lower that amount. Unless you know your level, assume that you need one gallon of water a day. Check your hike destination for water sources, and pack your own for the trail.

Food. Snacks on the trail are a good idea. Try to avoid foods that are high in sugar and fat like candy bars and potato chips. These food types are harder to digest and are low in nutritional value. Instead, bring along foods that are easy to pack, nutritious, and high in energy (e.g., bagels, nutrition bars, dehydrated fruit, gorp, and jerky).

First Aid

I know you're tough, but get 10 miles into the woods and develop a blister, and you'll wish you had carried that first-aid kit. Face it, it's just plain good sense. Many companies produce lightweight, compact first-aid kits. Just make sure yours contains at least the following:

- adhesive bandages
- moleskin or duct tape
- various sterile gauze and dressings
- white surgical tape
- an Ace bandage
- an antihistamine
- aspirin
- Betadine solution
- a first-aid book
- antacid tablets

- tweezers
- scissors
- antibacterial wipes
- triple-antibiotic ointment
- plastic gloves
- sterile cotton tip applicators
- syrup of ipecac (to induce vomiting)
- thermometer
- wire splint

Here are a few tips for dealing with and hopefully preventing certain ailments.

Sunburn. Take along sunscreen or sunblock, protective clothing, and a wide-brimmed hat. If you do get a sunburn, treat the area with aloe vera gel and protect the area from further sun exposure. Sunglasses can be a good way to prevent headaches and permanent eye damage from the sun, especially in places where light-colored rock or patches of snow reflect light up in your face.

Blisters. Be prepared to take care of these hike-spoilers by carrying moleskin (a lightly padded adhesive), gauze and tape, or adhesive bandages. An effective way to apply moleskin is to cut out a circle of moleskin and remove the center—like a doughnut—and place it over the blistered area. Cutting the center out will reduce the pressure applied to the sensitive skin. Other products can help you combat blisters. Some are applied to suspicious hot spots before a blister forms to help decrease friction to that area, while others are applied to the blister after it has popped to help prevent further irritation.

Insect bites and stings. You can treat most insect bites and stings by applying hydrocortisone 1% cream topically and taking a pain medication such as ibuprofen or acetaminophen to reduce swelling. Remove any stingers by using tweezers or scraping the area with your fingernail or a knife blade. Don't pinch the area, as you'll only spread the venom.

Some hikers are highly sensitive to bites and stings and may have a serious allergic reaction that can be life threatening. Symptoms of a serious allergic reaction can include wheezing, an asthmatic attack, and shock. The treatment for this severe type of reaction is epinephrine. If you know that you are sensitive to bites and stings, carry a prepackaged kit of epinephrine, which can be obtained only by prescription from your doctor.

Ticks. Ticks can carry diseases such as Lyme disease. If you know you're going to be hiking through an area littered with ticks, wear long pants and a long-sleeved shirt. You can apply a permethrin repellent to your clothing and a DEET repellent to exposed skin. At the end of your hike, do a spot check for ticks (and insects in general). If you do find a tick, grab the head of the tick firmly—with a pair of tweezers if you have them—and gently pull it away from the skin with a twisting motion. Sometimes the mouth parts linger, embedded in your skin. If this happens, try to remove them with a disinfected needle. Clean the affected area with an antibacterial cleanser and then apply a triple-antibiotic ointment. Monitor the area for a few days. If irritation persists or a target-like red rash develops, see a doctor for possible infection.

Poison ivy, oak, and sumac. These skin irritants can be found most anywhere in North America and come in the form of a bush or a vine, having leaflets in groups of three, five, seven, or nine. Learn how to spot the plants. The oil they secrete can cause an allergic reaction in the form of blisters, usually about 12 hours after exposure. The itchy rash can last from ten days to several weeks. The best defense against these irritants is to wear clothing that covers the arms, legs, and torso. For summer, zip-off cargo pants come in handy. There are also nonprescription lotions you can apply to exposed skin that guard against the effects of poison ivy/oak/sumac and can be washed off with soap and water. If you think you were in contact with the plants, after hiking (or even on the trail during longer hikes) wash with soap and water. Taking a hot shower with soap after you return home from your hike will also help to remove any lingering oil from your skin. Should you contract a rash from any of these plants, use an antihistamine to reduce the itching. If the rash is localized, create a light bleach/water wash to dry up the area. If the rash has spread, either tough it out or see your doctor about getting a dose of cortisone (available both orally and by injection).

Wild parsnip. While it may be related to the carrot, wild parsnip is not your friend, but its appearance might lead you to believe it's just another wildflower along the trail or the roadside, especially in open prairie areas. Wild parsnip is a single-stalked plant with myriad little yellow flowers at the top, arranged almost like a parasol. The plant can grow as high as 4 feet. Their danger lies in the juice within the plant. Exposure to it may result in a chemical burn. The liquid is absorbed into your skin, and when the UV rays from the sun trigger it, you can get some nasty burns or phytophotodermatitis. This can happen long after the exposure, and it can come back when it seems it's gone. It takes only a bit of the juice, and the ultraviolet light of even a cloudy day is sufficient to trigger the reaction. Discolored skin from a burn can last up to a couple of years, but the burning sensation only lasts a couple of days. Your clothing is the first line of defense, but be sure not to pick the flowers. (Most parks don't allow flower picking anyway.) But also be aware that in the cases of mowed trails, especially through prairie, there can be an abundance of wild parsnip juice after the mower has gone through.

Snakebites. Including this as a warning is most certainly a worst-case-scenario sort of item, so don't be alarmed. In Wisconsin we have twenty-one species of snakes. Two of them are indeed poisonous—the eastern Massasauga rattlesnake and the timber rattlesnake—but chances of seeing one in southeastern Wisconsin are pretty unlikely. They are endangered species. Simple rule: If is has a rattle, keep your distance.

If a *nonpoisonous* snake bites you, allow the wound to bleed a small amount and then cleanse the wounded area with a Betadine solution (10 percent povidone iodine). Rinse the wound with clean water (preferably) or fresh urine (it might sound ugly, but it's sterile). Once the area is clean, cover it with a triple-antibiotic ointment and a clean bandage. Remember, most residual damage from snakebites, poisonous or otherwise, comes from infection, not the snake's venom. Keep the area as clean as possible and get medical attention immediately.

Dehydration. Symptoms of dehydration include fatigue, headache, and decreased coordination and judgment. When you are hiking, your body's rate of fluid loss depends on the outside temperature, humidity, altitude, and your activity level. On average, a hiker walking in warm weather will lose four liters of fluid a day. That fluid loss is easily replaced by normal consumption of liquids and food. However, if a hiker is walking briskly in hot, dry weather and hauling a heavy pack, he or she can lose one to three liters of water an hour. It's important to always carry plenty of water and to stop often and drink fluids regularly, even if you aren't thirsty.

Heat exhaustion is the result of a loss of large amounts of electrolytes and often occurs if a hiker is dehydrated and has been under heavy exertion. Common symptoms of heat exhaustion include cramping, exhaustion, fatigue, lightheadedness, and nausea. You can treat heat exhaustion by getting out of the sun and drinking an electrolyte solution made up of one teaspoon of salt and one tablespoon of sugar dissolved in a liter of water. Drink this solution slowly over a period of one hour. Drinking plenty of fluids (preferably an electrolyte solution/ sports drink) can prevent heat exhaustion. Avoid hiking during the hottest parts of the day, and wear breathable clothing, a wide-brimmed hat, and sunglasses.

Hypothermia. Even in summer, a sudden rain and change in wind and temperature can cause you to get a deep chill. It starts with shivering, but more advanced signs include decreased coordination, slurred speech, and blurred vision. When a victim's temperature falls below 92 degrees, the blood pressure and pulse plummet, possibly leading to coma and death. On a 1-mile nature loop in a county park, this might not be a big deal. But when you are 5 miles out in the Kettle Moraine, you might be in serious trouble.

Frostbite. Hiking or snowshoeing is a good way get outdoors in winter. If temperatures are below freezing and a persistent chill attacks a localized area, say, your hands or your toes, the circulatory system reacts by cutting off blood flow to the affected area. Ice crystals start to form from the water in the cells of the neglected tissue. This is frostbite.

Prevention is your best defense against this situation. Most prone to frostbite are your face, hands, and feet, so protect these areas well. Wool is the traditional material of choice because it provides ample air space for insulation and draws moisture away from the skin. Synthetic fabrics, however, have made great strides in the cold-weather clothing market. Do your research. A pair of light silk liners under your regular gloves is a good trick for keeping warm.

Should your skin go numb and start to appear white and waxy, you may be developing frostbite. Do your best to get out of the cold entirely and seek medical attention—which usually consists of performing a rapid rewarming in water for 20 to 30 minutes.

Other Hazards

Besides tripping over a rock or tree root on the trail, there are some real hazards to be aware of while hiking. Even if where you're hiking doesn't have the plethora of poisonous snakes and plants, insects, and bears found in other parts of the United States, there are a few weather conditions and predators you may need to take into account.

Lightning. Thunderstorms can come up suddenly at any time, especially during the summer. Lightning is generated by thunderheads and can strike without warning, even several miles away from the nearest overhead cloud. If something is clearly building up, your first action should be to leave exposed peaks, bluffs, and ridges. Keep an eye on cloud formations and don't underestimate how fast a storm can build. The bigger they get, the more likely a thunderstorm will happen. Lightning takes the path of least resistance, so if you're the high point, it might choose you. Ducking under a rock overhang is dangerous, as you form the shortest path between the rock and ground. Avoid standing under the only tree or the tallest tree and stay away from anything metal you might be carrying. Move down off the ridge slightly to a low, treeless point and squat until the storm passes. If you have an insulating pad, squat on it. Be aware of tree roots, another channel for lightning to surprise you. Avoid having both your hands and feet touching the ground at once and never lie flat. If you hear a buzzing sound or feel your hair standing on end, move quickly, as an electrical charge is building up.

Hunting. Hunting is a popular sport in Wisconsin, especially during rifle season in November. Hiking is still enjoyable in those months in many areas, so just take a few precautions. First, learn when the different hunting seasons start and end in the area in which you'll be hiking. During this time frame, be sure to wear at least a blaze-orange hat, and possibly put an orange vest over your pack. Don't be surprised to see hunters in camo outfits carrying bows or rifles around during their season. If you would feel more comfortable without hunters around, hike in national parks and monuments or state and local parks where hunting is not allowed.

Navigation

Whether you are going on a short hike in a familiar area or planning a week-long backpack trip, you should always be equipped with the proper navigational equipment—at the very least a detailed map and a sturdy compass.

Maps. The maps in this book are enough to get you in and out of the woods, and most parks have maps at the trailhead or park office, or even posted at trail junctures. The Ice Age Trail has its own atlas and guide if you are interested in going beyond the handful of segments described in this book.

If you want to check out the high-tech world of maps, you can purchase topographic maps on CD-ROM. These software-mapping programs let you select a route on your computer, print it out, then take it with you on the trail. Some software mapping programs let you insert symbols and labels, download way-points from a GPS unit, and export the maps to other software programs.

Compasses and GPS devices. First off, the sun is not a substitute for a compass. So what kind of compass should you have? Here are some characteristics you should look for: a rectangular base with detailed scales, a liquid-filled housing, protective housing, a sighting line on the mirror, luminous alignment and back-bearing arrows, a luminous north-seeking arrow, and a well-defined bezel ring.

If you are a klutz at using a compass, you may be interested in checking out the technical wizardry of the GPS (Global Positioning System) device. There are many different types of GPS units available, and they range in price from $100 to $400. In general, all GPS units have a display screen and keypad where you input information. In addition to acting as a compass, the unit allows you to plot your route, easily retrace your path, track your traveling speed, find the mileage between waypoints, and calculate the total mileage of your route.

Before you purchase a GPS unit, keep in mind that these devices don't pick up signals indoors, in heavily wooded areas, or in deep valleys. Also, batteries can wear out or other technical problems can develop. A GPS unit should be used in conjunction with a map and compass, not in place of those items.

Pedometers. A pedometer is a small, clip-on unit with a digital display that calculates your hiking distance in miles or kilometers based on your walking stride. Some units also calculate the calories you burn and your total hiking time. Pedometers are available at most large outdoor stores and range in price from $20 to $40.

Trip Planning

Planning your hiking adventure begins with letting a friend or relative know your trip itinerary so they can call for help if you don't return at your scheduled time. Your next task is to make sure you are outfitted to experience the risks and rewards of the trail. This section highlights gear and clothing you may want to take with you to get the most out of your hike.

Day Hikes

- camera
- compass/GPS unit
- pedometer
- daypack
- first-aid kit
- food
- guidebook
- headlamp/flashlight with extra batteries and bulbs
- hat
- insect repellent
- knife/multipurpose tool
- map
- matches in waterproof container and fire starter
- fleece jacket
- rain gear
- space blanket
- sunglasses
- sunscreen
- swimsuit and/or fishing gear (if hiking to a lake)
- watch
- water
- water bottles/water hydration system

Equipment

Clothes. Adequate rain protection and extra layers of clothing are a good idea. In summer, a wide-brimmed hat can help keep the sun at bay. In the winter months the first layer you'll want to wear is a "wicking" layer of long underwear that keeps perspiration away from your skin. Wear long underwear made from synthetic fibers that wick moisture away from the skin and draw it toward the next layer of clothing, where it then evaporates. Avoid wearing long underwear made of cotton as it is slow to dry and keeps moisture next to your skin.

Footwear. Poor shoes will bring a hike to a halt faster than anything else. A lightweight hiking boot is better than a heavy, leather mountaineering boot for most day hikes and backpacking. Trail running shoes provide a little extra cushion and are often made in a high-top style that many people wear for hiking. These running shoes are lighter, more flexible, and more breathable than hiking boots. If you know you'll be hiking in wet weather often, purchase boots or shoes with a Gore-Tex liner, which will help keep your feet dry.

When buying your boots, be sure to wear the same type of socks you'll be wearing on the trail. If the boots you're buying are for cold-weather hiking, try the boots on while wearing two pairs of socks. Many outdoor stores have some type of ramp to simulate hiking uphill and downhill. Be sure to take advantage of this test, as toe-jamming boot fronts can be very painful and debilitating on a downhill trek. Once you've purchased your footwear, be sure to break them in before you hit the trail. New footwear is often stiff and needs to be stretched and molded to your foot.

Hiking poles. Hiking poles help with balance and, more importantly, take pressure off your knees. The ones with shock absorbers are easier on your elbows and knees. Some poles even come with a camera attachment to be used as a monopod.

Backpacks. No matter what type of hiking you do, you'll need a pack of some sort to carry the basic trail essentials. There are a variety of backpacks on the market, but let's first discuss what you intend to use it for. Day hikes or overnight trips?

If you plan on doing a day hike, a daypack should have some of the following characteristics: a padded hip belt that's at least 2 inches in diameter (avoid packs with only a small piece of nylon webbing for a hip belt); a chest strap (the chest strap helps stabilize the pack against your body); external pockets to carry water and other items that you want easy access to; an internal pocket to hold keys, a knife, a wallet, and other miscellaneous items; an external lashing system to hold a jacket; and, if you so desire, a hydration pocket for carrying a hydration system (which consists of a water bladder with an attachable drinking hose).

For short hikes, some hikers like to use a fanny pack to store just a camera, food, a compass, a map, and other trail essentials. Most fanny packs have pockets for two water bottles and a padded hip belt.

If you intend to do an extended, overnight trip—such as a thru-hike along the Ice Age National Scenic Trail—then you should look for a larger pack with an internal or external frame.

Cell phones. Many hikers are carrying their cell phones into the backcountry these days in case of emergency. That's fine and good, but please know that cell phone coverage is often poor to nonexistent in the more rural areas. More importantly, people have started to call for help because they're tired or lost. Let's go back to being prepared. You are responsible for yourself in the backcountry. Use your brain to avoid problems, and if you do encounter one, first use your brain to try to correct the situation. Only use your cell phone, if it works, in true emergencies. If it doesn't work down low in a valley, try hiking to a high point where you might get reception.

Hiking with Children

Hikes don't need to be long. Kids like to stop and point out bugs and plants, look under rocks, jump in puddles, and throw sticks. If you're taking a toddler or young child on a hike, start with a trail that you're familiar with. Trails that have interesting things for kids, like piles of leaves to play in or a small stream to wade through during the summer, will make the hike much more enjoyable for them and will keep them from getting bored.

You can keep your child's attention if you have a strategy before starting on the trail. Quiz children on the names of plants and animals. Pick up a family-friendly outdoor hobby like geocaching (www.geocaching.com) or letterboxing (www.atlasquest.com), both of which combine the outdoors, clue-solving, and treasure hunting.

Especially in Wisconsin, it seems weather can change dramatically in a very short time. Always bring extra clothing for children, regardless of the season. In the winter, have your children wear wool socks and warm layers such as long underwear, a fleece jacket and hat, wool mittens, and good rain gear. It's not a bad idea to have these along in late fall and early spring as well. Good footwear is also important. A sturdy pair of high-top tennis shoes or lightweight hiking boots are the best bet for little ones. If you're hiking in the summer near a lake or stream, bring along a pair of old sneakers that your child can put on when he or she wants to go exploring in the water. Remember when you're near any type of water, always watch your child at all times. Also, keep a close eye on teething toddlers who may decide a rock or leaf of poison oak is an interesting item to put in their mouth.

From spring through fall you'll want your kids to wear a wide-brimmed hat to keep their face, head, and ears protected from the hot sun. Also, make sure your children wear sunscreen at all times. Choose a brand without PABA—children have sensitive skin and may have an allergic reaction to sunscreen that contains PABA. If you are hiking with a child younger than six months, don't use sunscreen or insect repellent. Instead, be sure that their head, face, neck, and ears are protected from the sun with a wide-brimmed hat, and that all other skin exposed to the sun is protected with the appropriate clothing.

Avoid poorly designed child-carrying packs—you don't want to break your back carrying your child. Most child-carrying backpacks designed to hold a 40-pound child will contain a large carrying pocket to hold diapers and other items. Some have an optional rain/sun hood.

How to Use This Guide

Take a close look and you'll find that this guide contains just about everything you'll ever need to choose, plan for, enjoy, and survive a hike near Milwaukee. Stuffed with useful Milwaukee-area information, *Best Hikes Near Milwaukee* features forty mapped and cued hikes. Here's an outline of the book's major components:

Each section begins with an **introduction to the region,** in which you're given a sweeping look at the lay of the land. Each hike then starts with a short **summary** of the hike's highlights. These quick overviews give you a taste of the hiking adventures to follow. You'll learn about the trail terrain and what surprises each route has to offer. Many chapters also include a Kid Friendly recommendation that provides parents with a quick reference for keeping their youngster engaged.

Following the overview you'll find the **hike specs:** quick, nitty-gritty details of the hike. Most are self-explanatory, but here are some details on others:

Distance: The total distance of the recommended route—one-way for loop hikes, the round-trip on an out-and-back or lollipop hike, point-to-point for a shuttle. Options are additional.

Hiking time: The average time it will take to cover the route. It is based on the total distance, elevation gain, and condition and difficulty of the trail. Your fitness level will also affect your time.

Difficulty: Each hike has been assigned a level of difficulty. The rating system was developed from several sources and personal experience. These levels are meant to be a guideline only and may prove easier or harder for different people depending on ability and physical fitness.

> **Easy**—Five miles or less total trip distance in one day, with minimal elevation gain and paved or smooth-surfaced dirt trail.

> **Moderate**—Up to 10 miles total trip distance in one day, with moderate elevation gain and potentially rough terrain.

> **Difficult**—More than 10 miles total trip distance in one day, with strenuous elevation gains and rough and/or rocky terrain.

Trail surface: General information about what to expect underfoot.

Best season: General information on the best time of year to hike.

Other trail users: Such as horseback riders, mountain bikers, inline skaters, etc.

Canine compatibility: Know the trail regulations before you take your dog hiking with you. Dogs are not allowed on several trails in this book.

Land status: National forest, county open space, national park wilderness, etc.

Fees and permits: Whether you need to carry any money with you for park entrance fees and permits.

Schedule: Trail access hours, days, and seasons when applicable.

Maps: This is a list of other maps to supplement the maps in this book. USGS maps are the best source for accurate topographical information, but the local park map may show more recent trails. Use both.

Trail contact(s): This is the location, phone number, and website URL for the local land manager(s) in charge of all the trails within the selected hike. Before you head out, get trail access information, or contact the land manager after your visit if you see problems with trail erosion, damage, or misuse.

Special considerations: This section calls your attention to specific trail hazards, like a lack of water or hunting seasons.

The **Finding the trailhead** section gives you dependable driving directions to where you'll want to park. **The Hike** is the meat of the chapter. Detailed and honest, it's a carefully researched impression of the trail. It also often includes lots of area history, both natural and human. Under **Miles and Directions,** mileage cues identify all turns and trail name changes, as well as points of interest. **Options** are also given for many hikes to make your journey shorter or longer depending on the amount of time you have. The **Hike Information** section provides information on local events and attractions, restaurants, hiking tours, and hiking organizations.

Don't feel restricted to the routes and trails that are mapped here. Be adventurous and use this guide as a platform to discover new routes for yourself. One of the simplest ways to begin this is to just turn the map upside down and hike any route in reverse. The change in perspective is often fantastic, and the hike should feel quite different. With this in mind, it'll be like getting two distinctly different hikes on each map. For your own purposes, you may wish to copy the route directions onto a small sheet of paper to help you while hiking, or photocopy the map and cue sheet to take with you. Otherwise, just slip the whole book in your backpack and take it all with you. Enjoy your time in the outdoors and remember to pack out what you pack in.

How to Use the Maps

Overview map: This map shows the location of each hike in the area by hike number.

Route map: This is your primary guide to each hike. It shows all the accessible roads and trails, points of interest, water, landmarks, and geographical features. It also distinguishes trails from roads, and paved roads from unpaved roads. The selected route is highlighted, and directional arrows point the way.

Map Legend

Symbol	Description	Symbol	Description
(40)	Interstate Highway	∧	Arch
(45)	US Highway	▬	Bench
(144)	State Highway	⇃	Boat Ramp/Launch
(T)	County Road	⌣	Bridge
	Local Road	■	Building/Point of Interest
=======:	Unpaved Road/Mountain Bike Route	▲	Campground
+—+—+—+	Railroad	○	City/Town
▬▬▬▬▬	Featured Trail	⦙	Gate
- - - - -	Trail	▲	Mountain/Peak
▬▬▬	Paved/Bike Trail	🄺	Overlook/Viewpoint
··············	Snowmobile/Horse Trail	**P**	Parking
•—•—•—•	Power Lines	🛈	Park Office
|||||||||||	Boardwalk/Steps	🅰	Picnic Area
—··—··—	State Border	🚻	Restroom
⌇	Small River or Creek	⌐	Ridge/Cliff
⬭	Body of Water	×	Spot Elevation
	Marsh	🗼	Tower
⌀	Spring	①	Trailhead
[▲]	State Park/Forest/Natural Area	❓	Visitor/Information Center
[▲]	Other Park	🖼	Water
[▲]	Nature Area/Preserve/Wildlife Refuge/Recreation Area		

Trail Finder

Milwaukee Metro

Hike No.	Hike Name	Best Hikes with Kids	Best Hikes with Dogs	Best Hikes for Water Lovers	Best Hikes for Birders	Best Hikes for Great Views	Best Hikes for Geology Buffs	Best Hikes for Nature Lovers
1	Milwaukee Rotary Centennial Arboretum Trails	●		●		●		●
2	Three Bridges Park with Mitchell Park Trails	●	●	●	●	●		
3	Retzer Nature Center Trails	●			●	●		●
4	Muskego Park Trails	●	●					●

North of Milwaukee

Hike No.	Hike Name	Best Hikes with Kids	Best Hikes with Dogs	Best Hikes for Water Lovers	Best Hikes for Birders	Best Hikes for Great Views	Best Hikes for Geology Buffs	Best Hikes for Nature Lovers
5	Lion's Den Gorge Nature Preserve Trails	●	●	●	●	●	●	●
6	Harrington Beach State Park Trails	●	●	●		●		
7	Kohler-Andrae State Park—Dunes Cordwalk	●		●		●	●	
8	Kettle Moraine State Forest—Northern Unit: Greenbush Hiking Trails		●				●	●
9	Kettle Moraine State Forest—Northern Unit: Parnell Tower Hiking Trail	●				●	●	●

Hike No.	Hike Name	Best Hikes with Kids	Best Hikes with Dogs	Best Hikes for Water Lovers	Best Hikes for Birders	Best Hikes for Great Views	Best Hikes for Geology Buffs	Best Hikes for Nature Lovers
10	Kettle Moraine State Forest—Northern Unit: Butler Lake Hiking Trail			●		●	●	●
11	Kettle Moraine State Forest—Northern Unit: Summit Trail	●				●	●	
12	Kettle Moraine State Forest—Northern Unit: Zillmer Hiking Trails				●	●	●	●
13	Kettle Moraine State Forest—Northern Unit: Tamarack Circle Hiking Trail	●		●	●	●		●
14	Kettle Moraine State Forest—Northern Unit: New Fane Hiking Trails						●	●
15	Horicon National Wildlife Refuge Trails	●	●	●	●	●		
16	Horicon Marsh State Wildlife Area Trails	●		●	●	●		
17	Glacial Blue Hills Recreation Area with Ice Age Trail		●					
18	Ice Age National Scenic Trail: Cedar Lakes Segment						●	●
19	Kettle Moraine State Forest—Pike Lake Unit Trails	●		●	●	●		●
20	Ice Age National Scenic Trail: Holy Hill Segment					●	●	●

Hike No.	Hike Name	Best Hikes with Kids	Best Hikes with Dogs	Best Hikes for Water Lovers	Best Hikes for Birders	Best Hikes for Great Views	Best Hikes for Geology Buffs	Best Hikes for Nature Lovers
21	Ice Age National Scenic Trail: Monches Segment			●			●	●
West of Milwaukee								
22	Nashotah Park Green Trail	●	●					●
23	Aztalan State Park Trails	●		●				
24	CamRock County Park–Area 2 Trails			●				●
25	Kettle Moraine State Forest—Lapham Peak Unit: Meadow Trail	●	●					●
26	Kettle Moraine State Forest—Lapham Peak Unit: Kame Terrace Trail		●				●	
27	Kettle Moraine State Forest—Southern Unit: Scuppernong Trails		●			●		●
28	Kettle Moraine State Forest—Southern Unit: Scuppernong Springs Nature Trail	●		●				●
29	Ice Age National Scenic Trail and Bald Bluff Nature Trail		●			●	●	●
30	Kettle Moraine State Forest—Southern Unit: John Muir Trails						●	

Hike No.	Hike Name	Best Hikes with Kids	Best Hikes with Dogs	Best Hikes for Water Lovers	Best Hikes for Birders	Best Hikes for Great Views	Best Hikes for Geology Buffs	Best Hikes for Nature Lovers
31	Kettle Moraine State Forest—Southern Unit: Nordic Ski Trails				●	●	●	●
32	Ice Age National Scenic Trail: Whitewater Lake Segment					●	●	●
South of Milwaukee								
33	Geneva Lake Shorepath	●		●		●		
34	Richard Bong State Recreation Area Trails	●	●					●
35	Petrifying Springs County Park Trail	●	●					
36	Bristol Woods County Park Trails	●			●			●
37	Chain O'Lakes State Park Trails	●		●	●	●		●
38	Glacial Park Trails	●	●	●	●	●		●
39	Volo Bog State Natural Area Trails	●			●	●	●	●
40	Adeline Jay Geo-Karis Illinois Beach State Park Trails	●		●	●	●		

Retzer Nature Center. **Preamtip Satasuk**

Milwaukee Rotary Centennial Arboretum Trails

It's hard to imagine you are in the heart of Milwaukee as you stroll through this arboretum and along the Milwaukee River. The hike begins near the Urban Ecology Center, takes a loop through the prairie and wildflower section where oak savanna is being brought back, then follows the riverbank downstream under the North Avenue Bridge. A pedestrian bridge crosses the river, and the Beerline Trail goes all the way to Locust Street. Cross the river again and complete the loop with a pass through the woods.

Start: From the trailhead at the parking lot

Distance: 2.9-mile loop

Hiking time: 1.5 hours

Difficulty: Easy

Trail surface: Paved, dirt

Best season: Spring through fall

Other trail users: Bicyclists

Canine compatibility: Leashed dogs permitted

Land status: City park

Fees and permits: None

Schedule: Daily, sunrise to 10 p.m.

Maps: USGS Milwaukee; at Urban Ecology Center

Trail contact: Milwaukee County Park System, 9480 Watertown Plank Rd., Wauwatosa, WI 53226; (414) 257-7275; www.county parks.com

Special considerations: The city has referred to this as the safest park in Milwaukee, but it is not advised after dark. At the southern turn under the North Avenue Bridge, tall grasses contribute to a sense of seclusion here. It's not necessarily something to avoid as a solo hiker, but simply worth being aware of.

Finding the trailhead: From downtown Milwaukee take I-43 north to exit 74 for Locust Street. Turn right onto Locust Street and go 1.6 miles. Turn right onto Oakland Avenue, go 0.3 mile, and turn right onto East Park Place. Continue 0.2 mile to road's end and turn left into the last parking lot. The trailhead is marked by a large stone arch next to the lot. **GPS:** N43 4.022' / W87 53.564'

THE HIKE

The Milwaukee Rotary Centennial Arboretum takes its name from the Rotary Club of Milwaukee, which on its 100-year anniversary in 2013 helped make the arboretum's development possible with a contribution. It lies along the Milwaukee River in Riverside Park from Locust Street south to North Avenue. The multiuse, paved Oak Leaf Trail bounds it on the east side. Some of this terrain has been reclaimed from old industrial sites, and like Three Bridges Park, an Urban Ecology

Center is connected to it. Check out the Urban Ecology Center for activities and events and even guided hikes.

Pass through the stone arch and climb up the little hill before you. This will gradually become oak savanna but in the interim is awash with native Wisconsin wildflowers. The view toward the river is a nice reminder of how well a green space serves a city. Come back to the trail and follow it south (left if you are facing the hill from the stone arch); it curves around the hill and goes north with the river on your left. Keep on the path and go straight across the next intersection, then follow the path on a left curve down to the riverside. A canoe launch is there.

Take a left onto the East Bank Trail, a crushed-rock footpath along the river; you are heading south (river on right) below the sloping bank of the hill you were just on. Down in here the rest of the city is invisible, and simply a light breeze through the leaves is enough to hide the hum of distant traffic. It is quite a remarkable spot in Milwaukee. Follow the trail south through partial shade and brush, with occasional willow trees and cottonwoods on either side of you and views of the river to the right. Under the North Avenue Bridge a trail is available if you want to go up onto the street bridge. Otherwise, continue along, passing under the bridge. To your right is a narrow spot on the river, tossing up some rapids for paddlers (see FalconGuides' *Paddling Wisconsin*).

From humble beginnings: an oak sapling in the arboretum's oak savanna restoration. Preamtip Satasuk

After the North Avenue Bridge the terrain becomes covered in grasses, sometimes taller than the average person. The trail takes a wide curve to the left where there's a mural on a concrete wall on the left and then the path heads right, to a concrete path and steps up to a wide, concrete pedestrian bridge over the river. On the other side turn right, heading upstream now on a cedar-chip trail. This soon merges with a paved trail coming off the end of Riverboat Road on your left and passes under the North Avenue Bridge. This is the Beerline Trail, a multiuse trail still in development. The name comes from the rail line that passed through here back in the heyday of the big brewers, hauling in the raw ingredients for beer.

Follow the Beerline Trail north until you get to Gordon Park. Take the first trail on your right, which curls to the right around the park and closer to the trees on the river side of it. Follow this up to Locust Street. No need to cross Locust; take the sidewalk across and watch for the dirt trail to the right at the other end of the bridge. Follow it down and keep bearing right until you are actually passing under the Locust Street Bridge with the river on your right. The trail leads left down even farther until you are at river level. Take the East Bank Trail to the left, back under the bridge, and into the northern section of the arboretum. Pass a trail angling up to the left and forward—an option for you—and hike to a staircase on your left. Take this up into the arboretum onto a circle trail around an open area of oaks.

Follow the path away from the river toward a bridge on the far side. This is Susie's Bridge, and it takes you across the Oak Leaf Trail. Turn right on the other side and head straight for the back of the Urban Ecology Center. Go through to the street and turn right onto Park Place, crossing the bridge with a human sundial on it, where you can become the *gnomon* (that's the upright part of a sundial that casts the shadow, and a useful word for impressing trivia masters). The parking lot where you began is on the other side of the bridge and on the left.

Urban Ecology Center

Located in Riverside Park, this fantastic community-driven environmental center started as a park cleanup and educational project back in 1991. What began in a simple trailer now is a collection of classrooms in its very own building. And it keeps growing: Two other centers operate in Washington Park and Menomonee Valley (see the Three Bridges Park hike). Not only are they promoting and creating green space in the city of Milwaukee, but they are also passing that passion and enthusiasm to the kids. The centers work with schools on environmental education programs and provide some open-air classroom learning as well. But it's not just for students. A regular calendar of events are open to people of all ages and walks of life who care about their community and have a love of, or at least some curiosity about, nature. Join them on bird walks, walking tours, cleanup and invasive plant removal projects, and much more.

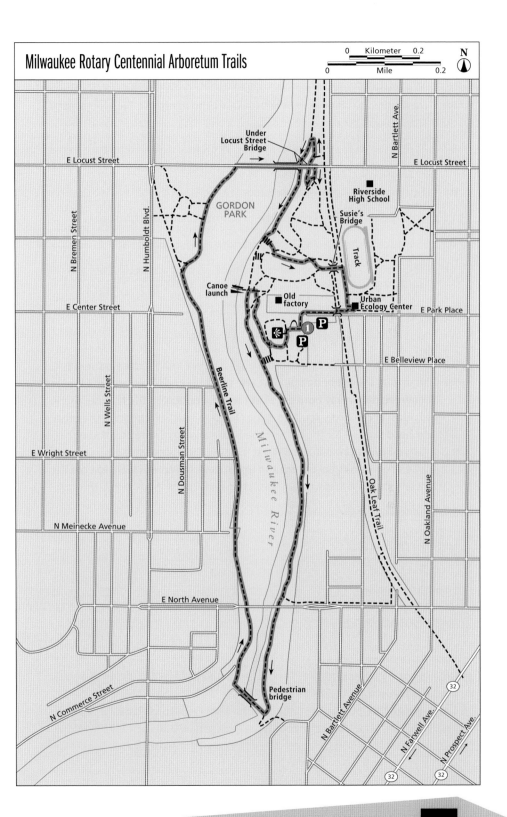

Milwaukee Rotary Centennial Arboretum Trails

0 Kilometer 0.2
0 Mile 0.2

N

E Locust Street

Under Locust Street Bridge

GORDON PARK

Riverside High School

Susie's Bridge

N Bartlett Ave.

E Locust Street

Track

Canoe launch

Old factory

Urban Ecology Center

E Park Place

N Bremen Street

N Humboldt Blvd.

E Center Street

①

P

P

E Belleview Place

Beerline Trail

N Wells Street

N Dousman Street

E Wright Street

Milwaukee River

Oak Leaf Trail

N Oakland Avenue

E Meinecke Avenue

E North Avenue

N Commerce Street

Pedestrian bridge

N Bartlett Avenue

N Farwell Ave.

N Prospect Ave.

32

32

32

MILES AND DIRECTIONS

0.0 Start from the stone arch at the trailhead and follow the path left around the hill.

0.2 Take the asphalt path north with the hill on your right and follow it to the canoe launch; take the trail to the left.

0.8 Pass under the North Avenue Bridge.

1.0 Cross the Milwaukee River on the pedestrian bridge and turn right.

1.2 Pass back under the North Avenue Bridge heading north.

1.8 At Gordon Park take the trail to the right angling across the park toward the river and the Locust Street Bridge.

2.0 Cross the Locust Street Bridge.

2.2 Take the dirt trail down to the right on the other side.

2.3 Follow the trail back toward the Locust Street Bridge and pass under it, then follow the curving trail down to river level and pass under the bridge again, heading south (with the river on your right).

2.5 Take the steps on the left up into the arboretum.

2.7 Cross the oak savanna area east to take Susie's Bridge across the Oak Leaf Trail, then turn right toward the Urban Ecology Center. Walk toward the river from the Urban Ecology Center on Park Place.

2.9 Arrive back at the parking lot and trailhead.

HIKE INFORMATION

Local Information
Visit Milwaukee, 648 N. Plankinton Ave., #425, Milwaukee, WI 53203; (414) 273-3950; visitmilwaukee.org

Local Attractions
Urban Ecology Center, 1500 E. Park Pl., Milwaukee, WI 53211; (414) 964-8505; www.urbanecologycenter.org
Oak Leaf Bike Trail, Milwaukee County Parks, 9480 Watertown Plank Rd., Wauwatosa, WI 53226; (414) 257-7275; county.milwaukee.gov/OakLeafTrail8289.htm

Three Bridges Park with Mitchell Park Trails

One of Milwaukee's newest parks, this reclaimed green space along the Menomonee River borrows a bit of the paved Hank Aaron State Trail and blazes some trails of its own. At one end of this hike lies the Menomonee Valley location of the Urban Ecology Center and at the other is Mitchell Park Horticultural Conservatory and its famous Domes, both worthy attractions. The hike starts in Mitchell Park, circling the lagoon, then crosses a bridge into Three Bridges Park on an out-and-back trek.

Start: From the parking lot corner in front of the Mitchell Park Domes
Distance: 2.7-mile series of loops
Hiking time: 1.5 hours
Difficulty: Easy
Trail surface: Mostly asphalt, some crushed rock
Best season: Spring through fall
Other trail users: Bicyclists
Canine compatibility: Leashed dogs permitted
Land status: City and county park
Fees and permits: None

Schedule: Daily, sunrise to 10 p.m.
Maps: USGS Milwaukee; on Urban Ecology Center website
Trail contact: Hank Aaron State Trail, 2300 N. MLK Jr Dr., Milwaukee, WI 53212; (414) 263-8559
Special considerations: Water is available outside the Urban Ecology Center, but there are no facilities along the trail. The paved portions in Mitchell and Three Bridges Parks are wheelchair accessible.

Finding the trailhead: From downtown Milwaukee take I-94 west toward Madison, then take exit 309B for 25th Street. Go left on 25th Street over the interstate and turn right onto St. Paul Avenue. Turn left onto 27th Street/WI 57, which becomes Layton Boulevard. Go 0.6 mile and turn left into the entrance for the Mitchell Park Domes. Parking is to the right, and the unmarked trailhead is on the sidewalk in front of the Domes. **GPS:** N43 1.539' / W87 56.775'

THE HIKE

While perhaps not very long for an urban hike, you could kill half a day here if you linger and visit the anchoring attractions at either end. A lot of effort has gone into creating Three Bridges Park, and the multiuse Hank Aaron State Trail passing through it is quite popular. It's an urban renewal and greenway success story, and offers good learning experiences for children via the Urban Ecology Center.

Beginning at the sidewalk along the southern side of the Domes complex, walk along the building, heading toward the Mitchell Park lagoon to the east. Pass the raised flower bed, and when you come to an asphalt path on the right, take it and follow it as it curves behind the row of greenhouses behind the Domes. At the next juncture follow the path right down to the side of the lagoon and stroll the path that circles it in a counterclockwise direction. The number of bird species and the presence of herons may surprise you. Upon completing a loop of the lagoon, go past the pavilion on your right, then follow the path right to where it angles up the hill toward picnic areas and an upper parking lot. Pass a volleyball sand pit on your right along the way.

Once back at the parking lot, go left to its end and follow the exit road out, looking for a bike path sign past a private entrance to a rail yard (Canadian Pacific). Take this paved asphalt path to the right across a pedestrian/bike bridge over the railroad tracks. There's a nice view toward the downtown skyline from here. Three Bridges Park begins here. This is also the Hank Aaron State Trail, and from the bridge it curves left, offering slow curves and gentle hills as you head west.

As you pass under the 27th Street bridge, you see the Menomonee River on your right, now running parallel to the park; you are walking upstream. Throughout here prairie grass and wildflowers grow on modest hills. Past the bridge, at about 1.0 mile, you reach a crushed-rock footpath on your right. Turn right; the

A view of the Menomonee River in Three Bridges Park. Preamtip Satasuk

> *The Milwaukee County Winter Farmers Market (www.mcwfm.org) is held Saturday mornings from November through April inside The Domes. Admission is free during that time.*

trail curves closer to the river and passes to the right of a stormwater rain garden (a connecting path curves like an S back to the bike path if you change your mind). At 1.3 miles return to the bike path and continue heading west on the asphalt, immediately passing a trail on the right. Continue straight west within the park; the bridge on your right crosses the river and connects to 33rd Court for bicyclists.

Just a few steps from the bridge path is a trail on the right that descends to a dovetail with a river observation platform to the left and a canoe launch to the right, both worth checking out. Just past this spur trail is another trail, also on the right. Take this; it continues west after curving around the hills of the community gardens to follow the river again. Pass under the 35th Street bridge and watch for a cedar-chip and dirt path into the brush on your right. Take this if you want a better view of the river for a short distance, but both footpaths come back out onto the asphalt path just before the final bridge over the river. Here you can go right, over the bridge, to get to the Hank Aaron State Trail segment on the north side of the river, or go left through a short underpass decorated with murals to access the Urban Ecology Center. But for the purposes of the hike, this is the turn-around point; return along the paved Hank Aaron Trail to the first bridge at the other end of the park.

Cross the bridge over the train tracks and take a right down the road, still on the paved path. A crosswalk leads left to the sidewalk past the front of the Domes and back to where you started near the parking lot.

The Domes

The Mitchell Park Horticultural Conservatory is best known by its casual name given by the three large central domes. Each is 85 feet high and 140 feet in diameter, and they are visible from I-94. They opened over a period of several years, with the final dome being inaugurated in 1967. Shaped a bit like beehives, the Domes are made of glass and light up at night. Each dome has its own thing going on: tropical plants in one, an arid environment in another featuring desert plants from Africa and the Americas, and a floral show in a third. The floral show changes seasonally, and a special holiday show is held in December. Plan for about an hour to visit The Domes.

Three Bridges Park with Mitchell Park Trails 33

Three Bridges Park with Mitchell Park Trails

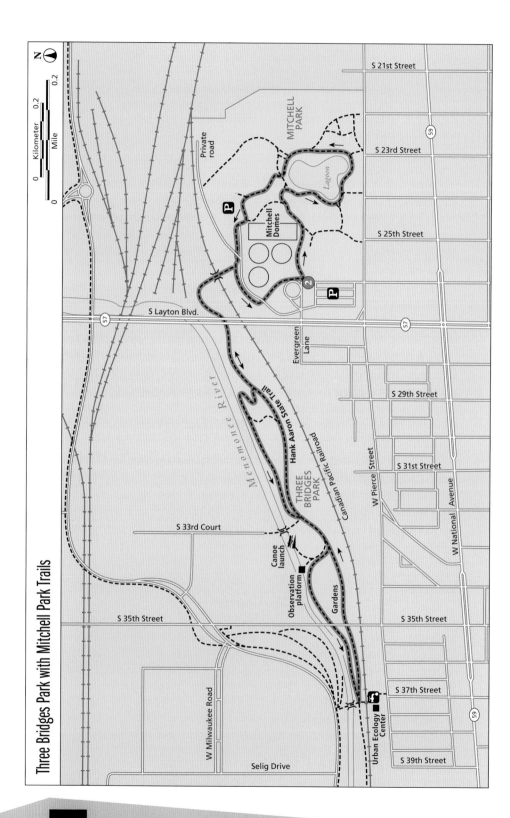

S 21st Street

MITCHELL PARK

S 23rd Street

Lagoon

S 25th Street

Private road

Mitchell Domes

S Layton Blvd.

Evergreen Lane

Menomonee River

Hank Aaron State Trail

Canadian Pacific Railroad

S 29th Street

S 31st Street

W Pierce Street

W National Avenue

THREE BRIDGES PARK

S 33rd Court

Canoe launch

Observation platform

Gardens

S 35th Street

S 35th Street

W Milwaukee Road

S 37th Street

Urban Ecology Center

Selig Drive

S 39th Street

N

0   Kilometer   0.2
0   Mile   0.2

MILES AND DIRECTIONS

0.0   Start from the trailhead and follow along the edge of the Domes complex.

0.5   Walk around the entire Mitchell Park lagoon, then head back uphill behind the greenhouses.

0.7   Cross the bridge over the railroad tracks and into Three Bridges Park.

1.0   Leave the paved Hank Aaron State Trail and take the footpath to the right along the river.

1.3   Come back onto the paved trail, turning right. Stay straight past the second trail bridge on your right.

1.4   Just steps after the spur trail to the river, pass another footpath on the right.

1.6   Take a cedar-chip trail on the right that enters the trees by the river.

1.7   Come out on the asphalt path again near the third trail bridge over the river. Go left through a short tunnel if you want to visit the Urban Ecology Center; otherwise, turn around and backtrack to the first bridge.

2.5   Cross the first bridge and take a right down the road past the Domes. Cross the road at the crosswalk and follow the sidewalk past the front of the Domes.

2.7   Arrive back at the trailhead and parking lot.

HIKE INFORMATION

Local Information
Friends of the Hank Aaron Trail, www.hankaaronstatetrail.org
Milwaukee County Parks, 9480 Watertown Plank Rd., Wauwatosa, WI 53226; (414) 257-7275; www.countyparks.com

Local Attractions
Mitchell Park Conservancy—The Domes, 524 S. Layton Blvd., Milwaukee, WI 53215; (414) 257-5611; www.milwaukeedomes.org
Urban Ecology Center—Menomonee Valley, 3700 W. Pierce St., Milwaukee, WI 53215; (414) 431-2940; www.urbanecologycenter.org

🌿 **Green Tip:**
Enjoy and respect this beautiful landscape.

3

Retzer Nature Center Trails

Centered around the nature center, the trail system offers a wide variety of landscapes in a relatively small area. Pass through pine forest and on to a meadow overlook where you can scan the horizon for miles around, then descend into one of the few places in this part of the state to see a type of wetland known as a fen. Wildflowers and birds are abundant and you'll cross a small stream toward the end of the hike.

Start: From the trailhead near the nature center
Distance: 3.0-mile circuit
Hiking time: 1.5 hours
Difficulty: Moderate due to steepness
Trail surface: Grass, packed soil, wood chips, some boardwalk
Best season: Spring through fall
Other trail users: None
Canine compatibility: Dogs not permitted

Land status: County park
Fees and permits: None
Schedule: Daily, sunrise to 10 p.m. The Environmental Learning Center is open daily 8 a.m. to 4:30 p.m.
Maps: USGS Hartland; at nature center
Trail contact: Retzer Nature Center, S14 W28167 Madison St., Waukesha, WI 53188; (262) 896-8007; www.waukeshacounty parks.com

Finding the trailhead: From downtown Milwaukee go west on I-94 to Waukesha and take exit 291 for CR TT. Go left (south) to US 18 and turn right. Follow this to CR DT and turn left. The next left is Madison Street, and the nature center entrance is on the right. Park in the lot near the learning center; the trailhead is to the left of the building as you approach. **GPS:** N43 0.91' / W88 18.68'

THE HIKE

This property was meant to be a retirement home for John and Florence Retzer. It started with a 90-acre purchase back in 1938, but in 1973 Florence left the land to Waukesha County, intending that it become a conservation park. They had already given it its start, planting thousands of trees and shrubs, bringing wildflowers back to land degraded by agriculture with the help of the Wisconsin Conservation Department. The following year, the nature center project began. Further land purchases in the 1980s brought the acreage to 335.

The Retzer Environmental Learning Center and the Charles Horwitz Planetarium make this a great place to take the family. The trails offer a hike through a rather uncommon ecosystem known as a fen, a wetland with an internal flow of water rich with calcium and magnesium. Other parks generally have wheelchair-accessible portions of trails, but Retzer Nature Center also provides braille on signs along its accessible, 800-foot, paved interpretive Adventure Trail.

As you approach the Environmental Learning Center, the trailhead and map board are on the left. Follow the asphalt path to a picnic area under pines. Go left of the picnic area on a wood-chip trail marked with color-coded posts. This is the Outer Hiking Loop (green). The trail immediately leaves the trees and starts off across meadows full of wildflowers on wide, mowed paths.

The first juncture shows the Prairie Vista Trail (yellow) on your right, a 0.3-mile loop with an overlook of the prairie and the hills far beyond the park. Return to the Green Trail, and as you crest the hill, take a connector trail to the outer trail (Winter Trail). Follow that down the hill along the edge of the woods to get to the Fen Boardwalk Trail. This 0.75-mile loop passes through these unusual wetlands partly on boardwalks and offers an elevated observation deck. Parts of the trail may be soggy at times. You will pass over a small river on a footbridge as the loop returns to the prairie.

Now backtrack up the hill and rejoin the Green Trail as it curves across the meadow. You cross the red Winter Trail just before entering the woods. Through here are more boardwalks over tiny streams and some moderate climbs. Watch on your left for the purple Orchard Trail, a 0.3 mile out-and-back spur trail past a barn to an observation point.

Wood-chip trails start in the forest and head out into open prairie. Preamtip Satasuk

Retzer Nature Center Trails

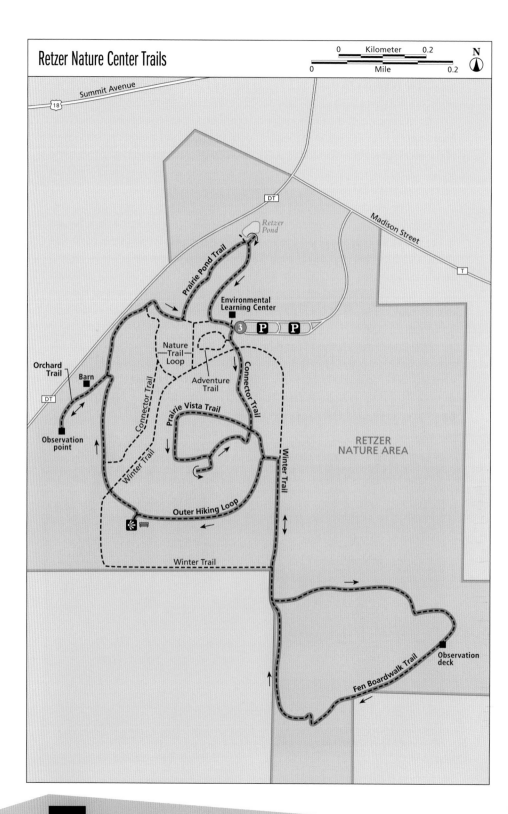

Summit Avenue

18

DT

Retzer Pond

Madison Street

T

Prairie Pond Trail

Environmental
Learning Center

3 P P

Nature
Trail
Loop

Orchard
Trail

Barn

DT

Connector Trail

Adventure
Trail

Connector Trail

Prairie Vista Trail

Observation
point

Winter Trail

Winter Trail

RETZER
NATURE AREA

Outer Hiking Loop

Winter Trail

Fen Boardwalk Trail

Observation
deck

Kilometer

Mile

0   0.2

0   0.2

N

Return to the Green Trail and continue along the several boardwalks. At the next trail juncture the red Nature Trail Loop joins from the right. Take the left path until you come to the blue Prairie Pond Loop trail on your left. This path takes you almost 0.3 mile out to a pond and back to the learning center and the trailhead.

MILES AND DIRECTIONS

0.0 Start from the trailhead near the Environmental Learning Center.

0.3 Turn right onto the Prairie Vista Trail for a 0.3-mile loop.

0.8 Turn left onto the Fen Boardwalk Trail.

1.2 Stop at the observation deck.

1.8 Return to the green Outer Hiking Loop trail.

2.3 Turn left onto the Orchard Trail for a short out-and-back.

2.7 Arrive at the Prairie Pond Loop trail.

3.0 Arrive back at the Environmental Learning Center.

HIKE INFORMATION

Local Information
Waukesha Pewaukee Convention & Visitor Bureau, N14 W23755 Stone Ridge Dr., Ste. 225, Waukesha, WI 53188; (262) 542-0330; www.visitwaukesha.org

Local Attractions
Friends of Retzer Nature Center, www.friendsofretzer.org
Waukesha County Historical Society & Museum, 101 W. Main St., Waukesha, WI 53186; (262) 521-2859; www.waukeshacountymuseum.org. Learn about native son and guitar legend Les Paul, among many other things.

4

Muskego Park Trails

The hardwood forest here is the subject of state scientific research, and the wetlands give a nice balance to the hike. A sort of open-air museum—or graveyard—of the agriculture days is an interesting distraction along the trail.

Start: From the trailhead at Picnic Area #4
Distance: 1.4-mile loop
Hiking time: 30 to 60 minutes
Difficulty: Easy
Trail surface: Wood chips, packed dirt
Best season: Year-round
Other trail users: Horses
Canine compatibility: Leashed dogs permitted, droppings pickup required

Land status: County park
Fees and permits: Daily entrance fee or yearly vehicle sticker
Schedule: Daily, sunrise to 10 p.m.
Maps: USGS Muskego; on park website
Trail contact: Muskego Park, S83 W20370 Janesville Rd., Muskego, WI 53150; (262) 679-0310; www .waukeshacountyparks.com

Finding the trailhead: From Milwaukee take I-43 south toward Beloit. Get off at the CR Y/Racine Avenue exit and go left (south) for 2.4 miles. Turn right onto CR L/Janesville Road; the park entrance is 1 mile on your right. Drive straight into Picnic Area #4, on your right. The trailhead is behind the restrooms and handicap parking space. **GPS:** N42 53.92' / W88 9.86'

THE HIKE

Another one of Waukesha County's fine parks, Muskego Park includes a 2-acre swimming pond with a sandy beach and a campground with twenty-four first-come, first-served sites. The trail itself passes through a 60-acre hardwood forest—primarily old-growth red and white oaks—which has been designated a Wisconsin Scientific Area. The birding is good with plenty of woodpeckers, and the cerulean warbler, considered threatened here in Wisconsin, is a prize for one's life list.

From the trailhead begin going right on the trail loop. Whereas dog owners are obliged to pick up their companion's droppings, horse riders aren't. Watch your step. The next trail coming in on your right is the Bridle Trail entrance; keep going straight. At 0.3 mile you come to a trail juncture. The path straight ahead is actually the cutoff trail that curves and goes straight up through the center of the loop, crossing a similar path that bisects the loop from east to west. At this juncture you should take the right branch to stay on the outer loop trail.

> *The name Muskego originates from the Potawatomi tribe, who named the area Mus-kee-Guaac before the arrival of European settlers. It was their word for "sunfish."*

The trail curls around the south end of the park, and on your left you will see wetlands with some open water. At 0.6 mile the trail passes right along the edge of the backyards of local residences. Keep along the brush line and head straight across to where the trail heads back into the woods. After another 0.1 mile you pass the second cutoff trail on your left. Stay right. Just around the next bend you start passing through old, rusting hulks of farm equipment and an antique truck.

Heavily wooded, the trails at Muskego are colorful in fall. Preamtip Satasuk

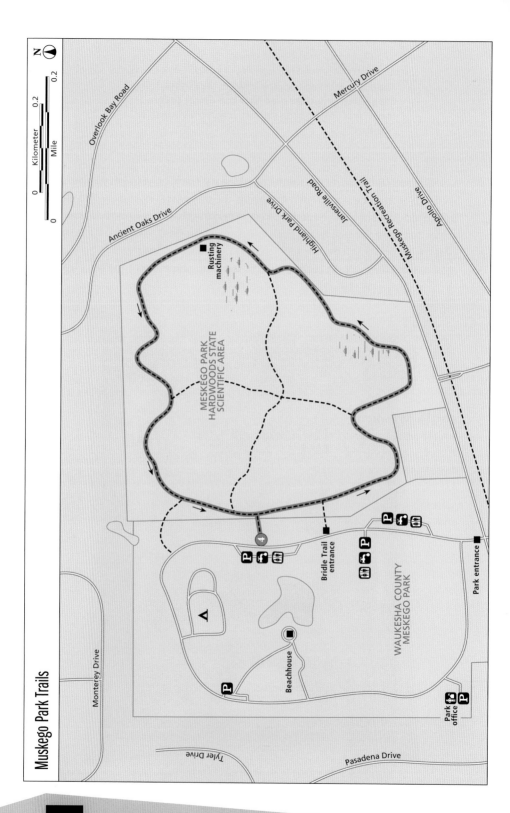

Muskego Park Trails

Overlook Bay Road

Mercury Drive

Apollo Drive

Ancient Oaks Drive

Janesville Road

Highland Park Drive

Muskego Recreation Trail

Rusting machinery

MESKEGO PARK HARDWOODS STATE SCIENTIFIC AREA

Bridle Trail entrance

Park entrance

WAUKESHA COUNTY MESKEGO PARK

Monterey Drive

Beachhouse

Park office

Tyler Drive

Pasadena Drive

N

Kilometer
0   0.2   0.2
Mile
0   0.2

At 1.3 miles a trail to the right heads out to the park road; stay left to continue on the loop. A couple hundred feet past this trail, you pass the outlet from the east-west cutoff trail on your left. The next trail on the right takes you back to the trailhead.

MILES AND DIRECTIONS

0.0   Start from the trailhead in Picnic Area #4.

0.3   Take the trail to the right at the juncture with the north-south cutoff trail.

0.6   Pass by the edge of some backyards.

0.7   Continue on the trail to the right at the juncture with the east-west cutoff trail.

1.3   Pass the spur trail to the park road on your right.

1.4   Arrive back at trailhead.

HIKE INFORMATION

Local Information
Visit Waukesha County, www.visitwaukeshacounty.com

Local Attractions
Minooka Park, 1927 E. Sunset Dr., Waukesha, WI 53186; (262) 896-8006; www .waukeshacountyparks.com. A fantastic dog park with some mountain biking trails as well.

Tamarack Circle Hiking Trail. Breamtin Satacyk

Lion's Den Gorge Nature Preserve Trails

This 73-acre park is named for a scenic gorge accessible by a bridge and stairs, but the Lake Michigan bluff views and beach access are worthy reasons to visit as well. And if that isn't enough, the hike ends on a boardwalk along the edge of a US Fish and Wildlife Service wetlands. The park is very popular for walking dogs as well as some great bird watching.

Start: From the trailhead at the parking lot loop
Distance: 2.2-mile loop
Hiking time: 1 hour
Difficulty: Easy, but some stairs to the beach
Trail surface: Dirt, crushed rock, grass, boardwalk
Best season: Summer through fall
Other trail users: None
Canine compatibility: Leashed dogs permitted
Land status: County park
Fees and permits: None

Schedule: Daily, 6 a.m. to 9 p.m.
Maps: USGS Cedarburg; at trail kiosk and on website
Trail contact: Ozaukee County Parks, 121 W. Main St., P.O. Box 994, Port Washington, WI 53074; (262) 284-9411; www.co.ozaukee .wi.us
Special considerations: Portable toilets are at the parking loop. Many of the trails are wheelchair friendly but not the beach entry, which is a series of stairs.

Finding the trailhead: From downtown Milwaukee take I-43 north about 20 miles and get off on exit 92 for CR Q/Ulao Road. Go right (east) for 0.7 mile and take the second left, onto CR C. Drive 1.4 miles and turn right onto High Bluff Drive, following it 0.4 mile into the park. The trailhead is at the eastern end of the parking loop. **GPS:** N43 20.264' / W87 53.267'

THE HIKE

For such a small park, this one packs a lot of beauty. The scenic overlooks of Lake Michigan are just for starters. Add beach access, wildflowers, nice forest walks, a gorge carved into the rock, a small stream, and a boardwalk along a notable wetlands. Start down the trail from the parking lot and at the first juncture, take the short spur trail to the right. The first thing you come to is the wide view of the mighty Lake Michigan. Enjoy the view, then retrace the few steps back to the main trail and head north with the lake on your right.

It's a short distance to the central kiosk with park information and a map, though really, none is necessary. Take the trail to the right and find another great vista point with a bench. The trail continues past this area along the top of the cliffs. The trail is not so close to the edge, but it is something to consider if you have kids. It's a steep slope to the lakeshore below.

As you continue north into the woods with some shade, you pass cutoff trails that cross the center of this loop. Keep straight ahead and pass another spur trail on the right out to yet another scenic overlook at about 0.8 mile. Back on the trail you come to a 60-foot wooden bridge over a smaller offshoot of the larger gorge. On the other side is a trail juncture. To the left is just another cutoff trail. Take the trail to the right and descend the stairs to lake level. Cross a footbridge and follow a narrow path alongside a creek, then come out on the beach. It's a nice place to linger.

When you are ready to go, backtrack over the footbridge, up the steps and to the trail juncture again. The bridge is now on your left, so take the trail to your right; it follows along the main gorge area on the Gorge Loop. The trail soon splits for the Cedar Loop, which is just a short alternate route along the point here. Take it through its namesake cedars, see the view, and arrive back on the Gorge Loop trail again.

The Gorge Loop comes to the Lion's Den Trail juncture; take the trail to the right. It hits the edge of the park boundary, where it straightens out and heads due south, all the way back to the kiosk, passing Trillium Trek Trail, Wetland Way,

The beach along Lake Michigan near the gorge. Preamtip Satasuk

Lion's Den Gorge Nature Preserve Trails

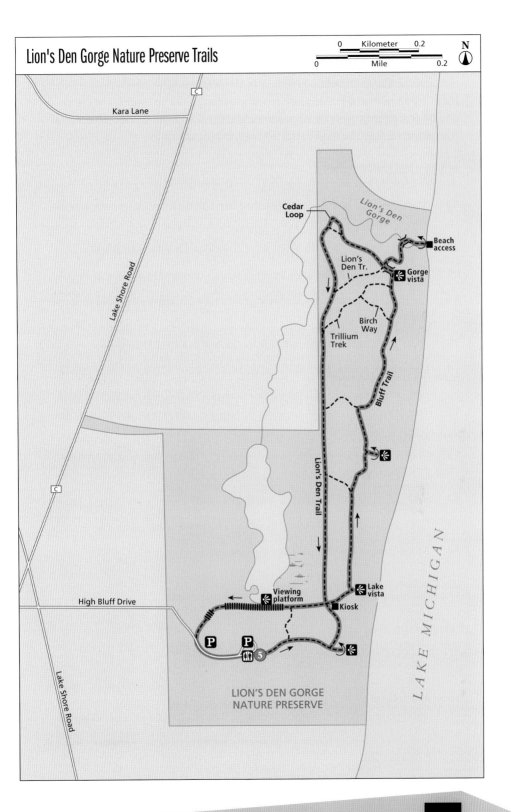

Kara Lane

Lake Shore Road

Kilometer
0
0.2

Mile
0
0.2

N

Lion's Den Gorge

Cedar Loop

Beach access

Lion's Den Tr.

Gorge vista

Birch Way

Trillium Trek

Bluff Trail

Lion's Den Trail

LAKE MICHIGAN

Viewing platform

Lake vista

High Bluff Drive

Kiosk

P

P

5

Lake Shore Road

LION'S DEN GORGE
NATURE PRESERVE

and Woodland Way on the left, in that order. Back at the kiosk, take the trail to the right and keep straight all the way to the boardwalk. On the right is a large observation platform in the marsh where you can spot a variety of birds, turtles, and frogs. Continue along the boardwalk and the trail beyond until you arrive at the park road. Take the road to the left back to the parking lot.

MILES AND DIRECTIONS

0.0 Start from the trailhead and take the Gentian Walk Trail to the right at the first juncture.

0.1 Stop at the first Lake Michigan scenic overlook on a short spur trail.

0.2 Come to the kiosk and take the Bluff Trail to the right to a scenic overlook.

0.8 Cross the gorge on a wooden bridge and take the trail to the right to some stairs.

1.0 Cross another footbridge and follow the trail out to the lakeshore.

1.1 Come back across the footbridge and up the stairs, and with the big bridge on your left, take the Gorge Loop trail to the right.

1.2 Take the Cedar Loop on the right for the view and come back out on the Gorge Loop trail again.

1.3 At the juncture with Lion's Den Trail, take the trail to the right and follow it all the way south to the kiosk.

1.9 Turn right to head toward the marsh boardwalk.

2.1 Exit the trail onto the park road and go left on the road.

2.2 Arrive back at the trailhead and parking lot.

HIKE INFORMATION

Local Information
Visit Port Washington, 126 E. Grand Ave., Port Washington, WI 53074; (262) 284-0900; www.visitportwashington.com

Local Attractions
1860 Lighthouse and Light Station Museum, 205 N. Franklin St., Port Washington, WI 53074; (262) 268-9150; www.portwashingtonhistoricalsociety.org/light station.htm

Harrington Beach State Park Trails

An often overlooked state park not far from the city, Harrington Beach offers the beauty of a one-mile, undeveloped sandy beach on the shores of Lake Michigan, a quarry lake, a cedar lowland forest, and historical landmarks from an old mining community.

Start: From the trailhead near the welcome center
Distance: 3.0-mile circuit
Hiking time: 2 hours
Difficulty: Easy with avoidable moderate sections due to trail surface
Trail surface: Mostly paved or crushed stone; some uneven packed dirt paths
Best season: Spring through fall
Other trail users: Bicyclists, park shuttle
Canine compatibility: Leashed dogs permitted except on Nature Trail
Land status: State park

Fees and permits: Vehicle admission sticker required; available for purchase at visitor center
Schedule: Daily, 6 a.m. to 11 p.m.
Maps: USGS Port Washington East; at park office and on website
Trail contact: Harrington Beach State Park, 531 CR D, Belgium, WI 53004; (262) 285-3015; http://dnr.wi.gov
Special considerations: The park's campground has 31 sites with electrical hookups, 33 rustic sites, and 5 walk-in sites. All are first-come, first-served, or reserve one at (888) 947-2757 or www.reserveamerica.com.

Finding the trailhead: From Milwaukee take I-43 north 35 miles to exit 107 and turn right onto CR D. Follow CR D for 1.2 miles to the park entrance on the right. Follow the park road 1.5 miles to the Ansay Welcome Center; the trailhead is to the left of the building. **GPS:** N43 29.81' / W87 47.67'

THE HIKE

Harrington Beach is just a short drive north of Milwaukee and offers a mile of sandy beach along Lake Michigan. It's especially popular during the hottest times of summer when cool lake breezes bring relief. The park's campground offers 69 sites, 31 of them with electrical hookups, as well as 5 hike-in sites and an accessible cabin. The hiking trail is mostly shaded and makes a loop of the park and Quarry Lake. To the right of the Ansay Welcome Center is the paved shuttle trail on which only the free shuttle circles the park until 7 p.m. The hike as marked, however, begins to the left of the welcome center. Only 200 feet into mixed forest from the trailhead, steps lead off the trail to the left, down to the beach, which stretches south from here nearly a mile.

From the top of the steps, the trail continues through the forest not far from the edge of the beach, with occasional benches and spur trails leading out onto the sand. At 0.3 mile the trail joins the shuttle path to the left. Watch for various signs indicating ruins of an old mining community. Just 100 feet down the shuttle path, take a paved path to the right to Quarry Lake for a 0.7 mile loop that returns to this same spot.

You can cut this loop for length, but it is quite scenic. Start the loop to the left and cross a footbridge. The crushed stone path follows the water's edge and passes a few outgoing spur trails. You cross another footbridge and, halfway around the lake, come to a fork in the trail. The path to the right is a spur trail to a lookout point with a picnic table. Take the trail to the left to continue and just keep going right at trail junctions until you return to the shuttle path and bridge.

Continue to the right on the shuttle path. The trail remains on this paved surface until 2.2 miles. If you prefer the asphalt, stay on it to the park road, then turn right to loop back to the parking lot. Otherwise, leave the pavement for a rugged wooded trail to a T intersection at 2.6 miles. Take the path to the right, which soon joins the lakeside path again coming from the right. At the next juncture

Beautiful Quarry Lake at the center of Harrington Beach State Park.

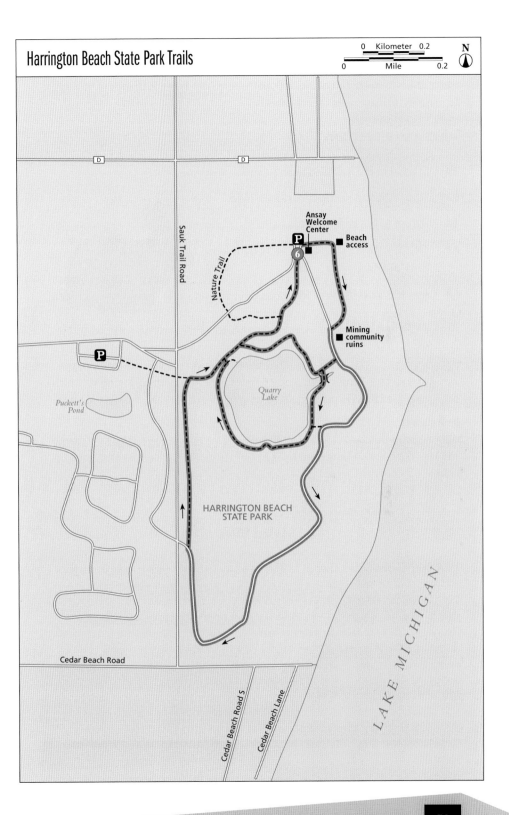

Harrington Beach State Park Trails

0   Kilometer   0.2

0   Mile   0.2

N

Sauk Trail Road

Ansay Welcome Center

Beach access

Nature Trail

6

Mining community ruins

Quarry Lake

Puckett's Pond

HARRINGTON BEACH STATE PARK

Cedar Beach Road

Cedar Beach Road S

Cedar Beach Lane

LAKE MICHIGAN

take the path to the left, back to the parking lot via cedar lowlands. You pass a trail to the left that is part of the optional Nature Trail. Take the branch to the right to finish in the parking lot at 3.0 miles.

MILES AND DIRECTIONS

0.0 Start from the trailhead near the Ansay Welcome Center.

0.3 Turn right to take the Quarry Lake loop.

1.2 Return to the paved shuttle path.

2.6 Take the wooded trail that veers right from the shuttle path.

3.0 Arrive back at the trailhead.

HIKE INFORMATION

Local Information
Friends of Harrington Beach State Park, www.friendsofharrington.org

Restaurant
HoBo's Korner Kitchen, 100 Main St., Belgium, WI 53004; (262) 285-3417; www .howdea.net/hobos-home.htm. A solid place for breakfast and reasonably priced food.

Seeing Stars

It's not often one gets a chance to visit an observatory. They are typically few and far between and often not even open to the public. So it's quite a bonus that Harrington Beach State Park actually has one. The observatory is operated by Northern Cross Science Foundation, a nonprofit organization based in southeastern Wisconsin with the primary aim of getting people enthused about astronomy. They've been at the park for years now, and the telescope they use keeps getting bigger. Currently they have a 20-inch telescope weighing in at just over 2,000 pounds. And while they started out in rather informal digs, since 2007 they have had a proper observatory building with a special roof design that allows it to roll along rails right off the building so the team has access to the whole sky. From summer into early fall, the group opens the observatory for public stargazing. Visit their website at www.ncsf.info to see when the next event is.

Kohler-Andrae State Park—Dunes Cordwalk

Set along a beautiful sandy beach on Lake Michigan, this state park protects a fragile ecosystem set among sand dunes. A cordwalk traverses the grass-covered rolling sands and offers views of the lake and rare plant species.

Start: From the Dunes Cordwalk trailhead at the southern parking lot
Distance: 2.8 miles out-and-back
Hiking time: 1.5 to 2 hours
Difficulty: Moderate due to surface and some steep sections
Trail surface: Cordwalk with some sandy patches, can be slippery
Best season: Year-round except when snow and ice are present
Other trail users: None
Canine compatibility: Dogs permitted on leashes except on Creeping Juniper Nature Trail or the beach south of the Sanderling Nature Center
Land status: State park

Fees and permits: Vehicle admission sticker required; available for purchase at park office
Schedule: Daily, 6 a.m. to 11 p.m.
Maps: USGS Sheboygan South; at park office and on website
Trail contact: Kohler-Andrae State Park, 1020 Beach Park Ln., Sheboygan, WI 53081; (920) 451-4080; http://dnr.wi.gov
Special considerations: There is little shade on this trail; take care on hot summer days. Also, this is a state natural area and as such has extra protections for some rare and fragile flora: Stay on the cordwalk at all times.

Finding the trailhead: From Milwaukee take I-43 north 48 miles to exit 120 for CR V. Turn right onto CR V and in 100 feet turn right again to stay on CR V. Follow CR V for 2 miles to the state park entrance, then drive 1.2 miles on Sand Dune Drive to the southern trailhead parking area for the Dunes Cordwalk. **GPS:** N43 39.48' / W87 43.46'

THE HIKE

The glaciers of the Wisconsin Glacial Episode carved out the basin of what is now Lake Michigan, depositing fine sand from its grinding work. When the waters of the previous glacial lake receded, the beaches emerged and winds created the dunes we see today. This park is actually the combination of two state parks, each named for a figure of Wisconsin industry whose families or companies donated land for their creation. The cordwalk, a series of narrow planks that traverses the sands, offers a chance for hikers to responsibly see the fragile dunes and their uncommon plants. The park also has a 0.25-mile marshland boardwalk and woodlands trail, parts of which are wheelchair accessible. For additional hiking consider the Black River Trail, which runs 2.5 miles through field and forest and is shared with mountain bikers and horse riders. The trailhead is off CR V at the north end of the property. If you are interested in staying overnight, the park offers 137 sites—52 with electrical hookups—as well as an accessible cabin.

There are three primary places to enter the cordwalk trail: from the north or south ends and in the middle, at the Sanderling Nature Center, which has exhibits about the geology, wildlife, and history of the region. Restrooms can be found inside; otherwise you can find toilets and water in the parking lots at either end of the trail.

Beginning at the southern trailhead, the cordwalk heads north, rising and falling over the dunes. At 0.1 mile you pass the trail to the group camp on your left. The trail continues around a large cottonwood 300 feet later; this tree and just a few other clumps of aspen or pine are the only shade the trail offers. Be aware also that sand sometimes drifts over portions of the trail.

The highest points offer great views of the lake to the east and the layout of the surrounding dunes. At 0.5 mile a spur trail goes left a short distance into the dunes to a bench in partial shade. At a fork at 0.7 mile take the left branch; you are on the first of two loops embedded in the length of the trail—Creeping

The cordwalk goes right through the dunes along Lake Michigan at Kohler-Andrae State Park.

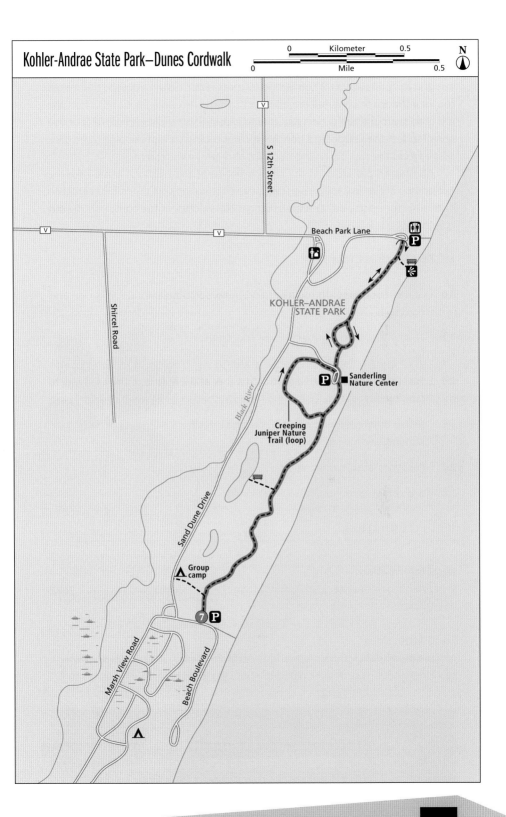

Kohler-Andrae State Park–Dunes Cordwalk

0 Kilometer 0.5

0 Mile 0.5

N

S 12th Street

V

V

V

Beach Park Lane

P

KOHLER–ANDRAE
STATE PARK

Shircel Road

Black River

P

Sanderling
Nature Center

Creeping
Juniper Nature
Trail (loop)

Sand Dune Drive

Group
camp

7 P

Marsh View Road

Beach Boulevard

Juniper Nature Trail, which offers some interpretive signage. At 1.0 mile you arrive at the parking lot for Sanderling Nature Center. Go left from the trail across the lot entrance to continue the hike north. At the next loop at 1.1 mile, take the left branch around to the next juncture to continue north. At 1.4 miles a spur trail goes 150 feet to the right to a bench with a sweeping view of the beach and lake. Just beyond the spur trail is the north lot and turnaround point.

The return path follows the second halves of the two loop trails. Take the left branch at the first loop, then cross the parking lot past the nature center to find the return path and Creeping Juniper Nature Trail in the corner on the left (southeast).

MILES AND DIRECTIONS

0.0 Start from the south trailhead and head north on the cordwalk.

0.7 Follow Creeping Juniper Nature Trail to the left.

1.0 Pass the Sanderling Nature Center and parking lot.

1.5 Reach the turnaround point at the park's north parking lot.

2.0 Pass the nature center again.

2.8 Arrive back at the trailhead.

HIKE INFORMATION

Local Information
Visit Sheboygan County, 3347 Kohler Memorial Dr., Sheboygan, WI 53081; (920) 459-0208; www.visitsheboygan.com

Local Attractions
Indian Mound Park, Panther Ave. and S. 9th St., (920) 459-3440. See Native American effigy mounds on a self-guided tour and explore wetlands on a boardwalk.

Green Tip:
Pass it down—the best way to instill good green habits in your children is to set a good example.

Kettle Moraine State Forest—Northern Unit: Greenbush Hiking Trails

This collection of skiing/hiking trails offers a wide range of courses. The outside loop offers a variety of scenery including hardwood forest, pine plantation, some rolling glacial terrain, and wetlands. Unlike some ski trails the outside loop does not have the relentless short but steep up-and-down climbs; it tends to be either level or more gradual with the climbs—except for the first 0.5 mile. As the trail turns back to the trailhead, Bear Lake and its marshes are visible. Watch for kettles and expect some moraines as the forest opens up more along the second half of the hike.

Start: From the beginning of the ski trails and the trailhead just inside the woods

Distance: 5.1-mile loop

Hiking time: 2.5 hours

Difficulty: Moderate due to distance and steep areas

Trail surface: Packed dirt, grass

Best season: Spring through fall

Other trail users: Skiers in winter

Canine compatibility: Leashed dogs permitted

Land status: State park

Fees and permits: Vehicle admission sticker required; available for purchase at park entrances, state forest headquarters, or Ice Age Visitor Center

Schedule: Daily, 6 a.m. to 11 p.m.

Maps: USGS Cascade; at park offices, Ice Age Visitor Center, and on website

Trail contacts: Kettle Moraine State Forest—Northern Unit, Forest Headquarters, N1765 Hwy. G, Campbellsport, WI 53010; (262) 626-2116; http://dnr.wi.gov/topic /parks/name/kmn; Ice Age Visitor Center, N2875 WI 67, Campbellsport, WI 53010; (920) 533-8322; http://dnr.wi.gov

Special considerations: Hiking and dogs are not allowed on ski trails when snow is present. Hiking is not allowed on the bike trails, and biking is not allowed on the hiking trails.

Finding the trailhead: From downtown Milwaukee follow I-43/WI 57 north for 24.4 miles and take exit 97 on the left to stay on WI 57 toward Plymouth for another 19.4 miles after it splits from I-43. Turn left onto WI 28, go 1.9 miles, and turn right onto CR V. Follow this 0.6 mile and take the first right onto CR E. Go 3.5 miles, then turn left onto WI 67. Go 5.3 miles and turn right onto Kettle Moraine Scenic Drive. Continue 1.6 miles, passing Greenbush Kettle and Greenbush Picnic Area, until you arrive at Greenbush Group Camp on the left. Enter the park and continue to the parking area on the left. Notice the wooden fence along the corner of the lot near a shelter house. Enter here; to the left a wide, grassy trail starts up the hill straight into the woods. Follow this for a short distance to the clearly marked ski trails trailhead. **GPS:** N43 44.945' / W88 6.175'

THE HIKE

From the trailhead follow all indicators for the Purple loop trail. This is the longest of the five color-coded routes through the woods, with Green being the most difficult and a bit shorter at 3.6 miles. As you come up the straight, grassy trail from the shelter area to the trailhead, take the trail to the left. Right away you cross the Ice Age Trail, which also comes up from the parking area but crosses and winds through the woods along the right side of the Purple Trail. This first stretch has a lot of moderately steep rising and falling, but this is the hardest portion of the hike in that respect, and it ends at 0.5 mile when you reach the Greenbush Picnic Area.

Come up a short ramp to this point; the Ice Age Trail joins the trail just before you arrive at the toilets. Take the trail to the right, away from the picnic area, and immediately the Ice Age Trail departs to the left and leaves the area. You stay on the purple ski trail, continuing straight on a wide two-track. The Pink Trail angles

Looking out over Bear Lake Marsh at the western end of the Greenbush Trails. Preamtip Satasuk

off on the right at a juncture 750 feet from the picnic area, and the Red Trail does the same another 100 feet farther. In both cases stay straight on the two-track.

Pass the 1.0-mile marker, a purple patch on a pole, and at 1.4 miles cross a bridle trail. At the next trail juncture, a connector to the Red Trail is straight ahead. Take the trail to the left to stay on the Purple and Green Trail. Much of the tree cover through here has been maple and aspen, but at 1.6 miles you pass under power lines in a clearing and head into pine plantation. At the next juncture 0.1 mile later, the Green Trail departs to the right; take the Purple Trail to the left. After the 2.0-mile marker, hike through a corridor of pine and, at the left bend in the trail, watch for a deep kettle in the woods to your right.

The trail is nice and level through this section, and at 2.7 miles you pass a bench. The trail rolls a bit following an S-curve and passing another kettle on the right. After 3 miles you can see Bear Lake through the trees on the left. A clear view of the Bear Lake Marsh opens up as you continue, and by 3.4 miles you also see a water-filled kettle on your right, so you have views of marshland on either side. Past the kettle on the right, you come to a juncture with the Green Trail at 3.6 miles. Stay left to stay on the Purple Trail and hike under the power lines once more 0.1 mile later. The view to the left is the last you will see of the marsh.

The trail continues into the woods but with low understory so you can see the rise and fall of the land. At 4.3 miles the trail rises up to the right onto a ridge, and at 4.7 miles you cross the bridle trail and immediately after, the connection to the Green Trail. Stay left and avoid any unmarked trails before finally arriving at the trailhead once more. Turn left to get back to the parking area.

MILES AND DIRECTIONS

0.0   Start from the trailhead, heading left.

0.5   At the Greenbush Picnic Area juncture, take the Purple Trail to the right.

Greenbush Kettle

An excellent example of a kettle, this roadside attraction is just south of Green-bush Recreation Area on the west side of the Kettle Moraine Scenic Drive. The kettle was formed by a large piece of ice from the retreating glaciers that was trapped beneath a pile of glacial deposits. When the ice melted, the rubble atop that ice sank into the kettle-like depression you see today. The Greenbush Kettle is quite symmetrical and deep, often accumulating water in the center, depending on the season and weather. A parking area, observation deck, and interpretive sign are right next to it.

Kettle Moraine State Forest–Northern Unit: Greenbush Hiking Trails

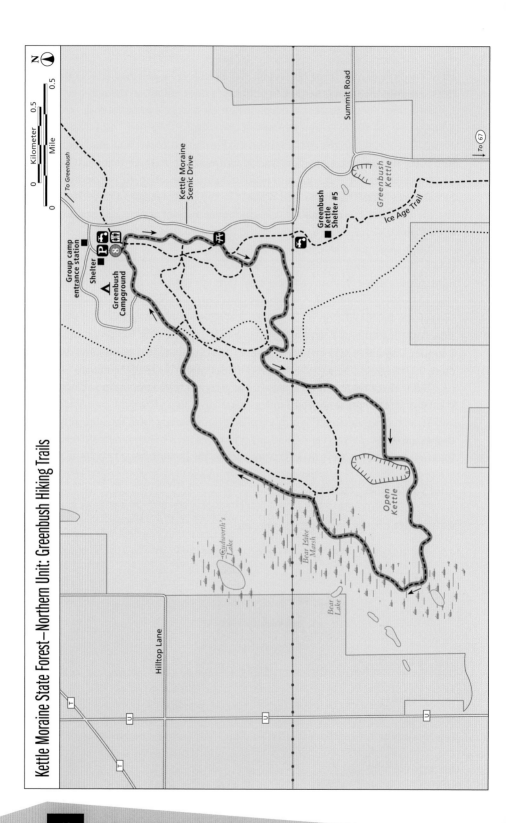

1.4 Go straight across the bridle trail and, at the trail juncture just after that, take the Purple Trail to the left.

1.7 Pass under the power lines and, at the juncture with the Green Trail, take the Purple Trail to the left.

3.6 On the right is a connecting trail to the green loop; stay left on the Purple Trail.

3.7 Pass under the power lines again.

4.7 Continue straight across the bridle trail and stay left where the Green Trail goes right a few steps later.

5.1 Arrive back at the trailhead. Go left down the path to the parking lot.

HIKE INFORMATION

Lodging
Camping available at Long Lake Recreation Area, (920) 533-8612, or Mauthe Lake Recreation Area, (262) 626-4305; register at park entrance stations or reserve at (888) 947-2757 or www.reserveamerica.com.

Organizations
Ice Age Trail Alliance, 2110 Main St., Cross Plains, WI 53528; (800) 227-0046; www.iceagetrail.org

9

Kettle Moraine State Forest—Northern Unit: Parnell Tower Hiking Trail

If you want a bird's-eye view of the Kettle Moraine, including some identifying signage of glacial features along the horizon, Parnell Tower is a must. You can go to the tower directly from the parking lot in minutes or, better yet, hike this fantastic rustic trail that joins the Ice Age National Scenic Trail briefly along the backs of some moraines before making a loop back to the tower.

Start: From the trailhead at the parking lot
Distance: 3.4-mile loop
Hiking time: 1.5 hours
Difficulty: Moderately strenuous due to rough surfaces and some steep climbs
Trail surface: Dirt, scattered rock, tree roots
Best season: Spring through fall, with great fall colors
Other trail users: None
Canine compatibility: Leashed dogs permitted
Land status: State park
Fees and permits: Vehicle admission sticker required; available for purchase at park entrances, state forest headquarters, or Ice Age Visitor Center
Schedule: Daily, 6 a.m. to 11 p.m.

Maps: USGS Cascade; at park offices, Ice Age Visitor Center, and on website
Trail contacts: Kettle Moraine State Forest—Northern Unit, Forest Headquarters, N1765 Hwy. G, Campbellsport, WI 53010; (262) 626-2116; http://dnr.wi.gov/topic /parks/name/kmn; Ice Age Visitor Center, N2875 WI 67, Campbellsport, WI 53010; (920) 533-8322; http://dnr.wi.gov
Special considerations: Parnell Shelter #4 is a simple wooden building with open windows and benches along the walls inside, located just off the Ice Age Trail on this hike. Staying here requires a prearranged permit from the state forest. Pack out what you pack in. Up to 10 campers are allowed for 1 night only.

Finding the trailhead: From downtown Milwaukee follow I-43/WI 57 north for 24.4 miles and take exit 97 on the left to stay on WI 57 toward Plymouth for another 19.4 miles after it splits from I-43. Turn left onto WI 28, go 1.9 miles, and turn right onto CR V. Follow this 5.3 miles, turn right onto CR A, and continue another 1.5 miles. Turn left onto Kettle Moraine Scenic Drive. The park entrance is 0.2 mile on the right. The trailhead is at the far end of the parking lot and is clearly marked. **GPS:** N43 41.861' / W88 5.410'

THE HIKE

Parnell Tower is a popular attraction in the Kettle Moraine, partly because it is so accessible, and partly because the view from the top of this 60-foot wooden structure is only rivaled by Dundee Mountain. On a clear day the 360-degree view can stretch as far as 25 miles. But to build up the anticipation, take the loop trail through the glacial terrain first.

From the parking lot the trail ascends on earth and wood-beam steps to a trail juncture and map board just 400 feet into a rich forest of tall hardwoods. From here it is another few minutes of hiking to reach the tower if you go straight; instead, take the trail to the left and follow along the backbone of a ridge. By 0.2 mile the path already starts to demand constant up-and-down hiking along the rugged trail surface. All around you are erratics of varying sizes. At 0.5 mile the trail goes up over another ridge and passes between two hills. The woods are dominated by maple, adding some great color in fall.

At 0.6 mile the trail meets the Ice Age National Scenic Trail, marked by yellow blazes on occasional posts. To the left the Ice Age Trail leads 4 miles to Butler Lake Trail and 7 miles to Dundee Shelter #3. Take the trail to the right, and for the next 0.25 mile, the Ice Age and Parnell Tower Trails are one. Pass the spur trail to Parnell Shelter #4, visible from the trail. Just past this trail is another map board. The Ice Age Trail continues straight, with just 3 more miles to Greenbush Kettle Shelter #5. Take the trail to the right, descending into mixed hardwood forest, with abundant rocks in the dirt trail to challenge your footing. The trail soon resumes its rise and fall, and at 1.4 miles the path descends steeply, crossing between two shallow kettles at the bottom. Cross a short clearing and then head back into the

Kettle Moraine Scenic Drive

When you follow directions to the various trailheads for the hikes here in the Kettle Moraine, you sometimes find yourself turning left or right from Kettle Moraine Scenic Drive onto . . . Kettle Moraine Scenic Drive. In some cases roads have two names, where the scenic drive overlaps a local name for a longer road. This route, designated a scenic drive by the state of Wisconsin, runs 115 miles from near Elkhart Lake in the north, down through the several units of the Kettle Moraine State Forest, to its end near Whitewater. The roads are paved but are often secondary roads or lettered county roads. You can make a nice day of it driving through, or find plenty to stop for along the way for several days—especially if you are hiking and camping. Historic sites are numerous as well. Old World Wisconsin, the Wade House, and Holy Hill Basilica lie along the route. Numerous hikes described in this book are also accessed along the way.

woods. Don't be surprised if you see an occasional horse rider through here; the equestrian trail is not far off to your left.

A white post with a purple tip stands just outside a pine plantation at 1.8 miles, and in the next clearing there is a map board. To your left only 20 to 30 feet is a clearing for power lines cutting through the woods. Soon the trail makes a turn to the right, starting the trek south to the tower. Look for a kettle to the left (east) when the leaves are scarce or gone. At 2.4 miles the trail descends into a deep depression, crosses the bottom of it, and then takes a direct run at the next steep climb. Halfway to the top the trail takes a gentler, though still strenuous, approach as it angles up the slope to the right. With the steepest climb behind you, the trail winds past another deep kettle with a view on your right—with spur trails to a closer look from the edge. From there the trail angles away to the left, coming to an old stone wall at 2.9 miles. The trail crosses through, follows along the wall, and crosses the wall again before leaving it behind.

Parnell Tower offers a commanding view of Kettle Moraine.

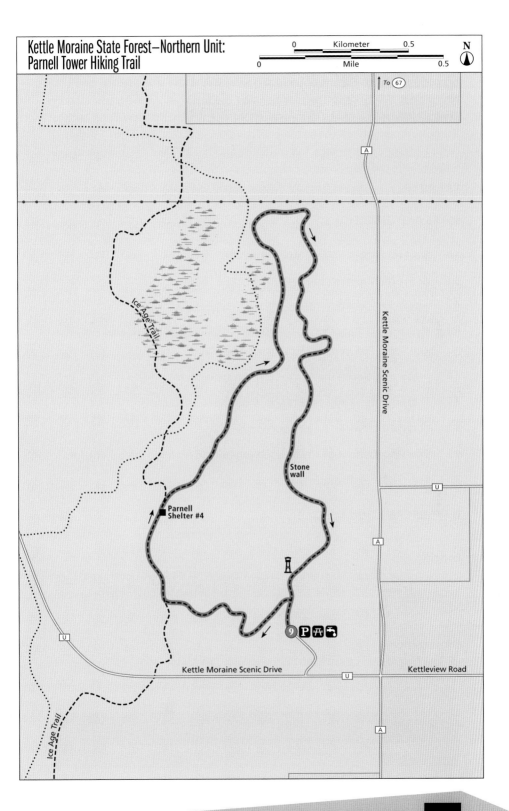

Kettle Moraine State Forest–Northern Unit:
Parnell Tower Hiking Trail

0   Kilometer   0.5
0   Mile   0.5

N

To 67

A

Kettle Moraine Scenic Drive

Ice Age Trail

Stone
wall

U

Parnell
Shelter #4

A

9 P 🎪 🏕

Kettle Moraine Scenic Drive

U

Kettleview Road

Ice Age Trail

U

A

From 3.1 miles the trail ascends steadily until you come to a bench; you are now 500 feet from the prize. The trail arrives out at the tower's base, and you have about 100 steps to the top. Signs on the top platform help you identify several landmarks and glacial formations. After enjoying the view, head back to the bottom; straight off the last step is the return trail. It starts down 150 feet of earth and wood-beam steps and continues another 350 feet to the original trail juncture with the map board. Go straight down the steps and you are back at the parking lot.

MILES AND DIRECTIONS

0.0   Start from the trailhead, heading uphill.

0.1   At the trail juncture, turn left.

0.6   Join the Ice Age Trail, turning right at the juncture.

0.9   Pass Parnell Shelter #4 and at the next juncture take a right where the Parnell Tower Trail departs from the Ice Age Trail.

1.9   Pass a map board; the trail turns south soon after.

2.9   Cross through a stone wall twice, then continue south.

3.2   Climb the tower for an amazing view.

3.3   Stay straight through the final trail juncture to return to the parking lot.

3.4   Arrive back at the trailhead and parking lot.

HIKE INFORMATION

Lodging
Camping available at Long Lake Recreation Area, (920) 533-8612, or Mauthe Lake Recreation Area, (262) 626-4305; register at park entrance stations or reserve at (888) 947-2757 or www.reserveamerica.com.

Organizations
Ice Age Trail Alliance, 2110 Main St., Cross Plains, WI 53528; (800) 227-0046; www.iceagetrail.org

🌰 **Green Tip:**
Donate used gear to a nonprofit kids' organization.

Kettle Moraine State Forest—Northern Unit: Butler Lake Hiking Trail

Despite the name of the trail, much of this trek is spent on the back and slopes of Parnell Esker in the forest south of the lake. For 1.3 miles of its length, the park's trail actually joins the Ice Age Trail, both heading out and on the final return, while passing a water-filled kettle and ending with a nice view of the namesake lake from the top of a moraine.

Start: From the trailhead at the end of the parking lot

Distance: 3.1-mile double loop

Hiking time: 1.5 hours

Difficulty: Moderate due to a lot of up and down

Trail surface: Packed dirt, tree roots, glacial till

Best season: Spring through fall, especially for fall colors

Other trail users: None

Canine compatibility: Leashed dogs permitted

Land status: State park

Fees and permits: Vehicle admission sticker required; available for purchase at park entrances, state forest headquarters, or Ice Age Visitor Center

Schedule: Daily, 6 a.m. to 11 p.m.

Maps: USGS Dundee; at park offices, Ice Age Visitor Center, on website, and posted at trail junctures

Trail contacts: Kettle Moraine State Forest—Northern Unit, Forest Headquarters, N1765 Hwy. G, Campbellsport, WI 53010; (262) 626-2116; http://dnr.wi.gov/topic/parks/name/kmn; Ice Age Visitor Center, N2875 WI 67, Campbellsport, WI 53010; (920) 533-8322; http://dnr.wi.gov

Special considerations: Hiking and dogs are not allowed on ski trails when snow is present. Hiking is not allowed on the bike trails, and biking is not allowed on the hiking trails.

Finding the trailhead: From downtown Milwaukee follow I-43/WI 57 north for 24.4 miles and take exit 97 on the left to stay on WI 57 toward Plymouth for another 19.4 miles after it splits from I-43. Turn left onto WI 28, go 1.9 miles, and turn right onto CR V. Follow this 6.5 miles, turn right to stay on it, and continue another 1.5 miles. Turn left onto Butler Lake Road/ Kettle Moraine Scenic Drive. The park entrance is 0.5 mile on the left. The parking lot is on the right as you enter, and the trailhead is at the far end of the lot. **GPS:** N43 39.784' / W88 8.202'

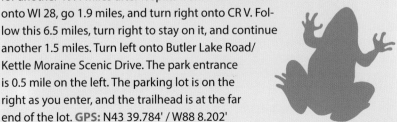

THE HIKE

What spans this park and the hike itself might appear to be a moraine, but the long, narrow mound of glacial till you see here heading southwest is actually an esker, part of the 4-mile Parnell Esker, to be exact. Butler Lake lies between two eskers, in fact, collecting the water flowing in from Flynn's Spring to the south. Surrounded by sedge meadow, the lake is part of a state natural area and home to at least two rare species: the unicorn clubtail dragonfly and the swamp spreadwing.

From the parking lot the hiking trail heads southwest with the esker rising up on your left side. White posts with purple tips mark the trail. Climb a short ramp up along the edge of the esker at 0.3 mile and come to the Ice Age Trail juncture. Go right here; the trails are united for the next 0.9 mile, primarily following along

Butler Lake's loop trail shares some mileage with the Ice Age National Scenic Trail. Preamtip Satasuk

the narrow back of the esker, often about 30 to 40 feet above the surrounding terrain. In addition to purple markers you can see yellow blazes marking the Ice Age Trail. At 0.6 mile the trail descends left, where you can see a water-filled depression on the right, and then climbs back onto the esker.

Pass the Mile 16 marker for the Ice Age Trail at 0.8 mile and watch for the kettles on either side. Soon you come to a high peak in the trail; the view all around is down. You are the king of all you survey. Past the 1.0-mile marker the canopy opens a bit, and at 1.1 miles you cross the equestrian trail and pass a map board. Just 500 feet later the Ice Age Trail splits off to the right, curling south to CR F, but you go left here. At 1.4 miles the trail passes around a kettle on the left and skirts a clearing. A sign indicates 1.5 miles just before the trail crosses the edge of the kettle and continues over the rolling terrain in a northwesterly direction. Cross the horse trail at 1.6 miles; soon after, the trail is unshaded and grassy. It follows a long, straight descent at 2.4 miles, heads back into the woods, and passes through a low area that can get a bit muddy. The trail then climbs again, returning to the Ice Age Trail juncture at 2.8 miles. Turn right and hike along the back of the esker again with a steep slope to your left. Just before you reach the parking lot, there is a bench with a nice view through the trees of Butler Lake.

From the bench continue to a wooden fence; the trail goes left and down a few earth-and-wood-beam steps to the parking lot. Across the park road, slightly to the right, are similar steps up the next ridge; this is the continuation of the Ice Age Trail if you want to extend the hike a bit. At the parking lot you are 4.6 miles from Parnell Tower, 7.5 miles from Greenbush Kettle Shelter #5, and 8.5 miles from Greenbush Group Camp.

Parnell Esker

Often it is said that the glaciers "retreated" at the end of the last ice age, but of course what is meant is they melted away (unlike their advance, which truly was movement forward across the land). Meltwater on the surface, even as the glaciers still advanced, found its way down into cracks and eventually formed flowing streams and rivers that passed through tunnels beneath the ice. As the waters rushed through, they deposited a mix of sand and gravel along the winding corridors. When the glaciers disappeared, those long, snaking mounds of sediment remained. Parnell Esker within Kettle Moraine is one such example, running nearly 4 miles and reaching a height of about 35 feet. The gap allowing passage from the parking lot at Butler Lake to the lake itself was likely human made, but other natural gaps as well as the varying heights are as the ice left them.

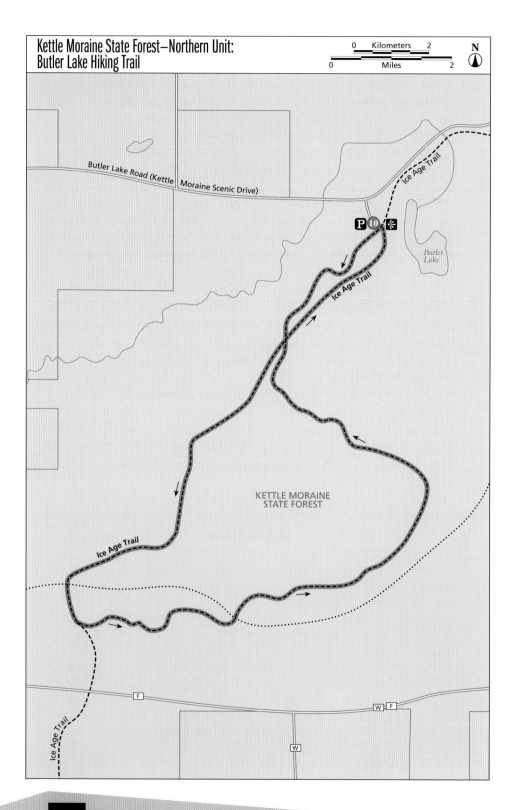

MILES AND DIRECTIONS

0.0 Start from the trailhead, following along the side of Parnell Esker.

0.3 At the juncture with the Ice Age Trail, go right.

1.1 Cross the equestrian trail.

1.2 Come to the Ice Age Trail juncture, departing to the right; go left on the purple-marked Butler Lake Trail.

1.6 Go straight across the equestrian trail.

2.8 Return to the first Ice Age Trail juncture and go right.

3.0 Pass the scenic overlook and descend the steps to the parking lot.

3.1 Arrive back at the trailhead and parking lot.

HIKE INFORMATION

Local Information
Butler Lake Flynn's Spring State Natural Area, http://dnr.wi.gov

Lodging
Camping available at Long Lake Recreation Area, (920) 533-8612, or Mauthe Lake Recreation Area, (262) 626-4305; register at park entrance stations or reserve at (888) 947-2757 or www.reserveamerica.com.

Organizations
Ice Age Trail Alliance, 2110 Main St., Cross Plains, WI 53528; (800) 227-0046; www .iceagetrail.org

Kettle Moraine State Forest—Northern Unit: Summit Trail

Short and sweet but also a bit steep. Situated inside Long Lake Recreation Area, this trail climbs the third-highest point in the entire Kettle Moraine—Dundee Mountain. Actually a moulin kame, this mound of glacial deposits rises 270 feet above the land. The views from the slope are exceptional, and at the top you can see the forest sloping away in all directions. The descending return trail crosses an esker and goes past an erratic. Some educational signage along the route enhances the experience and teaches some ice age geological vocabulary.

Start: From the trailhead along the loop for the campground's 900s sites

Distance: 1.0-mile lollipop (plus 0.8 mile round-trip from the lot to the trailhead)

Hiking time: 1 hour

Difficulty: Easy with some moderately steep stretches

Trail surface: Dirt, grass, rocks, roots

Best season: Spring through fall

Other trail users: None

Canine compatibility: Leashed dogs permitted

Land status: State park

Fees and permits: Vehicle admission sticker required; available for purchase at park entrance, state forest headquarters, or Ice Age Visitor Center

Schedule: Daily, 6 a.m. to 11 p.m.

Maps: USGS Dundee; at park office and on website

Trail contact: Long Lake Recreation Area Entrance Station; (920) 533-8612; http://dnr.wi.gov
   Kettle Moraine State Forest—Northern Unit, Forest Headquarters, N1765 Hwy. G, Campbellsport, WI 53010; (262) 626-2116; http://dnr.wi.gov

Special considerations: Getting to the trailhead requires a 0.4-mile walk from the parking area. Consider this extra 0.8 mile in addition to the trail length when planning your hike.

Finding the trailhead: From downtown Milwaukee follow I-43/WI 57 north for 24.4 miles and take exit 97 on the left to stay on WI 57 toward Plymouth for another 16.4 miles after it splits from I-43. Turn left onto CR W, go 11.2 miles, and turn left onto CR F. Follow this 1 mile and turn right onto Division Road/Kettle Moraine Scenic Drive. Continue 1.1 miles and enter the Long Lake Recreation Area on the left. Go past the entrance station to the first left—follow the arrow toward the campgrounds—and continue past the loops of campsites until you find the entrance to the 800s sites. Here on the right is a parking lot opposite the entrance (**GPS:** N43 39.656' / W88 9.858').

Park here and walk toward the 900s. At the first road juncture go left toward sites 922–967. At the next intersection go left again (it says Do Not Enter for cars). Pass a water fountain on the right and Site #946 on the left; the trail entrance is on the left side of the road. **GPS:** N43 39.440' / W88 10.069'

THE HIKE

The hike begins across a short, grassy stretch that gives way to crushed stone heading gradually uphill. Dundee Mountain is visible through the trees ahead and to the left. The trail is only partly shaded here. On your left, just 500 feet from the trailhead, is a trail on your left and interpretive sign #8 (this is your return trail). Go just a few paces past this trail to the next trail on your left that heads *up* the hill; turn left here onto a narrow footpath of crushed rock. The trail you started on continues straight ahead, past the Summit Trail another 0.5 mile south to CR F.

The path shows some earth and wood-beam steps, and a colony of aspen is on the left, but to the right (south) a great view unfolds as you climb, out to hills in the distance. A couple of benches at the park's Point 2 face what is a glacial outwash plain and moraines left behind by the Lake Michigan and Green Bay lobes of the most recent glaciers.

The trail continues through a bit of woods with a steep slope off the path on your left. When you come out from the canopy once again, you now have a view

A scenic overlook from the slope of Dundee Mountain.

north, on your left. At a wooden fence and some benches, stop and take in the view of Long Lake and out much farther to wind turbines on the horizon. Drumlins—conspicuously humpbacked hills—are also visible. Continue on, back into the woods, and soon you are on the very highest point of the kame. Land slopes away in all directions; you are straddling Dundee Mountain. If you are not significantly amazed by all this, consider that this is the third-largest pile of rubble formed *under* the ice of the glacier. Imagine how much higher the layer of ice over the entire landscape was.

The trail continues, still only about 0.5 mile from the trailhead, down the other side of the kame on a long S-curve of steps with nice views into the forest. The trail switches back and descends more steps, and at the Point 5 interpretive sign, you are standing on an esker, a serpentine ridge of deposits left by a meltwater river in an ice tunnel under the glacier. A short distance past that is an erratic, a boulder dragged here from somewhere else by the glacier. The trail comes to a clearing, curves left through a small field, and crosses terrain rising and falling like wave crests. Pass a wet kettle on the right and climb a steep but short ramp back up to Point 8. Take the trail to the right back out to the trailhead, then follow the park road back to the parking lot.

You Kame, You Saw, You Conquered

Kames such as Dundee Mountain are another type of glacial formation. Cracks and depressions formed in the massive sheets of ice when the glaciers finally began to melt and retreat, and glacial till—that material ground off the landscape by the force of the glacier moving across the earth—accumulated in these depressions. When the ice melted away, these tall, often oddly shaped hills were left behind. In Dundee's case it is a moulin kame. A moulin is a narrow, mostly vertical tube that allows meltwater on the glacier's surface to descend into the depths of the ice, providing lubricating water underneath the ice sheet, which can promote glacier movement. Sand and gravel carried down through a moulin and deposited at the bottom formed this kame. The basilica at Holy Hill sits atop the largest kame in the Kettle Moraine. Powder Hill, a close second, lies at the center of the Pike Lake Unit of the state forest. Hikes around both of them are included in this book.

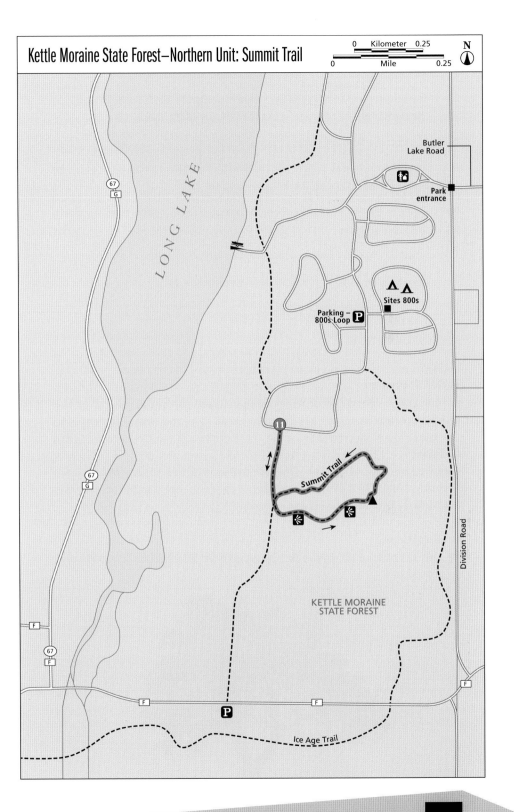

Kettle Moraine State Forest–Northern Unit: Summit Trail

0   Kilometer   0.25

0   Mile   0.25

N

LONG LAKE

67
G

67
G

F

67
F

Butler
Lake Road

Park
entrance

Sites 800s

Parking –
800s Loop

11

Summit Trail

KETTLE MORAINE
STATE FOREST

Division Road

F

F

F

F

Ice Age Trail

MILES AND DIRECTIONS

0.0 Start from the parking area and walk to campsite #946; the trailhead is to the right of the site (when facing the left side of the road).

0.4 Start up the Summit Trail.

0.6 Pass the return trail on the left, marked by Point 8 on a park sign, and take the next trail up and to the left, climbing the hill.

0.9 Arrive at the summit at the Point 4 interpretive sign, then continue down the S-curve steps.

1.3 Return to Point 8's trail juncture and go right, back to the campground.

1.4 Take the park road to the right back toward your car.

1.8 Arrive back at the parking lot.

HIKE INFORMATION

Local Information
Ice Age Visitor Center, N2875 WI 67, Campbellsport, WI 53010; (920) 533-8322; http://dnr.wi.gov

Lodging
Camping available at Long Lake Recreation Area, (920) 533-8612, or Mauthe Lake Recreation Area, (262) 626-4305; register at park entrance stations or reserve at (888) 947-2757 or www.reserveamerica.com.

Organizations
Ice Age Trail Alliance, 2110 Main St., Cross Plains, WI 53528; (800) 227-0046; www .iceagetrail.org

Kettle Moraine State Forest—Northern Unit: Zillmer Hiking Trails

A popular skiing route in winter, the Zillmer Trails, named for Raymond Zillmer, whose vision brought us the Ice Age National Scenic Trail, is also a fantastic place for a hike on the several color-coded trails. A creek runs through the park, and at the north end is a short spur trail out to the Ice Age Visitor Center—a nice place to take a break along the outer Yellow loop on which this trek is based. In addition to healthy forest and abundant glacial formations, the trail passes wetlands in its last mile.

Start: From the trailhead near the parking lot

Distance: 5.4-mile loop

Hiking time: 3 hours

Difficulty: Moderately difficult due to length and a lot of rolling ski trail terrain

Trail surface: Packed dirt, mowed grass

Best season: Spring through fall

Other trail users: Skiers in winter

Canine compatibility: Leashed dogs permitted

Land status: State park

Fees and permits: Vehicle admission sticker required; available for purchase at park entrances, state forest headquarters, or Ice Age Visitor Center

Schedule: Daily, 6 a.m. to 11 p.m.

Maps: USGS Kewaskum; at park offices, Ice Age Visitor Center, and on website

Trail contacts: Kettle Moraine State Forest—Northern Unit, Forest Headquarters, N1765 Hwy. G, Campbellsport, WI 53010; (262) 626-2116; http://dnr.wi.gov; Ice Age Visitor Center, N2875 WI 67, Campbellsport, WI 53010; (920) 533-8322; http://dnr.wi.gov

Special considerations: Hiking and dogs are not allowed on ski trails when snow is present. Hiking is not allowed on the bike trails, and biking is not allowed on the hiking trails.

Finding the trailhead: From Milwaukee take WI 145 north and take the exit onto US 41/45 north toward Fond du Lac. After 10.5 miles keep right and follow US 45 for another 25.2 miles. Turn right onto WI 67, drive 0.8 mile, and take the first right onto CR SS. Stay on CR SS for 1.8 miles; the Zillmer Trails entrance is on the left. Drive into the second parking lot; the trailhead is near the facilities and the handicap parking spots. **GPS:** N43 37.126' / W88 11.781'

THE HIKE

This nice network of nested trails is dedicated to Ray Zillmer, and you can see a boulder with his name on a plaque near the trailhead. The hike described here is the Yellow loop, the longest. The Red (3 miles) and Green (1.8 miles) head into the park's interior near the Zillmer Trail Shelter #6. They are hilly trails, but the distance and moderately steep climbs of the Yellow Trail still make it the most challenging. The 1.2-mile Brown Trail offers the least resistance, but you get what you work for.

Pass the parking lot shelter on its left side and be sure to take the trail to the right of Zillmer's plaque. The trails throughout the park are wide, often grassy, best for accommodating skiers. The moraines left behind by the glaciers created challenging terrain—at many places the trail rises and falls quickly and steeply. At the first turn the trail skirts the edge of the woods, looking out to the right over prairie, but by 0.25 mile the path heads into the trees. At 0.5 mile the Red and Green Trails split off to the left, and the Yellow Trail doesn't see them again until two-thirds of the way to the finish line.

At 0.7 mile the path enters thick hardwood forest, and without the benefit of sun, the trail shows packed dirt and scattered rock. Views now are of the land beneath your feet sloping away into deep ravines in several places. A brief passage through the open at 1.3 miles brings you past a bench marked on the map

A scenic overlook from a bluff along Zillmer Trails. Preamtip Satasuk

as a scenic overlook; perhaps this is true when the leaves aren't on the trees. Then it's back through the woods, mostly maple, some oak and hickory, and soon the trail is right along the narrow back of a ridge with land sloping on either side. The understory is low and broad-leafed like a glowing green sea.

At 1.9 miles a trail on the right offers a short connection to the Ice Age Visitor Center, which has facilities plus an abundance of information and some exhibits. It's about 1,000 feet to the front door from here. Otherwise, take the trail to the left up a steep hill and find a bench and scenic overlook on the left. Footpaths into the woods on the right are part of the short, double-loop system for the visitor center. Continue on the Yellow Trail down from the overlook. Cross a clearing where a pipeline passes unseen underground at 2.2 miles, and 0.1 mile later watch for a wet kettle on the right just before you cross a wooden bridge over Lake Fifteen Creek.

At 2.9 miles is a map board, and from the left the Red Trail joins the Yellow. Stay to the right. Not 1,000 feet later the Red Trail departs on the left again, heading toward the trail shelter; keep right again. Enter pine plantation for 0.25 mile starting at 3.2 miles; by 4.0 miles the trail is showing some moderately steep

The Father of the Ice Age Trail

Raymond T. Zillmer (1887–1960), a graduate of the University of Wisconsin and a lawyer from Milwaukee, felt very passionately about the natural beauty of Kettle Moraine. As a hiker and naturalist he understood its importance not only as an area of geological study, but also as an object of natural beauty and a destination for outdoor recreation. He was a member of both the Sierra Club and Alpine Club, and at one point was president of the Izaak Walton League, an organization dedicated to the outdoors and protecting natural resources. But most importantly perhaps, he founded what is now the Ice Age Trail Alliance.

Zillmer pushed to have many of the glacial formations we see today protected as a national scientific reserve. He started with Kettle Moraine, helping to find support for a state forest that now preserves more than 50,000 acres. Then he worked to create a trail that would give residents easy access to this remarkable display of the glaciers' work. Unfortunately he passed away before that dream came to fruition. In his will he left funds for the creation of the five shelter houses for distance hikers along the trail through Kettle Moraine's Northern Unit. But his passion had spread, and starting with that first trail, an army of volunteers started blazing trail along the area where the last advance of ice ended. Twenty years after Zillmer's death, President Jimmy Carter signed the law establishing the Ice Age National Scenic Trail, and decades later the Ice Age Trail Alliance and its many volunteers continue the work to complete what will be a 1,000-mile trek through Wisconsin.

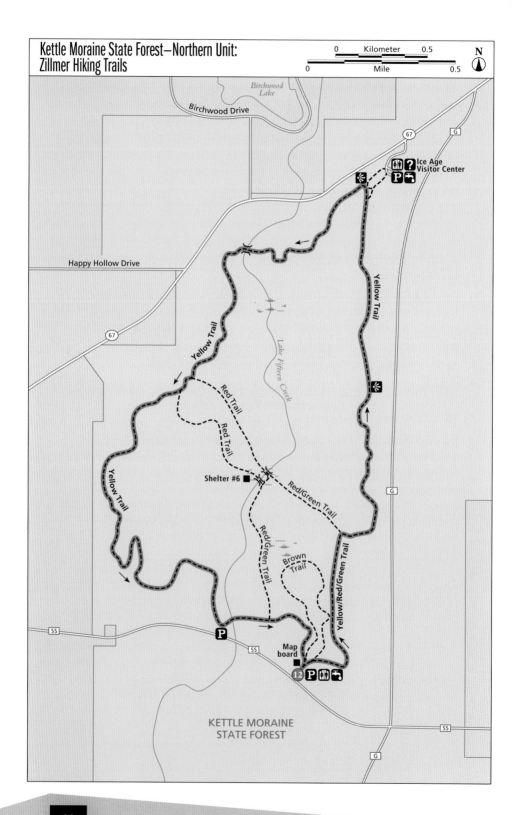

Kilometer

Mile

N

Birchwood Lake

Birchwood Drive

67

G

Ice Age
Visitor Center

Happy Hollow Drive

Yellow Trail

67

Yellow Trail

Lake Fifteen Creek

Yellow Trail

Red Trail

Red Trail

Shelter #6

Red/Green Trail

G

Red/Green Trail

Brown
Trail

Yellow/Red/Green Trail

SS

P

SS

Map
board

12 P

KETTLE MORAINE
STATE FOREST

G

SS

G

areas. Springs and rain can cause areas around the 4.5-mile mark to get a little soggy, and at 4.6 miles wetlands with open water appear to the left. The trail passes a parking lot with a wooden fence around it off CR SS, skirting the corner of the lot before descending left of it and crossing a culvert with a tiny stream running through it. At 5.0 miles the Red and Green Trails merge from the left and join the Yellow for the last 0.4 mile to the trailhead and parking lot.

MILES AND DIRECTIONS

0.0   Start from the trailhead for the Yellow Trail.

0.5   At the trail juncture with the Red and Green Trails, take the Yellow to the right.

1.9   Come to a juncture with a trail on the right, leading out to the Ice Age Visitor Center; take the left trail to continue the loop.

2.5   Cross Lake Fifteen Creek on a wooden bridge.

2.9   At the juncture with the Red Trail, take the trail to the right.

3.0   The Red Trail departs on the left again; take the Yellow Trail to the right.

3.6   Cross over a culvert and a small stream.

4.8   At an alternate gravel parking lot and wooden fence, follow the trail as it angles away to the left.

5.0   The Red and Green Trails join from the left; take the trail to the right.

5.4   Arrive back at the trailhead.

HIKE INFORMATION

Lodging
Camping available at Long Lake Recreation Area, (920) 533-8612, or Mauthe Lake Recreation Area, (262) 626-4305; register at park entrance stations or reserve at (888) 947-2757 or www.reserveamerica.com.

Organizations
Ice Age Trail Alliance, 2110 Main St., Cross Plains, WI 53528; (800) 227-0046; www .iceagetrail.org

13

Kettle Moraine State Forest—Northern Unit: Tamarack Circle Hiking Trail

A simple circle trail around Mauthe Lake includes two bridges over the East Branch of the Milwaukee River, which flows through the lake. Along the way is a mix of different kinds of forest, including some white cedars and tamaracks, that offers a nice habitat for birds. Unlike many other Kettle Moraine hikes, this one is quite flat. The last stretch of the trail passes through a developed park, including a playground and a swimming area.

Start: From the trailhead in the parking lot for the boat landing.
Distance: 2.3-mile loop
Hiking time: 1 hour
Difficulty: Easy, but sometimes floods
Trail surface: Crushed stone, dirt
Best season: Spring through fall
Other trail users: Bicyclists
Canine compatibility: Dogs not permitted
Land status: State park
Fees and permits: Vehicle admission sticker required; available for purchase at park entrances, state forest headquarters, or Ice Age Visitor Center
Schedule: Daily, 6 a.m. to 11 p.m.

Maps: USGS Kewaskum; at park offices, Ice Age Visitor Center, and on website
Trail contacts: Kettle Moraine State Forest—Northern Unit, Forest Headquarters, N1765 Hwy. G, Campbellsport, WI 53010; (262) 626-2116; http://dnr.wi.gov; Ice Age Visitor Center, N2875 WI 67, Campbellsport, WI 53010; (920) 533-8322; http://dnr.wi.gov
Special considerations: In periods of rainy weather, some portions of the trail may become soggy or even flooded. Contact the park to be sure. Signs are usually posted. No pets are allowed on the hiking-only sections of the trail, but are permitted on the bike path.

Finding the trailhead: From Milwaukee take WI 145 north and take the exit onto US 41/45 north toward Fond du Lac. After 10.5 miles keep right and follow US 45 for another 18 miles. In Kewaskum turn right onto Main Street/WI 28, drive 0.5 mile, and turn left onto CR S/Riverview Drive. Stay on CR S through a couple of turns over the next 6.3 miles. Then turn left onto CR GGG, which is still the scenic drive. Go 0.9 mile and enter Mauthe Lake Recreation Area on the left. At the fork past the entrance station, go left, following the park road to the boat landing parking lot. The trailhead is on the left as you enter the lot. **GPS:** N43 35.955' / W88 11.018'

THE HIKE

The Milwaukee River begins in several places northwest of the city itself, and the East Branch of the river rises up around Long Lake before passing through the kettle-formed Mauthe Lake. The lake was originally called Moon Lake, but the name was changed to honor William Mauthe, a former head of the Wisconsin Conservation Commission, the precursor of the Department of Natural Resources, whose efforts and leadership resulted in the acquisition of much of the land that makes up the Kettle Moraine State Forest today.

Start down the trail with the lake on your right; in 500 feet you cross a wide wooden bridge over the Milwaukee River's East Branch. For this first 0.5 mile, bicyclists and hikers share the same path. On the other side of the bridge, the water is no longer visible, but the land on either side is still soggy, showing wetland plant life and tall grasses. Go a little farther and maple trees start to offer a bit of shade on the trail, and at 0.3 mile the trail bends right and heads into pine forest, gaining a bit of elevation. The woods are loaded with red squirrels in this

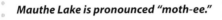

Mauthe Lake is pronounced "moth-ee."

Tamarack Trail circles Mauthe Lake and at times runs quite close to its edge. Preamtip Satasuk

park. Oak trees show in the woods and the trail is shaded more. The first trail juncture is at 0.5 mile, where the bike path continues straight while the narrow, crushed-rock footpath heads to the right. No pets are allowed on the hiking-only sections of the trail.

The brush is thick and the canopy thin, and you enter pine plantation just as you come to the park road to the state forest headquarters at 0.7 mile. Go straight across the road and pick up the footpath again. The pine plantation lasts 0.25 mile and then the brush thickens again as you pass through younger trees. Cross an arching wooden bridge over the incoming branch of the Milwaukee River at the 1.0-mile mark. Beyond here is the lowest segment of the trail and where you might find soggy footing. The crushed rock does help keep mud at bay, but not always. Flowers and ferns are more abundant along this section, and by 1.5 miles you see white cedars and stands of tamaracks.

As you come around the lake, you pass short spur trails out into the camping area on your left and skirt a park road at 1.7 miles; stay with the footpath right along the lake's edge. At 1.9 miles you enter a mowed area with water and pit toilets to the left and a bench overlooking the water on your right. Pass through some trees and then head into the larger recreation area with a playground and changing house for the swimming beach. Just before the beach house, take the asphalt path to the right; it heads around the building and straight into some cottonwoods. The path goes through this last strip of woods and returns to the parking lot and trailhead.

Tamaracks

Known in formal circles as *Larix laricina*, the tamarack is a variety of larch tree. Tamarack wood is durable and flexible, and Native Americans found many uses for it. The common name itself comes from an Algonquian word that means "tree used for snowshoes." While the tree has clusters of 1-inch-long green needles and bears small cones, it is not a true evergreen. In autumn the needles change to a bright yellow color and fall off. Tamaracks like wet areas, and the trail around Mauthe Lake definitely qualifies. Look for them in marshlands, bogs, and low areas.

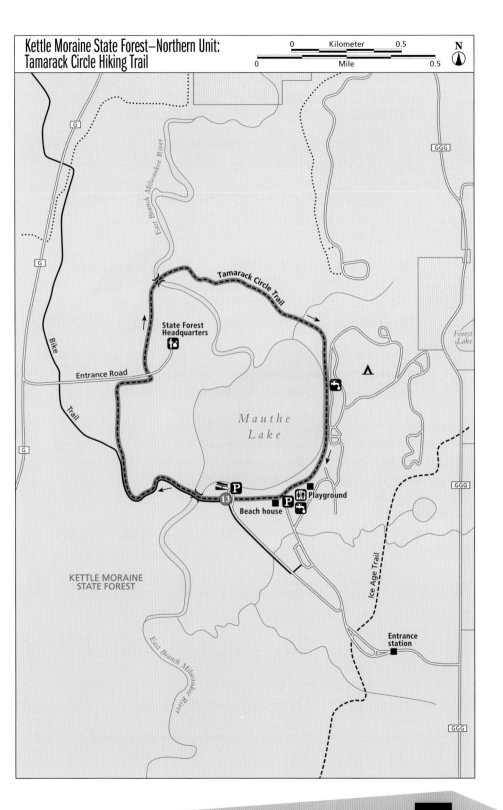

Kettle Moraine State Forest–Northern Unit:
Tamarack Circle Hiking Trail

MILES AND DIRECTIONS

0.0   Start from the trailhead on the left side (facing the lake) of the boat landing parking lot.

0.1   Cross the bridge over the East Branch Milwaukee River.

0.5   Leave the bike path and follow the footpath on the right.

0.7   Cross the park road and pick up the trail on the other side.

1.0   Take the bridge across the East Branch Milwaukee River again.

1.9   Pass through a mowed area with a bench on the right and a water fountain on the left, then continue on to a picnic area.

2.1   Pass the beach house and enter the woods.

2.3   Arrive back at the parking lot and trailhead.

HIKE INFORMATION

Lodging
Camping available at Long Lake Recreation Area, (920) 533-8612, or Mauthe Lake Recreation Area, (262) 626-4305; register at park entrance stations or reserve at (888) 947-2757 or www.reserveamerica.com.

Organizations
Ice Age Trail Alliance, 2110 Main St., Cross Plains, WI 53528; (800) 227-0046; www .iceagetrail.org

Kettle Moraine State Forest—Northern Unit: New Fane Hiking Trails

This is a compact ski area, compared to others in the Kettle Moraine, and as such offers a rugged but short trek through varying terrain—hardwood forest, a glimpse of wetlands, and some very nice ridges of glacial deposits. Dedicated bike trails keep the wheels off your heels, while the views of slopes, ravines, and kettles give you something to pause and admire.

Start: From the trailhead near the parking lot

Distance: 3.1-mile loop

Hiking time: 1.5 hours

Difficulty: Moderate due to a lot of up and down

Trail surface: Grass, packed dirt

Best season: Spring through fall

Other trail users: Skiers in winter

Canine compatibility: Leashed dogs permitted

Land status: State park

Fees and permits: Vehicle admission sticker required; available for purchase at park entrances, state forest headquarters, or Ice Age Visitor Center

Schedule: Daily, 6 a.m. to 11 p.m.

Maps: USGS Kewaskum; at park offices, Ice Age Visitor Center, on website, and on map board

Trail contacts: Kettle Moraine State Forest—Northern Unit, Forest Headquarters, N1765 Hwy. G, Campbellsport, WI 53010; (262) 626-2116; http://dnr.wi.gov; Ice Age Visitor Center, N2875 WI 67, Campbellsport, WI 53010; (920) 533-8322; http://dnr.wi.gov

Special considerations: Hiking and dogs are not allowed on ski trails when snow is present. Hiking is not allowed on the bike trails, and biking is not allowed on the hiking trails.

Finding the trailhead: From Milwaukee take WI 145 north and take the exit onto US 41/45 north toward Fond du Lac. After 11 miles keep right and follow US 45 for another 16.2 miles. Turn right onto CR H, drive 1.5 miles, and turn left onto Kettle Moraine Scenic Drive. Drive 3.4 miles and turn right onto County Line Drive; the park entrance is another 0.3 mile on your left. Go to the end of the parking lot near the shelter and find the trailhead to the right. **GPS:** N43 32.627' / W88 10.507'

THE HIKE

Start out through the grass in an open meadow along the longest of the routes: the Purple Trail. The trails are clearly marked with color-coded poles, and that's important. Several singletrack loops crisscross the hiking trail all the way around the loop. Junctures with the Green and Red Trails can be used as cutoffs, alternate routes, or simply some crisscrossing of your own if you want to extend the hike. A wide path from the left comes just after you leave the trailhead, but this is just a path to make it easier for skiers to take another lap. Stay straight and cross another similar path; this one is where the Green and Brown Trails depart to the left. Continuing on the Purple and Red, the trail reaches the end of the park property and takes a turn to the north. The woods are dominated by maple and a few other hardwoods and the occasional colony of aspen, and the trail gets some shade from the taller trees.

Mileage markers help you keep track of your progress. At 0.5 mile you come out from the canopy, but brush still lines the trail. The Green Trail comes out on your left, but you keep right. Head back into the shade; the fickle Green Trail departs to the left again as you keep right on the Purple path. The understory is thin enough that you can see deep into the woods at this point, and you can see deep ravines on either side at 0.9 mile. After 1.1 miles, you'll notice more pines in the forest and more scattered rocks on the trail. At 1.4 miles watch for

A clear view of a wet kettle along the New Fane Trails. Preamtip Satasuk

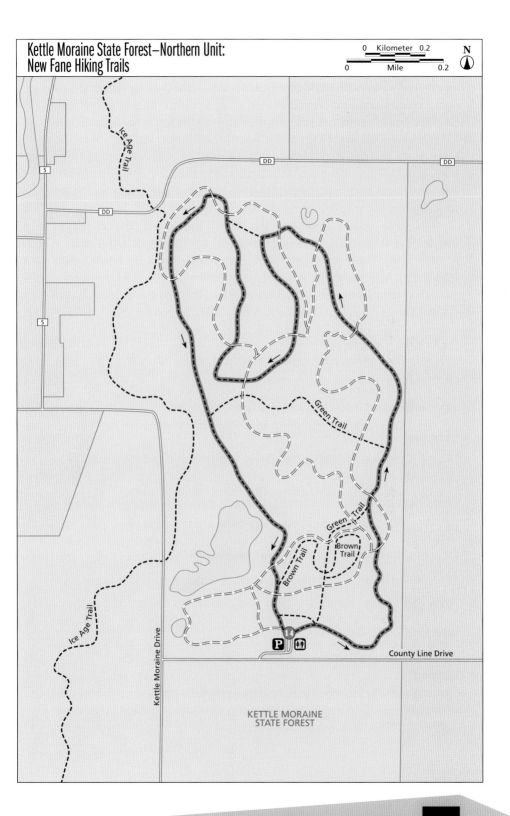

Kettle Moraine State Forest–Northern Unit:
New Fane Hiking Trails

0   Kilometer   0.2

0   Mile   0.2

N

Ice Age Trail

S

DD

DD

DD

S

Green Trail

Green Trail

Brown Trail

Brown Trail

Ice Age Trail

Kettle Moraine Drive

14

P

County Line Drive

KETTLE MORAINE
STATE FOREST

a water-filled kettle on the left. The trail takes a quick dip and brings you back up into the woods with thick canopy and brush. A marshy area lies off to your right. Come around a deep basin on your left and descend to another trail juncture. Red goes straight, but you take the Purple to the left; it heads south on a 0.7-mile-long loop and returns to the Red Trail again. (Go straight a short distance on the Red Trail if you want to skip the loop.) As you head south, a ravine is along the left side of the trail. The Purple path makes the turn, crosses a bike path, and heads back north to the Red through a bit of pine plantation. Go left when the Red Trail joins from the right, at about 2 miles.

Pass some cedars 0.1 mile after the 2.5-mile marker and come to another trail juncture as the Green once again joins the path from the left; stay straight. At 2.9 miles the trail descends to the edge of a marshy area just off to the right. After the 3.0-mile marker skip the path to the left that says Do Not Enter; it is the Brown Trail joining from the left. Shortly after this, again on the left, is the end of the trail. Follow it out to the left and into the parking and picnic area.

MILES AND DIRECTIONS

0.0   Start from the trailhead on the Purple ski trail.

0.5   Stay straight across the Green Trail joining from the left.

0.7   The Green Trail splits to the left; stay right.

1.3   At a juncture, the Red Trail continues straight ahead; take a left and stay on the Purple Trail.

2.0   The Purple Trail comes back to join the Red Trail; take the trail to the left.

2.6   Stay straight on the trail as the Green Trail meets from the left.

3.0   Pass the return trail of the Brown Trail; stay right here.

3.1   Take a left at the last trail juncture to arrive back at the trailhead and parking area.

HIKE INFORMATION

Lodging
Camping available at Long Lake Recreation Area, (920) 533-8612, or Mauthe Lake Recreation Area, (262) 626-4305; register at park entrance stations or reserve at (888) 947-2757 or www.reserveamerica.com.

Horicon National Wildlife Refuge Trails

One of Wisconsin's "Seven Natural Wonders" and an internationally recognized Ramsar site (Wetlands of International Importance), Horicon Marsh is 32,000 acres of protected wetlands, attracting hundreds of thousands of birds each year during migration. This hike follows two loops amid grasses and woods before ending along a boardwalk at the edge of the massive marsh. This hike spends less time along the edge of the waters than does the trek through the state-managed section in this book. But both are quite extraordinary, especially for bird watchers.

Start: From the trailhead in the Egret Trail parking lot
Distance: 4.3-mile series of loops
Hiking time: 2 hours
Difficulty: Easy
Trail surface: Crushed rock, boardwalks, grass
Best season: Spring through fall, especially during bird migration
Other trail users: None
Canine compatibility: Leashed dogs permitted
Land status: National wildlife refuge
Fees and permits: None
Schedule: Daily, sunrise to sunset

Maps: USGS Waupun North and South; at visitor center and posted on trail
Trail contact: Horicon National Wildlife Refuge, W4279 Headquarters Rd., Mayville, WI 53050; (920) 387-2658; www.fws.gov/refuge/horicon
Special considerations: Migration periods, May and September to November, see the most visitors, especially birders. Bring binoculars on your hike if you want to see birds; they aren't always close at hand. Field guides are a good idea as well.

Finding the trailhead: From Milwaukee take WI 145 north and exit onto US 41/45 north. Follow US 41 for 38.8 miles to WI 49 and take exit 87. Go left on WI 49 for 14.1 miles and turn left into the national wildlife refuge. Continue 1.5 miles to the parking lot for the Egret Trail on the right. The trailhead is across the road from the lot entrance next to a sign that reads Red Fox Hiking Trail. **GPS:** N43 37.111' / W88 40.248'

THE HIKE

While the marsh is lovely, it doesn't exactly lend itself to hiking, and one can only build so much boardwalk. This hike, however, offers more than 4 miles by trekking through some preserved prairie and even woodlands, with some nice places, often with benches, to admire the view from at least a marginally elevated perspective.

15

🍂 **Green Tip:**
*Consider citronella as an effective natural
mosquito repellent.*

Saving the marsh for the finale, take the Red Fox Hiking Trail and in about 250 feet come to the first trail juncture. The loop goes in either direction here; take the trail to the left through fields of wildflowers. Most of this is prairie, but over the next hill you pass through a small bit of forest. Watch for a bench with a nice overlook. At 0.6 mile the loop comes to a connecting trail to the next loop. Take this to the left, saving the other half of the Red Fox loop for your return.

A short distance later the next juncture is the Redhead Trail. Take it to the left as well and cross the park road. Along this segment there are a lot more wooded areas, but also a few areas of cattails and even a section of open water, with a bench where you can expect to spot some wildlife. The trail crosses a couple of short boardwalks, some more open water, and even a small hill, again a nice vantage point from which to really appreciate the size of the marsh. The trail crosses the park road and then passes a boulder and some prairie before it heads through trees and brush to the northern parking lot at 2.4 miles. Halfway across the lot on the right side is the next segment of trail, which is crushed rock at this point. Back in the open prairie, it is a little more than a half mile to the end of the

The boardwalk winds through the marsh at the national wildlife refuge at Horicon.

Redhead loop where you take the connector trail to the left, then follow the Red Fox Trail to the left soon after. When you get to the next juncture, take the trail to the left, crossing the boardwalk and coming back to the park road.

The final trail segment heads left along the park road, passing close by open water on your right. Soon the path heads into the woods on the right and comes out on a floating boardwalk, which heads out into the marsh, offering a couple of observation decks along the way, one of them actually shaded. At the end of the walk, a paved path connects back to the parking lot and the trailhead.

MILES AND DIRECTIONS

0.0   Start from the trailhead and take the left trail.

0.6   Take the connecting trail to the left to the next loop and go left there as well.

2.3   Cross the park road.

The Making of a Marsh

As you hike the area around Milwaukee and southeastern Wisconsin, it shouldn't come as much of a surprise that Horicon Marsh was another product of the last ice age. Before there was a marsh, there was a lake, Glacial Lake Horicon, in fact. First, the ice sheet carved away limestone to create a basin, leaving a few drumlins behind, which you can still see as islands in parts of the marsh. Then, as the Green Bay ice lobe melted, debris was deposited in the form of a moraine. This became the dam that gathered the icy waters. What is now the Rock River drained the lake slowly and wore away that natural barrier, but slowly enough that silt and peat could accumulate and eventually become this 32,000-acre marsh. But that wasn't the end of the story. European settlers came to the area and founded the town of Horicon. A local sawmill needed water power, so a dam was constructed in 1846 to build that marsh back into a lake again. The water levels rose dramatically, and the marsh was no longer. Enter the angry landowners who now needed snorkels if they wanted to see their land. The case went to the Wisconsin State Supreme Court, and in 1869 the court sided with the landowners, and the dam was removed. Soon after, it became apparent that massive amounts of birds were partial to the marsh, and despite some failed efforts to drain out plots of farmland in the early twentieth century, the marsh prevailed, and in 1927 the Horicon Marsh Wildlife Refuge Bill was passed by state government. Eventually the preserved lands grew to the current size, and now the northern two-thirds are managed as a national refuge while the southern portion is maintained by the Wisconsin Department of Natural Resources.

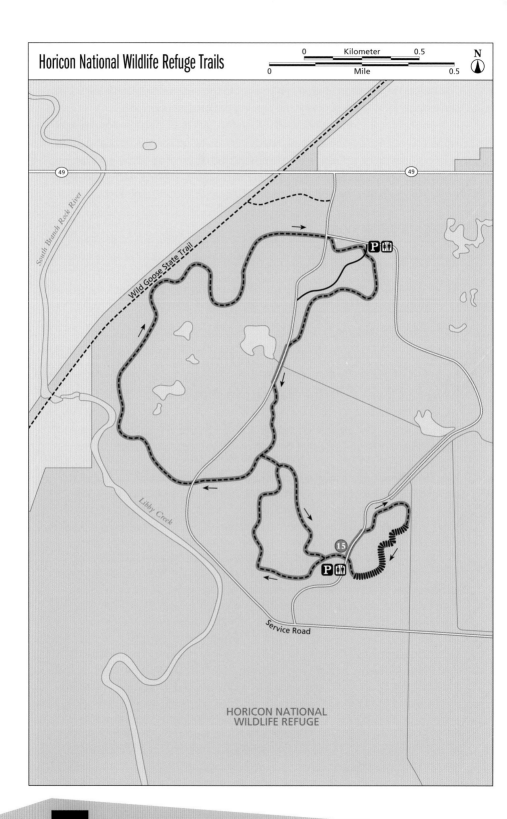

Horicon National Wildlife Refuge Trails

0   Kilometer   0.5

0   Mile   0.5

N

South Branch Rock River

Wild Goose State Trail

49

49

P

Libby Creek

15

P

Service Road

HORICON NATIONAL
WILDLIFE REFUGE

2.4 Enter the northern parking lot; the trail continues from the middle of the lot.

3.2 Take the connecting trail to the left, and go left again at the next juncture with the Red Fox Trail.

3.7 At the end of the Red Fox Trail, take the connector trail to the left and cross the road to the last trail segment.

4.0 Follow the trail along the road and onto a boardwalk as it curves to the right.

4.3 Arrive back at the trailhead and parking lot.

HIKE INFORMATION

Local Information
Friends of Horicon Marsh Education & Visitor Center, N7725 Hwy. 28, Horicon, WI 53032; (920) 387-7890; www.horiconmarsh.org

Local Attractions
Horicon Marsh Boat Tours, 311B Mill St., Horicon, WI 53032; (920) 485-4663; www .horiconmarsh.com. Boat and birding tours, canoe and kayak rentals.

Local Events
Horicon Marsh Bird Festival, http://horiconmarshbirdclub.com/bird-festival. The four-day event is held each year in early May.

Other Resources
Horicon Marsh Wildlife: An Introduction to Familiar Species by James Kavanagh, Waterford Press Ltd., 2013.

16

Horicon Marsh State Wildlife Area Trails

This hike gives several perspectives on the marsh, starting with a boardwalk along cattails and near open water, crossing an island popular for nesting birds, and climbing a hill with a view out over the entire marsh. While there are some forested segments here, much of the hike is level with the water on crushed-rock paths circling impoundments where waterfowl gather.

Start: From the trailhead next to the visitor center
Distance: 4.7-mile double loop
Hiking time: 2 hours
Difficulty: Easy
Trail surface: Crushed rock, dirt, grass
Best season: Spring through fall, especially during bird migration
Other trail users: None
Canine compatibility: Leashed dogs permitted
Land status: State park

Fees and permits: None
Schedule: Daily, 5 a.m. to 10 p.m.
Maps: USGS Waupun North and South; at visitor center and posted on trail
Trail contact: Horicon Marsh State Wildlife Area, N7725 WI 28, Horicon, WI 53032; (920) 387-7860; http://dnr.wi.gov
Special considerations: Binoculars and field guides are a good idea.

Finding the trailhead: From Milwaukee take WI 145 north and exit onto US 41/45 north. Follow US 41 for 24 miles and take exit 72 for WI 33. Turn left onto WI 33 and go 15.1 miles. Turn right onto WI 28/Clason Street and drive 1.9 miles. The visitor center is on the left, and the trailhead is to the left of the building. **GPS:** N43 28.430' / W88 36.068'

THE HIKE

Any hike should start with a visit to the Horicon Marsh Education and Visitor Center. Two floors of exhibits explain the origins of the marsh, its importance, and its residents (and migrants). The center overlooks the marsh and has a gift shop and an abundance of free information, such as birding checklists and park maps. You can get to the trails right out the back door.

From the parking lot, pass around the visitor center to the left to start on the trail. On your right is Bachhuber Impoundment, an area of open water set off by walkable dikes where you are likely to see a lot of waterfowl. A more recently added boardwalk runs parallel to the trail but is deeper into cattails if you prefer. Both come to Indermuehle Island, where you can follow a loop trail through the woods and possibly see nesting birds. A boardwalk trail off the island path connects south to an alternate parking lot along the highway.

Complete the loop of Indermuehle; the crushed-rock trail continues along the impoundment to the center of the park. Here you enter trees and brush, and the path goes to the left up the hill to where the visitor center used to be before the construction of the education center in 2009. At the top of the hill, step off the trail to find observation points giving you a wide view of the marsh and its enormity. A fixed spotting scope is available if you didn't bring binoculars.

Get back on the trail and continue south along this ridge, heading through brush and descending the hill until the path turns right, crosses the road, and continues on a trail from a parking lot there. This is the last stretch of woods; the trail then delivers you to open grasslands at the bottom of the hill you were just on at the observation point. The park service maintains roads through here, but where you are allowed to go is clearly marked. Trails venture out into the marsh with water on either side. At the end of the turn through the marsh, take the trail left into the woods, then turn left onto a service road and return to Bachhuber Impoundment. This time take a left onto the back of the dike and follow the path all the way around the impoundment back to the visitor center.

An observation deck offers a brilliant view of Horicon Marsh in the state wildlife area.

Horicon Marsh State Wildlife Area Trails

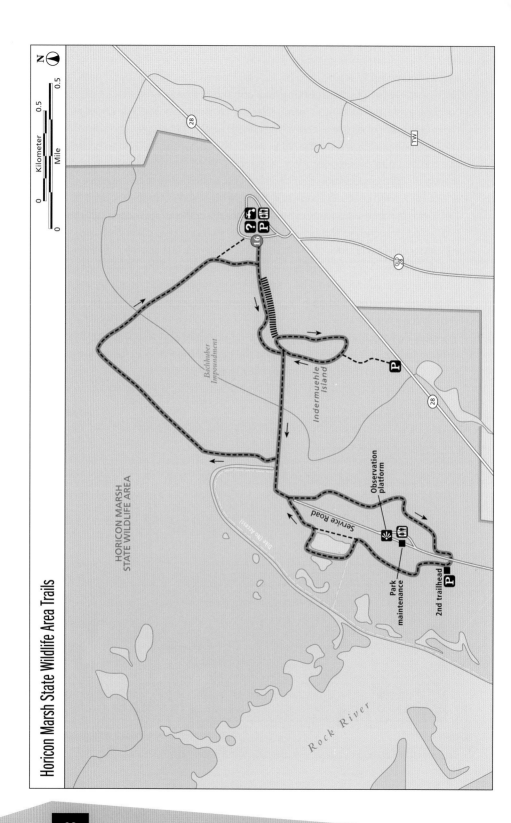

0.0 Start from the trailhead and take the path or boardwalk (they run parallel) along the water of the Bachhuber Impoundment and toward the woods straight ahead.

0.2 Take the loop trail into the trees on Indermuehle Island, then come around back to the main trail.

1.4 Pass the dike trail entering on the right as the trail heads straight into the woods and curves left up the hill.

1.9 Stop at the observation platform at the top of the hill, then continue down the trail along the southeast side of the ridge.

2.3 Cross the park road and the parking lot to find the next trailhead on the right.

2.8 Take the dike trail left out into the marsh and follow it around a half loop; turn left at the end of the half loop.

3.2 At a trail juncture in the woods, take the trail left and follow the curve to the right.

3.4 At the corner of the Bachhuber Impoundment, take the dike trail to the left, following it around the open water.

4.9 Arrive back at the trailhead just beyond the visitor center.

The Tour de Marsh

There's more ways to see the marsh, and hiking is merely one of them. Boat tours on pontoons are offered by a private outfitter, taking you into places you can't reach with your feet. Some tours are specifically for bird watching. If you are a paddler, the Horicon Marsh State Wildlife Area has a designated canoe trail (see FalconGuides' *Paddling Wisconsin*) that starts along the upper stretches of the Rock River, passes through the marsh proper, and ends up in the town of Horicon at a boat landing above the dam on the Rock River. Finally, there's pedal power: In memory of a local teacher and avid biker, Frank Dummann (1924–2007), a route map was created to outline the best course to bike or even drive around the entire marsh. The PDF maps for all exploration options are available at http://dnr.wi.gov/topic/lands/wildlifeareas/horicon.

Local Information

Friends of Horicon Marsh Education & Visitor Center, N7725 Hwy. 28, Horicon, WI 53032; (920) 387-7890; www.horiconmarsh.org

Local Attractions

Horicon Marsh Boat Tours, 311B Mill St., Horicon, WI 53032; (920) 485-4663; www .horiconmarsh.com. Boat and birding tours, canoe and kayak rentals.

Lodging

Dodge County Ledge Park, N7403 Park Rd., Horicon, WI 53032; reservations (920) 386-3700 ext. 1; www.co.dodge.wi.us/index.aspx?page=430. The park overlooks the marsh and offers camping.

Other Resources

Horicon Marsh Wildlife: An Introduction to Familiar Species by James Kavanagh, Waterford Press Ltd., 2013.

Glacial Blue Hills Recreation Area with Ice Age Trail

Laid out in a series of loops, part of the trail system is also the northern portion of the West Bend Segment of the Ice Age Trail. The loop trails pass through rough and rolling glacial terrain on a clearly marked hiking trail, but a network of mountain biking trails also crisscrosses the northern loop. Both loops start near the central parking area. The southern half, off-limits to bikers, is most scenic as it follows the back of an esker and circles a wet kettle before making the turn to head back to the parking lot.

Start: From the trailhead near the parking lot
Distance: 3.5-mile series of loops
Hiking time: 2 hours
Difficulty: Moderate due to some steep stretches and rugged trail surface
Trail surface: Dirt, sand, loose rock
Best season: Year-round, with great fall colors
Other trail users: Bicyclists in some areas but not on the Ice Age Trail portions
Canine compatibility: Dogs not permitted

Land status: City park
Fees and permits: None
Schedule: Daily, 6 a.m. to 9 p.m.
Maps: USGS West Bend; *Ice Age Trail Atlas*
Trail contact: Ice Age Trail Alliance, 2110 Main St., Cross Plains, WI 53528; (800) 227-0046; www .iceagetrail.org
Special considerations: There are no facilities here. Be aware of mountain bikers coming fast down the trail.

Finding the trailhead: From Milwaukee take WI 145 north to US 41/45. Go north about 22 miles to West Bend, staying on US 45, and take exit 71. Turn right onto Washington Street/WI 144, drive 0.3 mile, and turn left (north) onto 18th Avenue. Go 1 mile and turn left onto Jefferson Street (which becomes Beaver Dam Road). Go 0.6 mile; the parking lot is on the right. The trailhead is next to the parking entrance. **GPS:** N43 26.654' / W88 12.795'

THE HIKE

An esker, the long, often serpentine glacial deposit left behind by water flowing through ice tunnels, runs through much of this recreation area. The rough terrain makes for good hiking and mountain biking. In the northern half of this hike, the bikers have their own trails. As you complete the first loop and cross south to the next section of trail, the bikers don't follow.

From the parking lot the trail heads due north between ridges until a juncture where the Ice Age Trail, marked by yellow blazes on trees and posts, takes a right turn at 0.2 mile. The trail coming from the left is a white-blazed alternate trail for Ice Age Trail thru-hikers, and it functions as your return trail. A short distance up one of the bike trails on the right just past this juncture reveals a scenic overlook of open water below and to the east.

Back on the Ice Age Trail, the northern loop is crisscrossed by singletrack bike trails, and at 0.6 mile the Ice Age Trail departs to the right up toward CR D. Take the white-blazed trail to the left at this juncture to head back around to your starting point. The trail through here remains high, with fascinating looks into deeper ravines and kettles; the trees are primarily maples. Come back to the yellow-blazed trail at 1.3 miles and take it to the right and back to the parking lot.

The trail starts out straight between two parallel glacially formed ridges. Preamtip Satasuk

The next segment of trail begins across Beaver Dam Road to the south and is clearly marked as the Ice Age Trail. Head into the woods and at the juncture follow the trail to the left up the end of the esker. The trail heads south along the top of the esker; at 2 miles another park trail comes in from the right. Keep on the Ice Age Trail to the left, but remember this juncture for the return. The trail splits at 2.2 miles, once again offering an official white-blazed Ice Age Trail alternate path. Take the left trail, still marked by yellow blazes. (Be careful that you don't mistake the occasional unofficial footpath for the Ice Age Trail.) On the right lies a deep, water-filled kettle. At the next trail juncture, Park Avenue is ahead, just outside the woods. Take the white-blazed trail to the right; it crosses south of the deep kettle. This is your turnaround point.

The white-blazed trail heads north on the west side of that same big kettle area, then crosses through it before rejoining the yellow trail once more at 2.9 miles. At the next juncture take the trail to the left; it descends into a long, narrow valley between two ridges as it takes you back north. Just before you arrive at Beaver Dam Road, note the entrance to Hepburn Woods on the left, an optional bit of exploration, and then follow the trail as it bends right (east) and comes to the juncture. Take this to the left and cross the road to get back to the trailhead and parking lot.

Option: Extend the Hike

From the southernmost point of this hike, cross Park Avenue for an out-and-back segment on the Ice Age Trail. Houses are close on either side of this strip of woods, but the land continues to roll over moraine material. At the southern end of this segment, the trail turns to the right (west) and comes out onto a prairie-covered bluff overlooking a fast-food joint (Culver's, if you need a custard fix). The trail connects down to the street where the Ice Age Trail continues through West Bend. Hiking to here and back to Park Avenue adds 0.8 mile to your hike.

MILES AND DIRECTIONS

0.0 Start by heading north from the trailhead near the entrance of the parking lot.

0.2 At the trail juncture take the yellow-marked Ice Age Trail to the right.

0.6 Come to the juncture with the white-blazed trail where the yellow-blazed trail continues to the right; take the white-blazed trail to the left.

> *With about 1,400 caches within 10 minutes of town, West Bend calls itself the Geocaching Capital of the Midwest.*

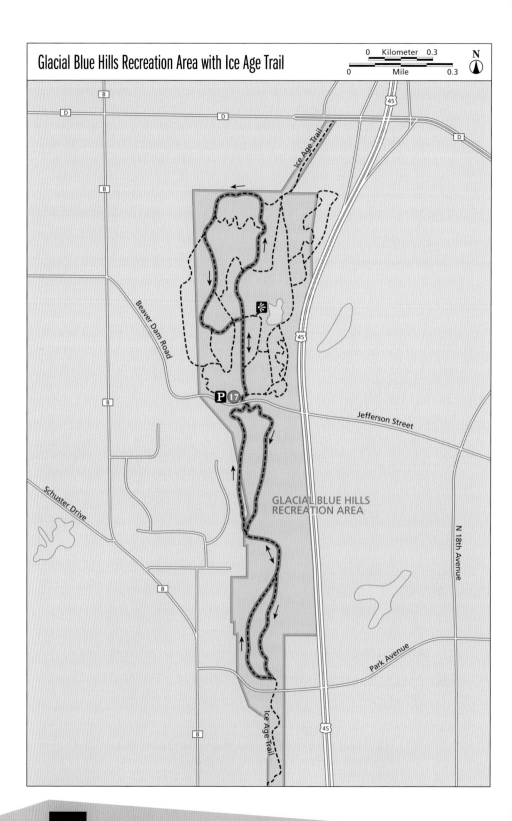

Glacial Blue Hills Recreation Area with Ice Age Trail

0   Kilometer   0.3

0   Mile   0.3

N

Ice Age Trail

45

D

B

D

B

Beaver Dam Road

45

P 17

Jefferson Street

Schuster Drive

GLACIAL BLUE HILLS
RECREATION AREA

N 18th Avenue

B

Park Avenue

Ice Age Trail

45

B

1.3   Return to the white and yellow split of the Ice Age Trail; take the trail to the right.

1.5   Cross the parking lot and Beaver Dam Road to the next Ice Age Trail trailhead.

1.6   After entering the woods again, take the trail to the left at the next juncture.

2.0   At a trail juncture, take the trail left, following the yellow blazes.

2.2   The trail splits again; take the trail to the left, still following yellow blazes.

2.5   Just before Park Avenue is a trail juncture; take it to the right on a trail marked with white blazes.

2.9   The white-blazed trail comes back to the yellow-marked trail. Take it to the left.

3.1   At the trail split, take the path to the left, leaving the yellow-blazed trail and heading to the first juncture near Beaver Dam Road.

3.5   Arrive back at the trailhead and parking lot.

HIKE INFORMATION

Local Information
West Bend Area Chamber of Commerce, 304 S. Main St., West Bend, WI 53095; (888) 338-8666; www.visitwestbend.com

Local Attractions
Museum of Wisconsin Art, 205 Veterans Ave., West Bend, WI; (262) 334-9638; www.wisconsinart.org

Green Tip:
Carry a reusable water container that you fill at the tap. Bottled water is expensive, lots of petroleum is used to make the plastic bottles, and they're a disposal nightmare.

Ice Age National Scenic Trail: Cedar Lakes Segment

This hike is along the Polk Kames, and thanks to a white-blazed alternate segment on the other side of the kames, this segment of the Ice Age Trail can be hiked round-trip without repeating too much ground. A couple of short stretches pass through rolling farmland, but most of it is in thick forest of oak, maple, and beech and follows the glacial formations. The trail loops around on the west side of the kames, passing a central pond before returning the way it came.

Start: From the trailhead by the parking area
Distance: 3.8-mile lollipop
Hiking time: 1.5 to 2 hours
Difficulty: Easy to moderate due to rustic trail surface
Trail surface: Dirt
Best season: Year-round
Other trail users: None
Canine compatibility: Leashed dogs permitted

Land status: State land
Fees and permits: None
Schedule: Daily, year-round
Maps: USGS Hartford East; *Ice Age Trail Atlas*; in a box at trailhead
Trail contact: Ice Age Trail Alliance, 2110 Main St., Cross Plains, WI 53528; (800) 227-0046; www.iceagetrail.org
Special considerations: There are no facilities at the trailhead.

Finding the trailhead: From Milwaukee take WI 145 north and exit onto US 41/45 north. Follow US 41 to WI 144 and take exit 66 for WI 144. Go north (right) on WI 144 for 0.3 mile and turn right onto CR NN/Arthur Road. Continue 0.7 mile; the parking lot is on the right. The trailhead is at the lot. **GPS:** N43 21.175' / W88 16.267'

THE HIKE

The trail heads south on a two-track along the edge of a field, but by 500 feet you are in the trees. Watch for a narrow, rustic footpath on the right marked with the yellow blaze of the Ice Age National Scenic Trail. Take this trail into the woods over gently rolling terrain through tall, stately hardwoods with sparse understory. A footbridge at 0.2 mile traverses a low, soggy spot at the edge of a small, marshy area on your left. The roll of the terrain starts to become a bit more strenuous, but never more than moderately so.

At 0.4 mile the trail comes alongside a ridge on your left and then angles slightly left between it and the next. These ridges are kames, glacial deposits formed at the bottom of downward-flowing water from a glacier, and you will see several throughout the hike. These are the Polk Kames, the largest collection of kames in Wisconsin. At 0.5 mile cross through an agricultural field—the trail is usually obvious but watch for the posts with yellow blazes—and after a row of trees, follow the trail as it angles left through more farmland before turning due east and returning to the forest. Be aware of thorny creeping plants along the trail; they like to scratch skin or snag clothing.

The trail follows a curve north and all the way around until it is heading south at the 1.0-mile mark. The ground slopes left as you traverse another kame. Smaller trees are overshadowed by towering oaks. Climb over another kame and descend to a footbridge over a low intermittent stream at 1.2 miles. Another footbridge follows. The thin understory allows you to really see the lay of the land, including a rather tall kame on the right. Pass along the southern edge of the kame and a marshy area on your left, cross another footbridge, and come to a trail juncture and map board at 1.4 miles. The trail on the right is marked with

One of several short boardwalks over low areas amid the kames. Preamtip Satasuk

white blazes, an alternate trail, but still officially the Ice Age Trail. Go left here on the yellow-blazed path. (You can go either way, though; the trails come together again less than a half mile later.)

The trail passes higher along the ridges, and you soon pass a bench and an interpretive sign about how a kame is formed. Cross a boardwalk at 1.7 miles, and 0.1 mile later come to the next juncture with the white-blazed trail. If you go straight, the Ice Age Trail continues 0.1 mile to Cedar Creek Road, which connects it west to the Slinger Segment. Take the white-blazed trail to the right and cross a boardwalk bridge. Highway noise becomes more apparent on the west side of the kames. Cross a farmer's access road to a field tucked into the woods on the right, then pass a rock wall that bears south from the edge of the trail. The trail comes out of the trees and follows the line between farm field and forest—shaded in the morning, exposed in the afternoon—heading a short distance before finding another bench and map board. Take the trail back into the woods.

Hike through another small clearing, and at 2.3 miles watch for a sign that reads Entering Sensitive Area. Down to the right is a water-filled kettle. The trail switches back, taking you down for a closer look, then crosses a boardwalk before coming back to the juncture with the yellow-blazed trail. Take it to the left and backtrack to the parking lot.

MILES AND DIRECTIONS

0.0 Start at the trailhead and head south across a field for 500 feet, then take the trail to the right.

0.2 Cross a footbridge along a marshy area.

0.5 Enter farm fields.

1.2 Cross a footbridge over an intermittent stream. Two more footbridges follow.

1.4 At the trail juncture with the white-blazed trail, go left.

1.8 Come to the second juncture and go right on the white trail.

1.9 Skirt an agricultural field.

> 🌿 **Green Tip:**
> *When hiking with your dog, stay in the center of the path and keep Fido close by. Dogs that run loose can harm fragile soils and spread pesky plants by carrying their seeds.*

Ice Age National Scenic Trail: Cedar Lakes Segment

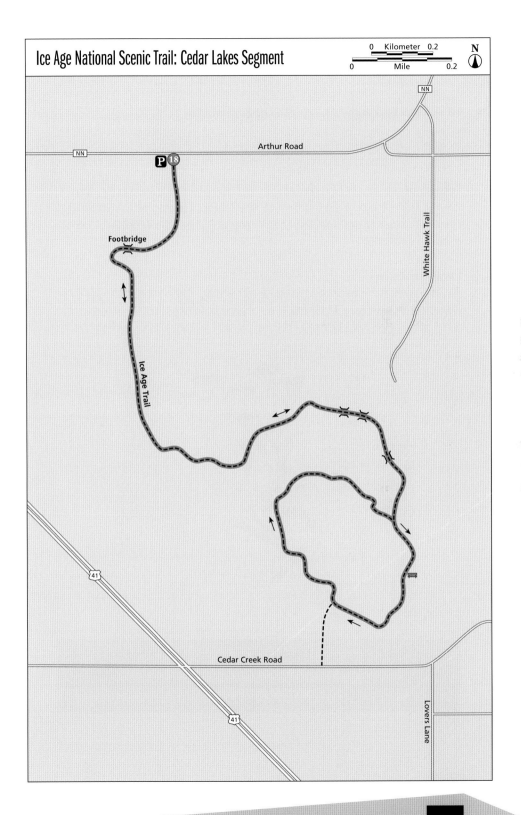

0   Kilometer   0.2

0   Mile   0.2

N

NN

Arthur Road

NN

P 18

White Hawk Trail

Footbridge

Ice Age Trail

41

Cedar Creek Road

41

Lovers Lane

2.4 Arrive back at the first trail juncture and turn left, back toward the parking lot.

3.8 Arrive back at the trailhead and parking lot.

HIKE INFORMATION

Local Information
Ice Age Trail Alliance, Washington/Ozaukee County Chapter, http://washington ozaukee.iceagetrail.org. Watch for trail events and check the website for current contact information.

Local Attractions
Held Meat Products, 480 Kettle Moraine Dr. N., Slinger, WI 53086; (262) 644-5135; www.heldsmarket.com. A popular local meat market with great beef jerky.

🌿 Green Tip:
Hiking and snowshoeing are great carbon-free winter activities!

Kettle Moraine State Forest—Pike Lake Unit Trails

This state park offers color-coded hikes through terrain characterized by glacial deposits. A 60-foot observation tower stands atop the second-highest point within the Kettle Moraine State Forest system, granting an incredible 360-degree view that is especially nice when fall colors arrive. The hike is primarily through rich forest, but abandoned farm equipment on the Green Trail shows this wasn't always the case. The Astronomy Trail is a unique feature, with interpretive signage along its length to give you perspective on the size of the universe. Pike Lake is a 522-acre spring-fed kettle, while Powder Hill at the park's center is an example of a kame—compressed sand and rock deposits left behind when the glacier melted.

Start: From the trailhead by the parking area
Distance: 4.3-mile loop (4.9 miles with spur trail to observation tower)
Hiking time: 2 hours
Difficulty: Moderate; some steep climbs, including steps up the observation tower
Trail surface: Gravel, dirt
Best season: Spring through fall, with great fall colors
Other trail users: None
Canine compatibility: Leashed dogs permitted
Land status: State park
Fees and permits: Vehicle admission sticker required; available for purchase at visitor center
Schedule: Daily, 6 a.m. to 10 p.m. Memorial Day to Labor Day; 7 a.m. to 8 p.m. otherwise

Maps: USGS Hartford East; trail map at park office, on website, and at trail junctures
Trail contact: Kettle Moraine State Forest—Pike Lake Unit, 3544 Kettle Moraine Rd., Hartford, WI 53027; (262) 670-3400; http://dnr.wi.gov
Special considerations: The park contains a segment of the Ice Age National Scenic Trail. The park office schedules free guided hikes year-round; check at the park office or website. This state park is part of the Wisconsin Explorers Program for kids; get materials at the park office. The 31 campsites are first come, first served, but it's best to reserve one at (888) 947-2757 or www.reserveamerica.com.

Finding the trailhead: From Milwaukee take WI 145 north and exit onto US 41/45 north. Follow US 41 to WI 60 and take exit 64B west toward Hartford. At 3.6 miles turn left onto Kettle Moraine Scenic Drive. Stop at the park office first if you do not have your vehicle permit. Otherwise, continue 0.9 mile; the parking lot is on the left. The trailhead is at the north end of the lot (on the right when facing the lake). **GPS:** N43 18.527' / W88 19.296'

THE HIKE

The Pike Lake Unit of Kettle Moraine State Forest is one of three stand-alone units that don't fall into the two larger Northern and Southern Units. Like Lapham Peak Unit, it is one of the more accessible of the state parks within the Kettle Moraine State Forest and has much to recommend it, including a campground, hiking/skiing trails, fishing, a swimming beach, and one particularly commanding view. At the center is Powder Hill, a moulin kame (see Dundee Mountain in the Summit Trail) that rises to an elevation of 1,350 feet, putting it 350 feet above the level of the lake, the second-highest point in Kettle Moraine. A 60-foot observation tower at the peak provides a look at the highest point, Holy Hill, out on the horizon. The site's naturalist leads scheduled hikes, and the Ice Age National Scenic Trail winds through the property. There's even a cool Astronomy Trail with facts about the planets on signs laid out to show the scale of our solar system. What's not to love?

The trail system is color coded, and the Brown Trail gives you the most mileage plus the expected climb up to the tower for the view. All trails begin at the parking area for the beach. A paved loop trail suitable for wheelchairs lies closer to the lake. All other trails start together a bit farther back from the water, but on the same north side of the lot. Follow a two-track across the mowed park area from the trailhead into the woods on crushed stone. The park's bike trail shares the trail for a short distance, but at 0.6 mile the hiking trail takes a right turn,

The trail at Pike Lake passes through rich hardwood forest. Preamtip Satasuk

leaving pedal traffic behind. The path crosses open prairie and then the park road before heading into thick woods at 0.9 mile. The understory is moderate, however, allowing you to see deep into the trees.

The next trail juncture on your right is the Green Trail, and is worth noting. This trail cuts across to the return trail of the Brown Trail, and along the way you can see old farm equipment, a reminder that the forest here was once cleared out for agriculture. Continue left on the Brown Trail and pass a spur trail to the park road on your left, but stay straight and pass along the edge of a wet kettle on the right. An unofficial connector trail crosses over to the Black Forest Nature Trail, an interpretive loop. This Black Trail intersects the Brown at 1.4 miles. At 1.5 miles is another juncture where the black loop is the trail on the right; the trail straight ahead is both the Ice Age Trail and a direct trail to the tower, which would bypass the rest of the brown loop. Take the trail to the left to stay on the longer Brown Trail, which is now sharing the path with the Ice Age Trail and Black Trail. The Black Trail departs on the left a short distance later; take the trail to the right to follow the Brown Trail.

Cross Powder Hill Road; the Ice Age Trail splits off to the left (watch for the yellow blazes on signs and trees). Fifty feet later the White Trail joins from the right, heading south past the campground and to the southern return path of the brown, shaving 1.4 miles off the hike. Stay on the main path through these two junctures and pass a short trail to a parking lot and facilities on the left. At a juncture at 2.1 miles, the end of the Astronomy Trail (part of the blue loop) is on the right. Take the Brown Trail to the left.

Follow the long loop through the east end of the property, crossing an orange-coded snowmobile trail and a white-blazed spur trail to the Ice Age Trail on the left. When the trail makes the turn west again, it comes to the Blue Trail at 3.0 miles (take the trail to the left), passes the interpretive sign for the Sun (the trailhead of the Astronomy Trail), and crosses the campground road, the White Trail (coming from the right), and finally Powder Hill Road.

The Astronomy Trail

One of the biggest hits for the kids in the Pike Lake Unit is the Astronomy Trail. Beginning near the camping overflow lot in the eastern side of the park, this 0.5-mile trail offers interpretive signage about our solar system. Starting with the Sun sign, the trail—which overlays part of the Blue Trail on the park map—is arranged so that each planet is posted at its relative distance from the sun. In other words, Mercury through Mars come rather quickly, and the greater distances of the remaining planets may surprise some. (While Pluto may have lost its official planet status, it is still out here on its own board.) There is a trail quiz available at the trailhead along with pencils. Kids who complete the quiz can pick up a little prize in the office.

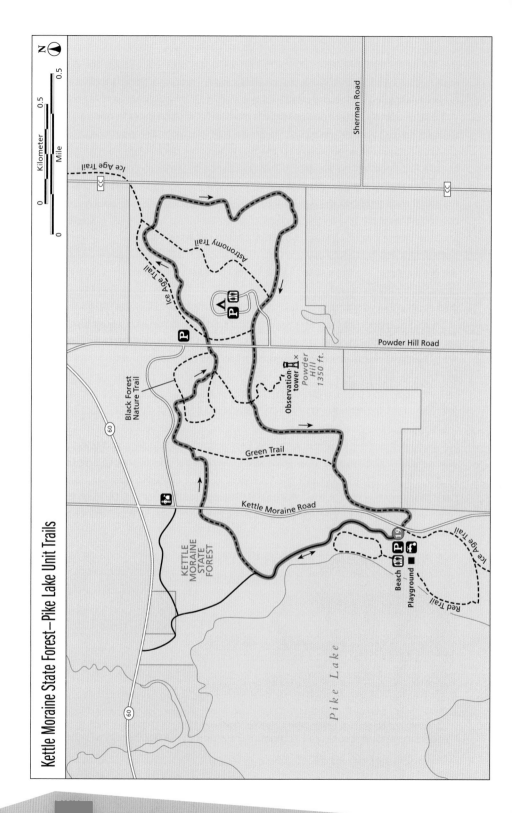

Kettle Moraine State Forest—Pike Lake Unit Trails

North of Milwaukee

N

Kilometer
0   0.5

Mile
0   0.5

Ice Age Trail

CC

Sherman Road

Astronomy Trail

Ice Age Trail

P

P

Powder Hill Road

CC

Black Forest
Nature Trail

Observation
tower
Powder
Hill
1350 ft.

Green Trail

60

Kettle Moraine Road

KETTLE
MORAINE
STATE
FOREST

Beach
Playground

P

Ice Age Trail

Red Trail

Pike Lake

60

At 3.4 miles is another juncture—the direct route for the tower and the Ice Age Trail that you passed earlier—coming in from the right. Take the trail left up a steep hill to a clearing and climb the tower. The view is extensive, as far as 25 miles on a clear day, and you can see Holy Hill to the south.

Backtrack to the trail juncture and take the Brown Trail (and the Ice Age Trail) to the left; this is also the segment of the Ice Age Trail heading south. Pass the connecting Green Trail on your right and then a park service building as the trail winds its way back toward the lake. The trail crosses Kettle Moraine Scenic Drive again to reach the parking lot. To the left is a 0.5-mile Red Trail loop in thick brush that leads closer to the lake, as well as the continuing Ice Age Trail. These might be a letdown after the Brown Trail, however.

MILES AND DIRECTIONS

0.0   Start from the trailhead, walking away from the parking lot.

0.6   Leave the bike trail, going right on the colored trails.

0.9   Cross Kettle Moraine Scenic Drive.

1.1   Reach the Green Trail juncture and go left.

1.5   Pass the Ice Age Trail and observation tower cutoff; go left.

1.6   Cross Powder Hill Road.

2.1   Reach the Astronomy Trail (Blue Trail loop) juncture; go left.

3.2   Cross Powder Hill Road again.

3.4   At a trail juncture either go left to climb the tower (adds 0.6 mile round-trip) or stay straight to skip it.

4.3   Cross Kettle Moraine Scenic Drive and arrive back at the trailhead and parking lot.

HIKE INFORMATION

Local Information
Hartford Chamber of Commerce, 1246-A E. Sumner St., P.O. Box 270305, Hartford, WI 53027; (262) 673-7002; www.hartfordchamber.org

Local Attractions
Wisconsin Auto Museum, 147 N. Rural St., Hartford, WI 53027; (262) 673-7999; www.wisconsinautomuseum.com

20

Ice Age National Scenic Trail: Holy Hill Segment

Hike a portion of the Ice Age National Scenic Trail as it passes through forest and prairie over moraines and kames. Then have a look at the Holy Hill Basilica on top of a 1,335-foot kame. From the top you can see all the way to Milwaukee.

Start: From the trailhead at the parking lot on the left of Station Way Road

Distance: 5.6 miles out-and-back (6.3 miles with the Stations of the Cross hike to the basilica, and an additional 0.4 mile for the Erratic Spur)

Hiking time: 2.5 to 3 hours

Difficulty: Moderate to difficult due to steepness and trail surface

Trail surface: Packed dirt with tree roots and loose stones; steps and asphalt for the basilica climb

Best season: Spring through fall

Other trail users: None

Canine compatibility: Dogs permitted on Ice Age Trail, but not on basilica climb

Land status: Public easement

Fees and permits: None

Schedule: Daily, no schedule for the Ice Age Trail, but basilica grounds close at 5 p.m.

Maps: USGS Merton, *Ice Age Trail Atlas*

Trail contact: Ice Age Trail Alliance, 2110 Main St., Cross Plains, WI 53528; (800) 227-0046; www.iceagetrail.org

Finding the trailhead: From Milwaukee take I-94 west and exit onto WI 16 west. At Hartland take exit 181 for WI 83 north. Follow this north through Hartland to WI 167/Holy Hill Road and turn right. At Station Way Road (past the Holy Hill entrance) take a right; in about 0.2 mile the parking lot is on your left. The trailhead is on the left as you enter the parking lot. The northbound trailhead is across Station Way Road from the lot. **GPS:** N43 14.90' / W88 19.53'

THE HIKE

A National Shrine of Mary, Holy Hill Basilica is built atop a glacial formation called a kame, formed by debris deposited by a stream that once rushed straight down from the thick sheet of ice above. This segment of the Ice Age Trail approaches from the north, passes around the kame, and heads south. Parking at the trail's southern end on Donegal Road is not permitted, but there is a small parking lot on Shannon Road just west of the northern trailhead. Additional parking/trailhead options include parking next to the trailhead on the north side of Holy Hill Road/WI 167 or in the lot at the basilica (which closes at 5 p.m.) or at St. Mary of the Hill Parish. The best option is to park in the middle of the hike on Station Way Road and hike the northern and southern halves each as an out-and-back.

Another short option is to hike the Stations of the Cross. Plenty of steps and some stretches of asphalt climb the kame past the fourteen stations to the basilica above. A visit to the top of the structure is free (donations welcome), and the view is worth the effort. You can see glacial drumlins in the distance, and on a clear day downtown Milwaukee is on the horizon. It should also be noted that this trail is incredible during the fall color season, when the views from the basilica's steeple are in Technicolor. The basilica itself is one of the most important Christian pilgrimage sites in the Midwest.

The trailhead is marked at the head of the southern half of this segment of the Ice Age Trail—the harder of the two halves. The trail makes some strenuous climbs and descents over smaller kames and moraines as it weaves its way through the forest, offering at least one good view of the basilica through the branches. Watch the trees for yellow blazes, which designate the official path. Blue blazes are spur trails that are worth exploring. The trail ends at Donegal Road, and an on-road path to the east connects it to the next segment of the national scenic trail.

From its perch atop a towering kame, Holy Hill Basilica offers an excellent view of the countryside and several glacial drumlins.

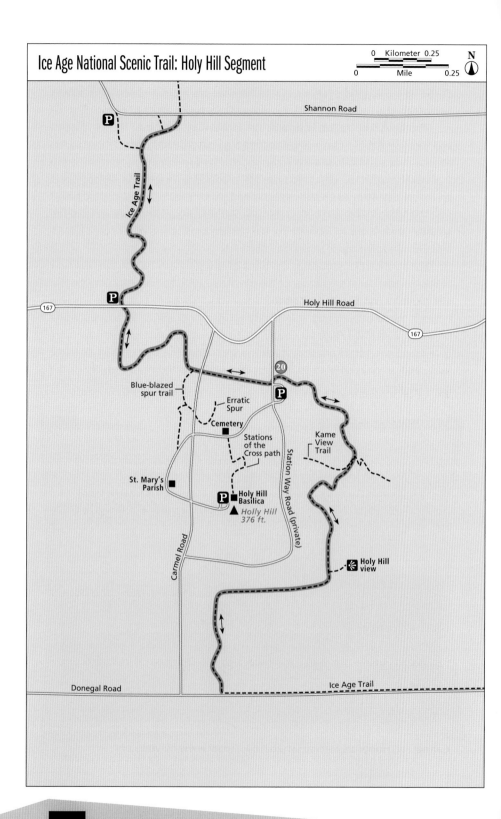

Ice Age National Scenic Trail: Holy Hill Segment

0   Kilometer 0.25

0   Mile   0.25

N

Shannon Road

P

Ice Age Trail

P

167

Holy Hill Road

167

20

Blue-blazed
spur trail

Erratic
Spur

Cemetery

Stations
of the
Cross path

P

Kame
View
Trail

St. Mary's
Parish

Station Way Road (private)

P

Holy Hill
Basilica

Holly Hill
376 ft.

Holy Hill
view

Carmel Road

Donegal Road

Ice Age Trail

The northbound half of this trail starts across Station Way Road. The narrow footpath passes through open woods, with milder inclines than those to the south, crossing Carmel Road at 0.2 mile. Just after crossing the road, watch for a blue-blazed trail on the left (blue indicates a spur on the Ice Age Trail). This trail leads to the St. Mary's parking lot and will also connect you to the Erratic Spur, which climbs steeply about 0.1 mile to a tremendous view from the top of a kame. The huge erratic boulder there is worth the climb alone. This out-and-back would add another 0.4 mile to the hike.

From the blue-blazed trail juncture, continue through the forest another 0.5 mile to Holy Hill Road. Directly across the road the trail resumes, this time through more open prairie and brush. The path continues 0.6 mile to the turn-around point at Shannon Road. Just before you reach that point, however, a spur trail leads west (left) about 0.1 mile to the Shannon Road parking lot, providing still another place to start this hike.

MILES AND DIRECTIONS

0.0   Start from the trailhead in the parking lot off Station Way Road.

0.4   Pass the Kame View Trail.

1.4   Turn around at Donegal Road.

2.8   Return to the trailhead and head north.

3.1   Cross Carmel Road.

3.5   Cross Holy Hill Road.

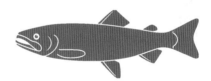

4.2   Turn around at Shannon Road.

5.6   Arrive back at the trailhead.

HIKE INFORMATION

Local Information
Ice Age Trail Alliance, Washington/Ozaukee County Chapter, http://washington ozaukee.iceagetrail.org. Watch for trail events and check the website for current contact information.

Local Attractions
The Basilica of the National Shrine of Mary, Help of Christians, at Holy Hill, 1525 Carmel Rd., Hubertus, WI 53033; (262) 628-1838; www.holyhill.com

Ice Age National Scenic Trail: Monches Segment

This segment of the Ice Age National Scenic Trail passes through the Carl Schurz Forest over glacial moraines and then descends into wetlands and lowland forest to follow the Oconomowoc River. The hike is even more impressive when fall colors hit their peak.

Start: From trailhead off County Road Q

Distance: 3.2 miles point-to-point (or 6.4 miles out-and-back)

Hiking time: 1.5 to 2.5 hours

Difficulty: Moderate to difficult due to trail surface and steepness

Trail surface: Packed dirt with roots and rocks, several boardwalks

Best season: Any season, but wet periods can be muddy

Other trail users: Foot traffic only

Canine compatibility: Leashed dogs permitted

Land status: Public easement

Fees and permits: None

Schedule: Open daily

Maps: USGS Merton; *Ice Age Trail Atlas*

Trail contacts: Ice Age Trail, Waukesha/Milwaukee County Chapter, http://waukeshamilwaukee.iceagetrail.org; Ice Age Trail Alliance, 2110 Main St., Cross Plains, WI 53528; (800) 227-0046; www.iceagetrail.org

Finding the trailhead: From downtown Milwaukee take I-94 west to WI 16. Get off in Hartland at exit 183 and go straight across Merton Avenue following Hartbrook Drive (parallel to WI 16) to North Avenue/CR E. Take this right (north) and remain on CR E all the way through Monches to where it intersects with CR K and CR Q 4 miles later. Turn left onto CR Q; the trailhead is immediately on the left. (The southern trailhead and parking lot are 0.3 mile to the west of CR E on Funk Road, 2.6 miles south of Monches.) **GPS:** N43 11.58' / W88 20.79'

THE HIKE

This trail segment connects the Loew Lake (to the north) and Merton (to the south) Segments of the Ice Age Trail. The northern portion of this segment of the Ice Age Trail is primarily up and down moraines through the forest dedicated to Wisconsin conservationist Carl Schurz. The southern portion follows along the marshy edge of the Oconomowoc River, which drains marshland here in the Kettle Moraine area. If you see yellow blazes on the trees, you are on the official Ice Age Trail. Blue blazes indicate spur trails, while unmarked trails lead elsewhere. Remember that the trail passes over private land. Respect the privilege of its use by staying on the path and leaving nothing behind but footprints. You can hike this route one-way with a pickup at the other end, or do it as an out-and-back. The trail is mostly shaded and uneven with rocks and tree roots. Mosquitoes can be an issue closer to the river. Footbridge planks can be slippery like ice when wet.

Starting from the northern trailhead, the trail heads immediately uphill. At 0.3 mile be careful to duck a wire across the trail about 5 feet off the ground; this is to keep horses off the path. A memorial boulder is just beyond. At the juncture at 1.1 miles, go left at the bench and watch for yellow blazes. The trail comes to the river at 1.5 miles and passes through a narrow stretch of trees and brush between the river on the left and farmland on the right. Just 0.1 mile later you cross the river on a bridge and some boardwalks with tree roots between them. Take care.

The northern trailhead of the Monches Segment. Preamtip Satasuk

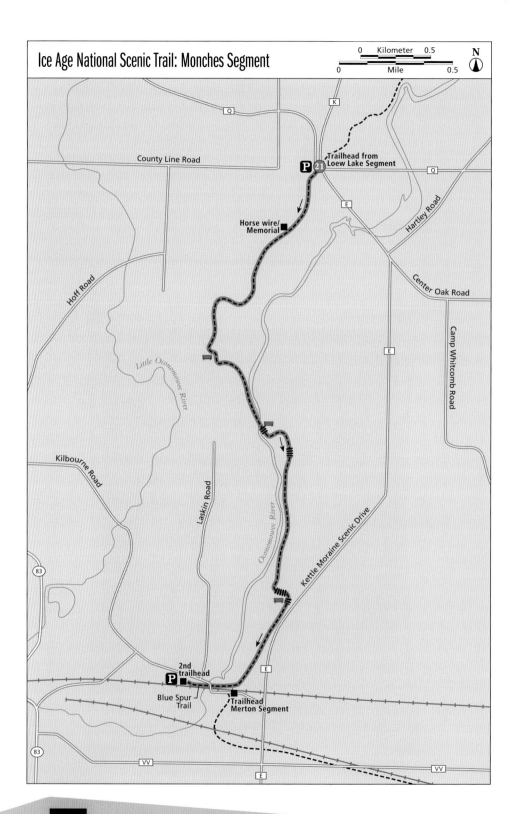

0   Kilometer   0.5

0   Mile   0.5

N

Q

K

County Line Road

P 21 Trailhead from Loew Lake Segment

Q

E

Horse wire/ Memorial ■

Hartley Road

Hoff Road

Center Oak Road

Little Oconomowoc River

E

Camp Whittomb Road

Kilbourne Road

Laskin Road

Oconomowoc River

83

Kettle Moraine Scenic Drive

2nd trailhead
P ■

E

Blue Spur Trail

■ Trailhead Merton Segment

83

VV

E

VV

The trail moves away from the river on the other side. At the next juncture follow the trail marker to the right. Cross a boardwalk over a soggy low spot at 1.8 miles. The trail nears the river once more, and heads south. The trail then comes into the open as it bends west and heads under power lines until coming out on a crushed limestone path to Kilbourne Road. To the left is the railroad viaduct. Take Kilbourne Road to the right and cross the river. On the left side of the road is the short blue segment of trail that takes you to the Ice Age Trail parking lot.

MILES AND DIRECTIONS

0.0   Start from the northern trailhead.

0.3   Pass under a horse wire.

1.1   Follow the trail to the left of the bench.

1.6   Cross the Oconomowoc River.

1.8   Use the boardwalk to cross a muddy area.

2.7   Cross a brook.

3.1   Cross Funk Road.

3.2   Arrive at the Ice Age Trail parking lot.

HIKE INFORMATION

Local Information
Monches Area Attractions, www.monchesfarm.com/areaattractions.htm

Local Attractions
Monches Farm, 5890 Monches Rd., Colgate, WI 53017; (262) 966-2787; www.monchesfarm.com. Get your green thumb on: The farm sells perennials, garden art, and more.

> 🌿🌰 **Green Tip:**
> *Keep to established trails as much as possible. If there aren't any, stay on surfaces that will be least affected, like rock, gravel, dry grasses, or snow.*

Scuppernong Springs Nature Trail. Preamtip Satasuk

Nashotah Park Green Trail

The variety of landscape in this park—including marshland, lakes, and hardwood forest—offers great habitat for birds and other wildlife, and the rolling landscape gives you scenic overlooks of the water and a little extra exercise.

Start: From the trailhead at Picnic Area #2

Distance: 3.4-mile loop

Hiking time: 1.5 to 2 hours

Difficulty: Easy to moderate due to some steepness

Trail surface: Grass, wood chips, packed dirt

Best season: Spring through fall

Other trail users: None

Canine compatibility: Leashed dogs permitted, droppings pickup required

Land status: County park

Fees and permits: Daily entrance fee or yearly vehicle sticker

Schedule: Daily, sunrise to 10 p.m.

Maps: USGS Oconomowoc East; on park website

Trail contact: Nashotah Park, W330 N5113 CR C, Nashotah, WI 53058; (262) 367-1022; www.waukeshacountyparks.com

Special considerations: The trails are groomed for skiing in the winter, but the park offers alternative trails for hiking or snowshoeing. There is a dedicated dog exercise area.

Finding the trailhead: From downtown Milwaukee follow I-94 west just past downtown Delafield and take CR C (exit 285) north 4 miles to the park entrance on the left. Drive to Picnic Area #2. The trailhead is down the hill toward the woods behind the pavilion. **GPS:** N43 6.68' / W88 24.54'

THE HIKE

For a park of 443 acres, Nashotah has quite a variety of habitats. With lakes, wetlands, savanna, meadow, cedar glades, and hardwood forest, the park is home to a variety of plants and animals, in particular songbirds.

There is a map board at the trailhead as well as most trail junctures throughout the hike. To the left of the trailhead is the entrance to the alternate Blue Trail, an easy 1.5-mile loop along the edge of Forest Lake. The Red and Green Trails start together into the forest, but the Red parts to the right at the first juncture at 0.2 mile, where there is another map board. The Red is the most strenuous but extends only 1 mile.

On the Green Trail you continue south alongside and above Forest Lake but soon descend to lake level. The trail makes a turn west and at 0.7 mile comes to a connector trail. The Green Trail goes steeply down to the right here. If you prefer to skip the incline, stay straight; the connector trail reconnects with the Green Trail less than 0.2 mile later. It's a horse apiece. One horse will be slightly more tired.

Back on the Green Trail you enter a clearing just before the next juncture. Here the Green Trail goes straight across while another trail leads right, downhill to the connector trail to the inner Red loop. Follow this trail on the right a short distance until it reconnects to the Green Trail. At 1.4 miles you see the entrance to the dumbbell-shaped, self-guided nature trail. The Green Trail continues past, skirting the edge of the park property and showing Grass Lake through the trees to the right. The hike turns east around the top of the lake; at 2.2 miles you reach the Red Trail again, which can take you directly back to the picnic area. Otherwise, continue left on the Green Trail, completing the final loop through mostly meadow, passing the park office on your left before arriving back at the parking lot.

Nashotah Park's trails are especially popular with dog owners.

Nashotah Park Green Trail

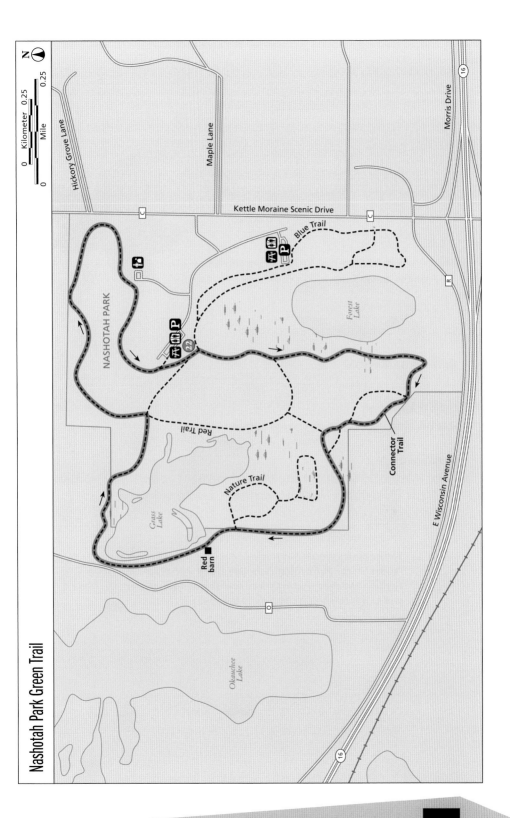

N

Kilometer
0   0.25

0   0.25
Mile

Hickory Grove Lane

Maple Lane

Morris Drive

16

Kettle Moraine Scenic Drive

Blue Trail

NASHOTAH PARK

Forest Lake

R

Red Trail

Connector Trail

Nature Trail

E Wisconsin Avenue

Grass Lake

Red barn

Okauchee Lake

16

22

MILES AND DIRECTIONS

0.0 Start from the trailhead in Picnic Area #2.

0.2 Pass the Red Trail juncture, staying left (south) on the Green Trail.

0.7 Go right at the trail juncture, following a short curve that reconnects to the Green Trail.

1.4 Reach the entrance to the Nature Trail on your right.

2.2 Arrive at another Red Trail juncture; stay left on the Green Trail.

3.0 Pass the park office.

3.4 Arrive back at the trailhead and parking lot.

HIKE INFORMATION

Local Information
Visit Waukesha County, www.visitwaukeshacounty.com

Restaurants
Sunny Side Up, 159 State Rd 67, Ste B, Dousman, WI 53118; (262) 965-5745. Great breakfasts and authentic Mexican fare.

> *The name Nashotah has Native American origins, meaning "twins" in the Potawotami language, and with a similar spelling and meaning in Ojibwa and Menominee. Upper and Lower Nashotah Lakes lie to the south of the park.*

Aztalan State Park Trails

Set along the banks of the slow-moving Crawfish River, Aztalan is a lovely spot to enjoy a summer day, so it's not really a surprise that people settled here over 1,000 years ago. A northern community in a much larger empire, this site is now both a state park and an active archaeological site. The trails are wide, mowed paths following the river and taking a turn along Native American earth mounds. Mowing patterns may change from time to time to accommodate projects or ecological wear and tear, but the small size of the park and the clear view of the lay of the land are such that it doesn't matter. Interpretive signs and an audio tour tell the story—what we know of it—of a people who were long gone even before Wisconsin's current resident native cultures.

Start: From the trailhead in the lower parking lot
Distance: 1.8-mile loop
Hiking time: 1 hour
Difficulty: Easy
Trail surface: Mowed grass, cedar chips, some dirt
Best season: Spring through fall
Other trail users: None
Canine compatibility: Leashed dogs permitted only in designated areas
Land status: State park
Fees and permits: Vehicle admission sticker required; available for purchase at self-registration station
Schedule: Daily, 6 a.m. to 10 p.m.
Maps: USGS Jefferson; at trailhead and on website
Trail contact: Aztalan State Park, N6200 Hwy Q, Lake Mills, WI 53551; (920) 648-8774; http://dnr.wi.gov
Special considerations: Before your visit, consider downloading the podcast from the state park website. A PBS video and a 37-minute streaming audio program are there as well.

Finding the trailhead: From downtown Milwaukee take I-94 west toward Madison for 43 miles. Take exit 267 for WI 26 and turn left. Go 0.9 mile on WI 26, then turn right onto Milwaukee Street, and continue 0.4 mile. Take a slight left onto CR B and stay on it for 4.4 miles. Turn left onto CR Q and go 0.6 mile to the state park entrance on the left. The trailhead is at the lower parking lot, closer to the river.
GPS: N43 3.805' / W88 51.712'

THE HIKE

We may never know the full story of the people and culture of this riverside community. Even the location name Aztalan was given by European settlers who saw earth mounds and associated them with the Aztec pyramids. Timothy Johnson found the site in 1835 when Wisconsin was still a territory, but it had been abandoned for nearly 1,000 years by that time. Local treasure and trinket hunters damaged, destroyed, or carried off many objects that may have given us some clue about the culture. None of the regional native tribes made such mounds around the time the site became known.

What's here now are a couple of large earth mounds—both are reconstructed—a rebuilt stockade, and a row of marker mounds. All of it stands in a field of prairie grass bordered by trees and brush along the Crawfish River. A canoe launch near the parking area attracts paddlers, and in truth the previous residents would have valued the water connection south to the Rock River and on to the Mississippi. The hike is simple, and while the setting is beautiful, the mystery and the mounds are a big part of the attraction.

The hike starts from the lower parking lot, down past the service building and nearly to the river. Another lot lies out near the road overlooking the site.

The mounds at Aztalan were reconstructed with the help of careful observations by Increase Lapham, Wisconsin's first scientist.

Start from the lower lot and head north along the river through the woods. The trail can get soggy along here in wet periods, but this is the only part of the hike that offers shade. Halfway to the north end of the park you get a glimpse of the stockade on your left. Continue north; the trail follows a curve out into the open grassy field, then cuts diagonally across the park to the upper parking lot. If official mowed paths allow it, take a path to the right with a more perpendicular route to the county road so that you can walk past the marker mounds there.

From the upper lot take in the lay of the land, then hike southeast to the stockade, down one side and up the other to get to the first mound. You can climb to the top of it. From that mound cross to the south, where there is a step mound. Walk east to stop at the interpretive pavilion, then complete the hike at the lower parking lot and picnic area.

From Cahokia to Aztalan?

Much of the Aztalan archaeological site was compromised by artifact hunters and smoothed over by early farming. Fortunately, early Wisconsin scientist and naturalist Increase Lapham did a detailed accounting of the site in 1850, which was published by the Smithsonian Institute five years later. Much of the reconstruction is based on his early drawings. Since that time digs have uncovered a variety of artifacts including stone and bone tools, refuse and food remains, parts of homes, and animal and even human bone fragments that have prompted some to ponder if there wasn't cannibalism here at one time (though it may also simply be evidence of burial rites). Pottery fragments from the Woodland and Mississippian cultures are also present, compelling Dr. Samuel Barrett, who led the first proper archaeological dig in the state here at Aztalan in 1919, to theorize that these people were part of the culture that built the large earthen pyramids at Cahokia, North America's largest archaeological site north of Mexico, located just east of St. Louis.

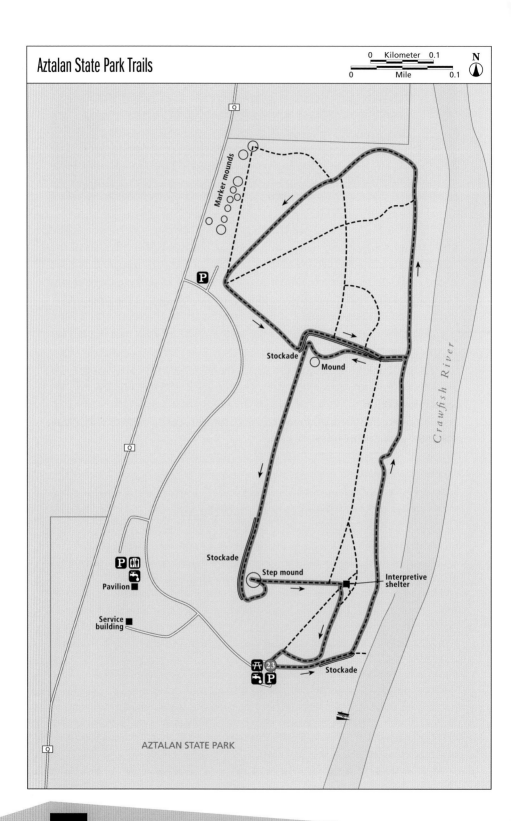

Aztalan State Park Trails

0 Kilometer 0.1
0 Mile 0.1

N

Marker mounds

P

Q

Stockade

Mound

Crawfish River

Stockade

P

Pavilion

Step mound

Interpretive shelter

Service building

Stockade

P

23

AZTALAN STATE PARK

MILES AND DIRECTIONS

0.0 Start from the trailhead at the riverside lot.

0.4 Pass the end of the stockade on your left.

0.6 Follow the trail as it bends west and heads toward the road before angling southwest toward the upper parking lot.

0.9 From the upper lot follow the trail down toward the river, along the left side of the stockade, then back up the other side.

1.1 Arrive at the foot of the large earth mound.

1.4 Cross the field south to the step mound.

1.5 Stop at the interpretive shelter, then turn right to head for the parking lot.

1.8 Arrive back at the trailhead and parking lot.

HIKE INFORMATION

Local Information
Lake Mills Area Chamber of Commerce, 200C Water St., Lake Mills, WI 53551; (920) 648-3585; www.lakemills.org

Local Attractions
Aztalan Historical Museum, N6284 CR Q, Lake Mills, WI 53551; (920) 648-4362; www.orgsites.com/wi/aztalan

CamRock County Park—Area 2 Trails

CamRock Park is unconventional in that it is spread out over three areas and connected by a 2.4-mile paved trail between Cambridge and Rockdale (thus the name CamRock). Area 2 has the longest of the hikes. The trail has a small prairie portion at the center of the park, but the rest is through hardwood forest and along the edge of that forest where you find wetlands and Koshkonong Creek.

Start: From the trailhead near the park entrance
Distance: 2.2-mile circuit
Hiking time: 1 hour
Difficulty: Easy
Trail surface: Dirt, grass
Best season: Spring through fall
Other trail users: Mountain bikers; skiers in winter
Canine compatibility: Leashed dogs permitted for a fee

Land status: County park
Fees and permits: None for hikers; skiers, bikers, and pet owners must pay a self-pay daily fee
Schedule: Daily, 6 a.m. to 10 p.m.
Maps: USGS Rockdale; on website and map board at trailhead
Trail contact: Dane County Parks, 5201 Fen Oak Dr., Madison, WI 53718; (608) 224-3730; www.countyofdane.com

Finding the trailhead: From downtown Milwaukee take I-94 west toward Madison for 43 miles. Take exit 267 for WI 26 and turn left. Go 6.9 miles on WI 26, then take the US 18 ramp and turn right onto US 18. Go 8.4 miles and turn left onto Park Road. Continue 0.8 mile and turn right onto US 12. Go 0.6 mile and turn left onto Spring Street, which becomes CR B. Go 1.9 miles and look for CamRock Park Area 2 on the right. The trailhead is near the park entrance on the right as you drive in. **GPS:** N42 58.688' / W89 1.380'

THE HIKE

At one time, Koshkonong Creek was dammed to create a millpond. When that dam was removed in 2000, the creek once again became a lively running waterway. The former pond bed has developed into wetlands. Both contribute to the attractiveness of this hike.

The trail begins into the woods and heads left at the first trail intersection, through the center of the park, where the path spends a short time amid a prairie restoration. The native wildflowers here are abundant, and the colors can be incredible, especially in summer. Turn right at 0.2 mile, then follow the Prairie Loop to the right, circling the prairie area and coming back to the juncture. Expect a lot of butterflies through here in summer as well.

Continue on the trail into the woods, but stay on the straight path when you come to a couple of crossing paths, the second of which comes in through a gate on the left and connects to a bridge over the creek. The trail is slightly uphill at this point. Pines through here contribute a blanket of needles on the path, and you pass a few spur trails, shortcuts out to facilities and the playground, for example. The path curves to the south, and the woods become dominated by hardwoods, especially maple—which makes for some good fall colors—and some oak. It's downhill to a curve, where you can see wetlands off on the left and there is a bench to enjoy a shaded perch overlooking the cattails.

The trail makes a turn back to the northeast, with the creek just to the left, and there is a spot to get a closer look at the water. Your path crosses the bridge path again, and you can duck out here to the left to have a look at the creek. That path connects to the CamRock Trail on the other side, connecting the two communities of Cambridge and Rockdale.

Continuing on the woodland trail, you skirt the edge of the prairie once again but soon head back into the shade. Through this final turn of trail along the northern edge of Area 2, you have more opportunities to see into the wetlands, including a nice observation deck at the 1.8-mile mark. Expect some good birding here, and really, throughout the park. After the observation deck the trail makes a turn back toward where you started; at the next juncture take the trail to the left to find the parking lot.

What was once a millpond is now a wetlands area.

CamRock County Park–Area 2 Trails

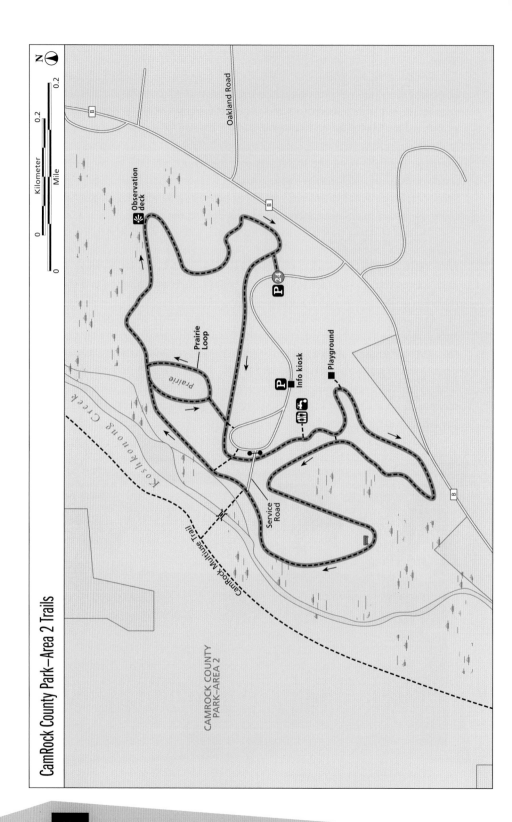

- Observation deck
- Prairie Loop
- Prairie
- Koshkonong Creek
- Oakland Road
- CamRock Multiuse Trail
- Service Road
- Info kiosk
- Playground
- CAMROCK COUNTY PARK–AREA 2

N

Kilometer
Mile

MILES AND DIRECTIONS

0.0   Start from the trailhead near the parking lot entrance and take the first left turn just inside the woods.

0.2   At the trail juncture, take the trail to the right onto the Prairie Loop, then return to the juncture.

0.5   Cross the service road/bike trail, passing the gate on the left.

0.6   Pass a cutoff trail on the right and follow the trail south to skirt the wetlands on your way to the creek.

1.4   Pass the trail bridge over the creek on your left; continue straight on the hiking trail.

1.6   The Prairie Loop connects on the right; continue on the path through the woods.

1.8   Come to an observation deck on the left.

2.2   At the final trail juncture, take the trail on the left and arrive back at the trailhead and parking lot.

HIKE INFORMATION

Local Information

Cambridge Area Chamber of Commerce, 102 W. Main St., Cambridge, WI 53523; (608) 423-3780; www.cambridgewi.com
Visit Cambridge, www.visitcambridgewi.com

Local Attractions

Glacial Heritage Area, Department of Natural Resources, (608) 275-3320; www.glacialheritagearea.org. A network of trails, waterways, parks, and natural areas, all mapped out for the outdoor enthusiast.

25

Kettle Moraine State Forest—Lapham Peak Unit: Meadow Trail

Just as much meadow as it is forest, this trail gives a taste of what you might find at the venerable Lapham Peak Park and shows some signs of Native American culture—the unusually bent marker trees believed to indicate trails or water sources.

Start: From the trailhead at Evergreen Grove parking area
Distance: 2.0-mile loop
Hiking time: 1 hour
Difficulty: Easy with some moderate climbs
Trail surface: Grass
Best season: Spring through fall
Other trail users: Skiers in winter
Canine compatibility: Leashed dogs permitted
Land status: State park
Fees and permits: Vehicle admission sticker required; available for purchase at visitor center
Schedule: Daily, 7 a.m. to 9 p.m. (until 10 p.m. in winter)

Maps: USGS Oconomowoc East; at park office and on website
Trail contact: Kettle Moraine State Forest—Lapham Peak Unit, W329 N846 CR C, Delafield, WI 53018; (262) 646-3025; trail information line: (262) 646-4421; http://dnr.wi .gov
Special considerations: Hiking is not allowed when snow is present. This is part of a much larger trail system with more challenging hikes, including a segment of the Ice Age Trail that passes through the park. A 1.5-mile paved accessible trail also starts near the map board. Visit the observation tower at the center of the park.

Finding the trailhead: From downtown Milwaukee go west on I-94 to exit 285 for CR C. The exit ramp curves back east; turn right (south) onto CR C and drive 0.8 mile to the park entrance on the left. At the first intersection past the park office, take a right into the Evergreen Grove parking area. The trailhead is on the left (east) as you enter the lot. **GPS:** N43 2.43' / W88 24.16'

THE HIKE

Lapham Peak is a regular hiking mecca. Trails are color coded and can be mixed and matched. The park signage clearly shows the colors as does the trail map, which even lists step-by-step trail difficulty if you want to avoid the leg burners. The two trails included in this guide tend toward easier hikes, and the Meadow Trail is coded green.

From the trailhead enter the meadow and take the trail going right. At 0.2 mile the trail goes slightly uphill out of the open meadow, passing a cutoff trail on the left that would shorten the loop by more than half. Go right along the trees; the trail brings you back out into the open meadow with scattered clumps of trees. At 0.5 mile the Ice Age National Scenic Trail, a rustic footpath marked with yellow blazes on posts and trees, crosses your path. The trail bends left and heads south just inside the park along CR C and then turns left into a trail juncture. The much longer (and more difficult) Black and Blue Trails continue straight ahead. Go left to stay on the Green Trail. Another 0.1 mile later the trail descends to the Black and Blue Trails coming from the right (east) again. Stay left to join them and continue downhill. Once again you cross the Ice Age Trail 0.1 mile later. If taken to the right, the Ice Age Trail would lead you on a rugged path uphill to

Woodland sunflowers along the Meadow Trail.

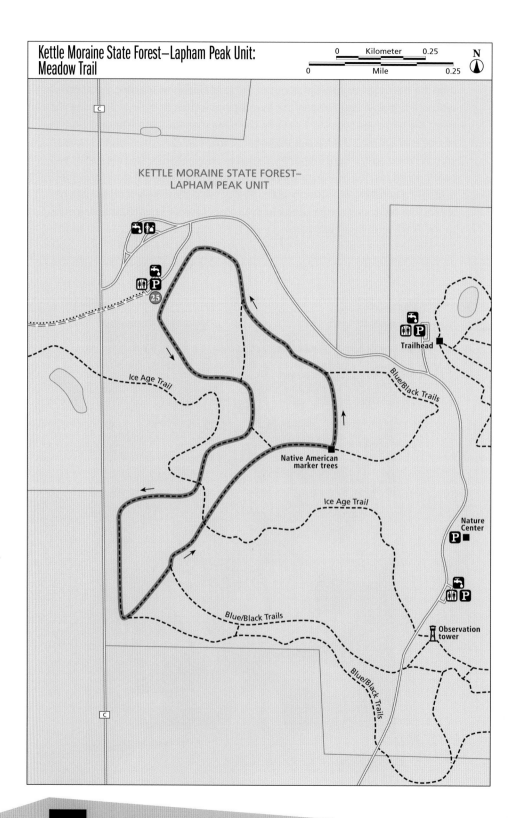

Kettle Moraine State Forest–Lapham Peak Unit: Meadow Trail

KETTLE MORAINE STATE FOREST–
LAPHAM PEAK UNIT

Ice Age Trail

25

Trailhead

Blue/Black Trails

Native American
marker trees

Ice Age Trail

Nature
Center

Blue/Black Trails

Observation
tower

Blue/Black Trails

the 45-foot observation tower on top of Waukesha County's highest point. This side trip would be about 0.6 mile one-way, with almost a 250-foot change in altitude.

Continuing from the Ice Age Trail crossing, you come to another cutoff trail at 1.2 miles. At 1.3 miles look for Native American marker trees (bent as saplings to mark trails) and the accompanying storyboard. Go left at the juncture nearby; going straight leads to two steep climbs on the Black and Blue Trails before they loop around and rejoin the Green Trail. Going left at the next juncture, the Green, Black, and Blue Trails descend to the meadow area once again and loop around to the trailhead.

MILES AND DIRECTIONS

0.0 Start from the trailhead and head right.

0.5 Cross the Ice Age Trail.

0.9 Take the Green Trail left at the fork.

1.1 Cross the Ice Age Trail again.

1.4 Just past the Native American marker trees, stay with the Green Trail going left.

1.5 Rejoin the Blue and Black Trails.

Wisconsin's First Scientist: Increase A. Lapham

The park bears his name, but who was this man often referred to as the state's first scientist? Lapham was born in Palmyra, New York, in 1811, but in 1836, he came to Wisconsin, then still a territory. As a naturalist he cataloged the plants as well as shells, writing his first book about both in the Milwaukee area. When Wisconsin became a state in 1848, Lapham also founded the Wisconsin Natural History Association. He made maps of the state and published books and papers about nature, history, and geology in Wisconsin. When it seemed development might destroy the intriguing mounds and artifacts of Aztalan, Lapham made careful notes and observations about the site, which would one day help archaeologists reconstruct what farmers and trinket hunters eventually destroyed. Meteorologists may also thank him: He pushed the US government and the Smithsonian Institute to develop some kind of weather forecasting system. From this we have the US Weather Service. His is the highest point in Waukesha County, right here in the park bearing his name.

1.7 Pass the cutoff trail on the left.

2.0 Arrive back at the trailhead.

HIKE INFORMATION

Local Information
Visit Delafield, 421 Main St., Delafield, WI 53018; (262) 646-8100; www.visit delafield.org
Friends of Lapham Peak, www.laphampeakfriends.org

Local Attractions
Ten Chimneys, S43 W31575 Depot Rd, Genesee Depot, WI 53127; (262) 968-4161; www.tenchimneys.org. A National Historic Landmark, this mansion, which belonged to a couple of early twentieth-century Broadway stars, is an award-winning museum.

Kettle Moraine State Forest—Lapham Peak Unit: Kame Terrace Trail

Hike over glacial terrain amid hardwood forests in this extensive trail system, part of the Kettle Moraine State Forest. Don't miss the Butterfly Garden at the center of the loop, and the 45-foot observation tower at the center of the park.

Start: From the trailhead at the Homestead Hollow parking area
Distance: 2.0-mile loop
Hiking time: 45 minutes to 1 hour
Difficulty: Moderate due to some short climbs
Trail surface: Grass, packed dirt
Best season: Spring through fall
Other trail users: Skiers in winter
Canine compatibility: Leashed dogs permitted
Land status: State park
Fees and permits: Vehicle admission sticker required; available for purchase at visitor center
Schedule: Daily, 7 a.m. to 9 p.m. (until 10 p.m. in winter)

Maps: USGS Oconomowoc East; at park office and on website
Trail contact: Kettle Moraine State Forest—Lapham Peak Unit, W329 N846 CR C, Delafield, WI 53018; (262) 646-3025; trail information line: (262) 646-4421; http://dnr.wi.gov
Special considerations: Hiking is not allowed when snow is present. This is part of a much larger trail system with more challenging hikes, including a segment of the Ice Age Trail that passes through the park. A 1.5-mile paved accessible trail also starts near the map board. Visit the observation tower at the center of the park.

Finding the trailhead: From downtown Milwaukee go west on I-94 to exit 285 for CR C. The exit ramp curves back east; turn right (south) onto CR C and drive 0.8 mile to the park entrance on the left. Take the park road 0.7 mile to the Homestead Hollow parking area on the left. The trailhead and a trail map kiosk are to the right of the restrooms. **GPS:** N43 2.38' / W88 23.56'

THE HIKE

Lapham Peak is named for Wisconsin's first great scientist and naturalist, Increase Lapham. The "peak" is a glacial formation known as a kame. Meltwaters flowed straight down a hole in the 1-mile-thick ice sheet, carrying debris and depositing it in a cone shape. The kame terrace was created by a large glacial river flowing past the kame. Within the park's 1,000 acres is some fascinating and rugged topography—and over 17 miles of trails to explore it. Plus, the Ice Age Trail passes through the park.

Heading into the woods on the Kame Terrace Trail.

Getting in Shape

Unless you want to be sore—and possibly have to shorten your trip or vaca-
tion—be sure to get in shape before a big hike. Some of the hikes in this book
are simple strolls on flatland, but anything involving Kettle Moraine State Forest
or the Ice Age Trail may challenge you more than you expect. If you're terribly
out of shape, start a walking program early, preferably eight weeks in advance.
Start with a 15-minute walk during your lunch hour or after work and gradually
increase your walking time to an hour. You should also increase your elevation
gain. Walking briskly up hills really strengthens your leg muscles and gets your
heart rate up. If you work in a storied office building, take the stairs instead
of the elevator. If you prefer going to a gym, walk the treadmill or use a stair
machine. You can further increase your strength and endurance by walking with
a loaded backpack. Stationary exercises you might consider are squats, leg lifts,
sit-ups, and push-ups. Other good ways to get in shape include biking, running,
aerobics, and, of course, short hikes. Stretching before and after a hike keeps
muscles flexible and helps avoid injuries.

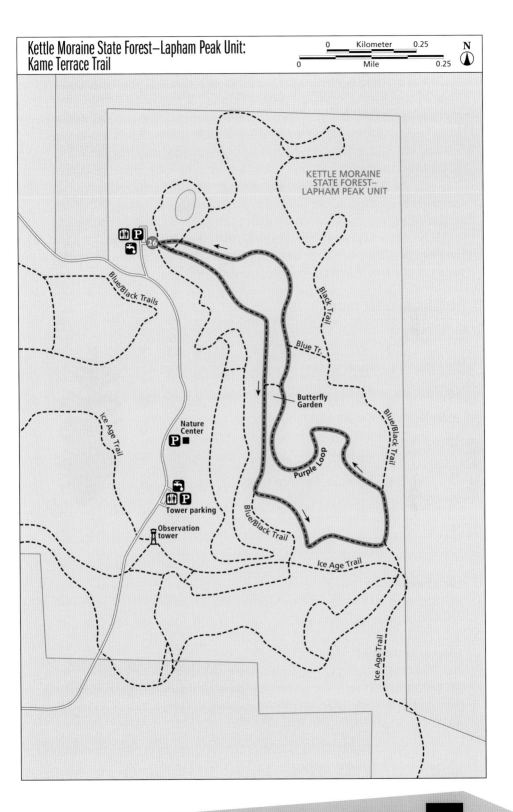

Kettle Moraine State Forest–Lapham Peak Unit: Kame Terrace Trail

0   Kilometer   0.25

0   Mile   0.25

N

KETTLE MORAINE
STATE FOREST–
LAPHAM PEAK UNIT

Blue/Black Trails

Black Trail

Blue Tr.

Blue/Black Trail

Butterfly
Garden

Purple Loop

Ice Age Trail

Nature
Center

Tower parking

Observation
tower

Blue/Black Trail

Ice Age Trail

Ice Age Trail

26

All trails are marked with color-coded symbols; the wavy purple one that resembles the Pepsi logo marks the gentler Kame Terrace Trail. The trail follows a wide, mowed path up the hill behind the map board. When it meets the woods you face a very steep but short climb to the top of the hill. At 0.3 mile a juncture shows the connecting trail to the right and a cutoff trail through a meadow to the left, which leads to the Butterfly Garden. Keep straight past this juncture and at 0.5 mile take the left path at a fork in the trail. (The more challenging Black and Blue Trails follow the path to the right.) At 0.8 mile the Kame Terrace Trail descends to another juncture with the Blue and Black Trails on the right. Stay left and at the next juncture take the left path. You'll descend a bit and come back to the open meadow, passing through the Butterfly Garden and crossing the juncture for the cutoff trail. On the other side of the meadow, the trail reenters the woods and makes its way down to the trailhead once more.

MILES AND DIRECTIONS

0.0 Start from the trailhead on a wide, mowed path.

0.3 Pass the Butterfly Garden.

0.5 Go left at the fork; the Black and Blue Trails continue straight.

0.8 Stay left and briefly rejoin the Black and Blue Trails; turn left at the next juncture.

1.5 Pass the Butterfly Garden once again.

2.0 Arrive back at the trailhead.

HIKE INFORMATION

Local Information
Visit Delafield, 421 Main St., Delafield, WI 53018; (262) 646-8100; www.visit delafield.org

Local Attractions
Ten Chimneys, S43 W31575 Depot Rd, Genesee Depot, WI 53127; (262) 968-4161; www.tenchimneys.org. A National Historic Landmark, this mansion, which belonged to a couple of early twentieth-century Broadway stars, is an award-winning museum.

Kettle Moraine State Forest—Southern Unit: Scuppernong Trails

A scenic overlook gives a view for miles, and rolling hills through pine forest invigorates the spirit. Popular with joggers, these trails offer three levels of difficulty dependent on inclines.

Start: From the trailhead at the parking lot
Distance: 5.4-mile loop
Hiking time: 2.5 hours
Difficulty: Moderate due to some steep portions
Trail surface: Packed dirt, crushed rock, some grass
Best season: Spring through fall
Other trail users: Foot traffic only; skiers in winter
Canine compatibility: Leashed dogs permitted
Land status: State park
Fees and permits: Vehicle admission sticker required; available for purchase at state forest office or self-pay tube
Schedule: Daily, 6 a.m. to 11 p.m.
Maps: USGS Eagle; at trailhead, state forest office, and on website
Trail contact: Kettle Moraine State Forest—Southern Unit, S91 W39091 Hwy. 59, Eagle, WI 53119; (262) 594-6200; http://dnr.wi.gov
Special considerations: No hiking or dogs allowed when snow is present. Parts of the park are open to hunters during gun deer hunting season at the end of November.

Finding the trailhead: From Milwaukee take I-94 west toward Madison. Get off at exit 282 and take WI 67 south (left) to CR ZZ. You will pass CR ZZ on the right and continue another 0.3 mile to take CR ZZ on the left going east. The park entrance is 0.4 mile on the left. The trailhead is at the north corner of the parking lot. **GPS:** N42 56.45' / W88 27.70'

THE HIKE

Not to be confused with Scuppernong Springs Nature Trail, this collection of three forest loops passes across higher ground. Also, unlike the nature trail, this park has pit toilets and drinking water. This trail doubles as a cross-country ski trail, and the short climbs up and over the roller-coaster terrain make it popular also for cross-country runners. Colored map boards are located at each trail juncture. The Green Loop is the outermost of the three color-coded trails. The Red Loop is the easiest of the three, getting you back to the trailhead in 2.3 miles; the Orange Loop makes it a 4.2-mile hike.

The trail enters from the parking lot bearing left into the woods and passing a park service road. At the first juncture, just 150 feet in, take the path to the right, a somewhat sandy and pine-needle-strewn lane. At the juncture at 0.7 mile, a hard right would take you to the D. J. Mackie group picnic area, where you can find water near the parking lot. The Red Loop is to the left. The Green and Orange Loops take the trail that bends a bit to the right.

At 1.5 miles you cross the Ice Age National Scenic Trail, which passes through this park on its 1,000-plus-mile journey across Wisconsin. The trail is marked with yellow blazes on trees and trail posts. Continue to the right on the wider path. At 2.3 miles the Orange Loop leaves this path to the left. Cross the Ice Age Trail again at 3.1 miles. At 3.5 miles the Red and Orange Loops intersect the trail from the left. Another 300 feet farther on your right is the 0.4-mile lollipop Observation Loop, with a scenic overlook at the far end. Returning back to this juncture,

Heading into pine plantation on the Scuppernong Trails.

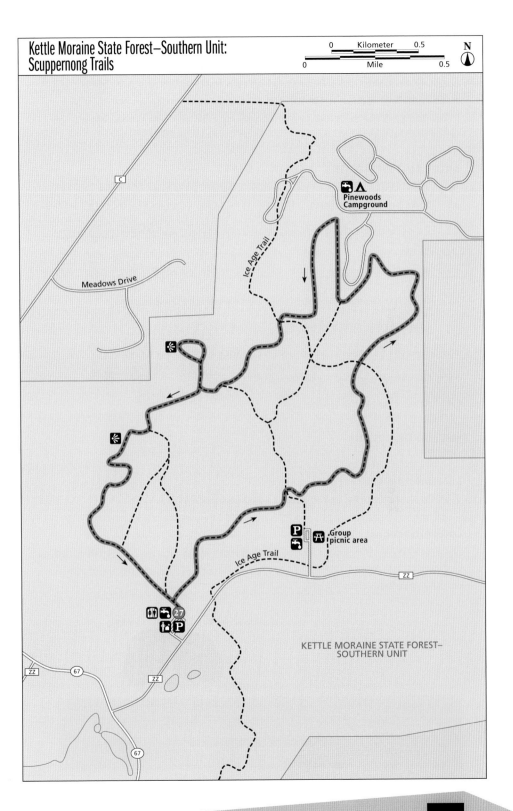

Kettle Moraine State Forest–Southern Unit:
Scuppernong Trails

0   Kilometer   0.5

0   Mile   0.5

N

C

Ice Age Trail

Pinewoods
Campground

Meadows Drive

Ice Age Trail

Group
picnic area

ZZ

27

KETTLE MORAINE STATE FOREST–
SOUTHERN UNIT

ZZ   67

ZZ

67

continue right on the Green Loop. At the next intersection the Red and Orange Loops go straight (and shortly split into two trails again) and the Green Loop goes right. This section is the most challenging, climbing to an overlook at 4.6 miles. You pass the split Red and Orange Loops on your left as the Green Loop returns to the trailhead.

MILES AND DIRECTIONS

0.0 Start from the trailhead.

0.7 Pass the trail to the group picnic area on the right and the Red Loop on the left.

1.5 Cross the Ice Age Trail.

2.3 Meet the Orange Loop juncture; continue on the Green Loop.

3.1 Cross the Ice Age Trail again.

3.5 Take the Observation Loop, then continue on the Green Loop.

4.6 Check out another scenic overlook.

5.4 Arrive back at the trailhead.

HIKE INFORMATION

Local Information
Visit Waukesha County, www.visitwaukeshacounty.com

Local Attractions
Old World Wisconsin, W372 S9727 WI 67, Eagle, WI 53119; (262) 594-6301; old worldwisconsin.wisconsinhistory.org. A re-creation of life in the nineteenth-century Wisconsin countryside.

🌿 Green Tip:
Pack out your dog's waste or dispose of it in a trash can or a hole dug into the ground.

Kettle Moraine State Forest—Southern Unit: Scuppernong Springs Nature Trail

In woods full of springs and patches of scenic wetland follow a self-guided nature trail with a booklet that has more to say about the human history of this spot.

Start: From the trailhead at the parking lot

Distance: 1.5-mile loop

Hiking time: 45 minutes

Difficulty: Easy to moderate when muddy

Trail surface: Packed dirt, sand, and boardwalks

Best season: Spring through fall

Other trail users: None

Canine compatibility: Dogs not permitted

Land status: State park

Fees and permits: Vehicle admission sticker required; available for purchase at state forest office or self-pay tube

Schedule: Daily, 6 a.m. to 11 p.m.

Maps: USGS Eagle; at state forest office and on website

Trail contact: Kettle Moraine State Forest—Southern Unit, S91 W39091 Hwy. 59, Eagle, WI 53119; (262) 594-6200; http://dnr.wi.gov

Special considerations: Mosquitoes can be a nuisance, as can soggy trails. Parking lot is plowed in winter.

Finding the trailhead: From downtown Milwaukee take I-94 west toward Madison. Get off at exit 282 and take WI 67 south (left) to CR ZZ and go right. The parking lot is on the left opposite the Ottawa Lake Recreation Area. Find the trailhead at the east end of the parking lot. **GPS:** N42 56.14' / W88 28.45'

THE HIKE

Scuppernong means "sweet-scented land" in the native Ho-Chunk language. Native Americans occupied the site no doubt for its abundant freshwater. A booklet, available at the trailhead, guides you past numbered posts along the trail and narrates a bit of cultural history.

Just inside the woods from the trailhead, the trail forks; take the path to the right. Much of the trail is shaded, but with the abundance of springs and low spots, you can expect some mud to contend with. At 0.2 mile you encounter railroad ties, part of an old railroad bed that extends about 300 feet along the trail.

Another 200 feet later you find a concrete wall from the old marl works. (Marl is a lime-rich soil used for mortar and as fertilizer.) A spur trail walks right around it and back onto the main trail.

At 0.3 mile you cross a bridge over the Scuppernong River and then the trail becomes a little sandy as it climbs gently to higher ground. Three hundred feet later the trail forks again. To the left is a cutoff trail to the return path of the loop. Take the path to the right and enter a bit of prairie where you'll likely find abundant wildflowers. A spur trail to the right at signpost #6 leads down the hill onto an unmaintained path through brush to the edge of a spring creek.

Continuing on the main trail another 200 feet, you come to a steep spur trail down to the right to a wooden platform overlooking one of the springs. Staying on the main trail, head downhill and pass a park maintenance road on the right as the trail begins to curve east. At 0.7 mile you pass a concrete wall just above the springs. The trail curves north and passes boardwalk spur trails into the marshy springs area to the left. At 0.8 mile is a long, straight boardwalk left out into the springs area. The other end of the cutoff trail is at 0.9 mile, and if you go left onto it, you will get a nice view of the water from a boardwalk bridge. Hotel Spring is just north of the bridge. Continue on the main trail, passing a spur trail on the right that heads up out of the park to the highway. Stay straight on a series of boardwalks; the trail then meanders through the woods back to the trailhead.

Hotel Spring is one of several points in the nature trail's interpretive booklet, available online for download. Preamtip Satasuk

Kettle Moraine State Forest–Southern Unit: Scuppernong Springs Nature Trail

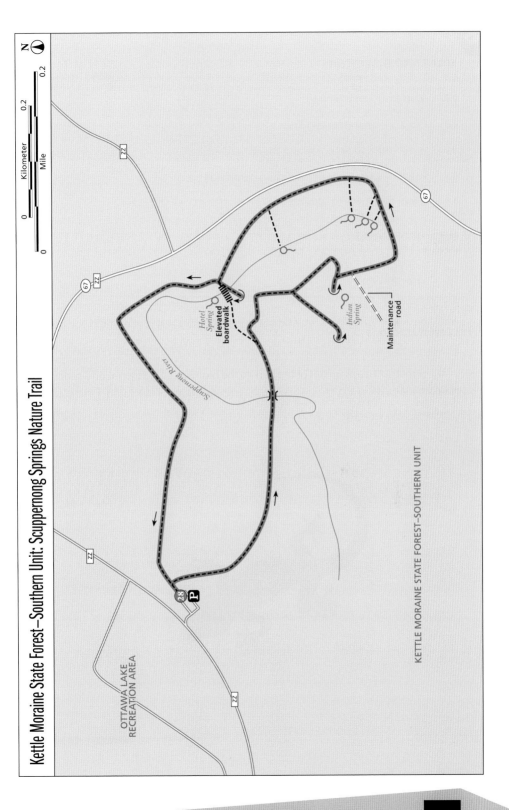

OTTAWA LAKE
RECREATION AREA

KETTLE MORAINE STATE FOREST–SOUTHERN UNIT

Hotel
Spring
**Elevated
boardwalk**

Scuppernong River

*Indian
Spring*

Maintenance
road

N

Kilometer

Mile

28

MILES AND DIRECTIONS

0.0   Start from the trailhead.

0.3   Cross the Scuppernong River.

0.7   Reach the concrete wall and the springs area.

0.9   Pass the elevated boardwalk and cutoff trail.

1.5   Arrive back at the trailhead.

HIKE INFORMATION

Local Information
Visit Waukesha County, www.visitwaukeshacounty.com

Local Attractions
Old World Wisconsin, W372 S9727 Wisconsin 67, Eagle, WI 53119; (262) 594-6301; oldworldwisconsin.wisconsinhistory.org. A re-creation of life in the nineteenth-century Wisconsin countryside.

Ice Age National Scenic Trail and Bald Bluff Nature Trail

Bald Bluff may seem a misnomer, as much of this hike is through rich forest. The nature trail and area (registered as a state natural area) are under the jurisdiction of the Southern Unit of the Kettle Moraine State Forest, which offers a narrative guide-book you can borrow at the trailhead, but this trail is also part of the Blue Spring Lake Segment of the Ice Age National Scenic Trail. The terrain is rugged, and loose rock and sand can make the steep portions a bit challenging. But a scenic overlook at the top of the bluff and a quirky granite erratic known as the Stone Elephant add to the attraction.

Start: From the trailhead by the gravel parking area
Distance: 3.4 miles out-and-back
Hiking time: 1.5 hours
Difficulty: Moderate due to some steep areas and rugged surface
Trail surface: Dirt, sand, loose rock
Best season: Year-round
Other trail users: None
Canine compatibility: Leashed dogs permitted
Land status: State park
Fees and permits: Vehicle admission sticker required; available for purchase at state forest office
Schedule: Daily, 6 a.m. to 11 p.m.

Maps: USGS Little Prairie; *Ice Age Trail Atlas*; at state forest office and on website
Trail contacts: Kettle Moraine State Forest—Southern Unit, S91 W39091 Hwy. 59, Eagle, WI 53119; (262) 594-6200; http://dnr.wi.gov; Ice Age Trail Alliance, 2110 Main St., Cross Plains, WI 53528; (800) 227-0046; www.iceagetrail.org
Special considerations: Use proper footwear; the trail surface can be quite uneven and slippery in spots. No facilities on this trail; drive south 2 miles on CR H to the state park's Nordic Trails for water and restrooms.

Finding the trailhead: From downtown Milwaukee head south on I-43 about 33 miles and turn right onto WI 20/North Street. Follow WI 20 for 9.4 miles and take a slight right onto US 12. Turn right onto CR H/Kettle Moraine Scenic Drive and continue 3.5 miles to the parking lot on the right. The trailhead is at the lot. **GPS:** N42 50.756' / W88 36.582'

THE HIKE

The proper name on the sign is Kettle Moraine Oak Opening Bald Bluff Unit State Natural Area, but anyone you ask is going to say Bald Bluff. This nicely forested section of the state forest offers a pleasant thru-hike on the Ice Age Trail if you prefer, but the out-and-back to an erratic is a better option to avoid needing a second vehicle. The trailhead is actually on a spur trail to the Ice Age Trail and thus is marked with blue blazes rather than the usual yellow blazes that designate the national scenic trail. For a bit of narrative of what you are seeing here, check the box at the lot for a self-guided interpretive brochure. Donations for trail maintenance and renting the little booklet are welcome.

The trail starts with some mowed grass but quickly gives way to the sandy, rock-strewn, and tree-root surfaces common along the trail. That's glacial till you are walking on, piled up by retreating glaciers over 10,000 years ago. Pass 300 feet along the edge of the oak-dominated woods and the trail bends left into the trees, granting good shade. Come to the intersection with the yellow-blazed trail and follow it to the left. A sign indicates distances on the larger trail: 2.7 miles to Shelter #3, 5.7 miles to La Grange, and 6.9 miles out to US 12, the distance of a thru-hike on this segment of the Ice Age Trail. The canopy opens up, and in 0.25 mile the trail switches back rather steeply and you arrive at the top of the bluff. Two benches backed by oak forest face a view for miles to the southwest.

The trail passes briefly along the top of an open bluff with a nice view. **Preamtip Satasuk**

Legend has it that Abraham Lincoln once camped in the field west of the parking lot as a volunteer in the Illinois militia in 1932 during the Black Hawk War.

Continue along the trail back into the woods, descending through a lot of brush and hardwoods. The understory soon thins out so you can see the roll of the terrain better. From here the trail does a lot of up-and-down climbing on a potentially ankle-turning surface. Wild berries are common and OK for picking. Ravines are deep on either side of the path as you walk along the top of the ridge. At 0.8 mile continue out into open prairie filled with wildflowers in season and a few young oaks. Just beyond is pine plantation, changing the sound and smell of your surroundings.

At 1.1 miles cross a snowmobile trail, and 750 feet later notice the glacially formed depressions on both sides. Past here the trail goes up and left with the slopes on either side. Just before the crest of the hill at about 1.3 miles, the trail gets its steepest, and you may slide a bit on the loose ground as you descend the other side (and again on the return route).

The rise and fall tapers off a bit, and at 1.7 miles is the sign for the Stone Elephant. A spur trail turns left off the Ice Age Trail a very short distance to a large erratic. This may be the most challenging part of the hike: trying to imagine how someone thought this looked like an elephant. At any rate it is a traveler, and no one knows just how far it journeyed with the last advance of glaciers. Contemplate this as you backtrack to the parking lot.

A Stone's Throw

In many places within the Kettle Moraine you will encounter *erratics*. The term is used to describe any piece of rock that has been carried along by the movement of glaciers and differs from the bedrock where it is found. This can mean pieces as small as a pebble, but is most often applied to very large boulders, as the immense weight and size and a long journey make quite an impression. Throughout Wisconsin there are examples of erratics made of a type of stone only found far north in Canada or perhaps from the Lake Superior basin. These long-range rocks must be composed of a very hard substance to avoid being ground down by the journey. Sandstone, for example, wouldn't travel well. The largest known erratic in the world is the Okotoks Erratic, or "Big Rock," a 16,500-ton chunk of quartzite in Alberta, Canada. A number of drifting diamonds have also been uncovered in Wisconsin, the first on a farm near Eagle in 1876, and the largest, a 21.5-carat spherical diamond, in Theresa, not far from a couple of hikes in this book.

Ice Age National Scenic Trail and Bald Bluff Nature Trail

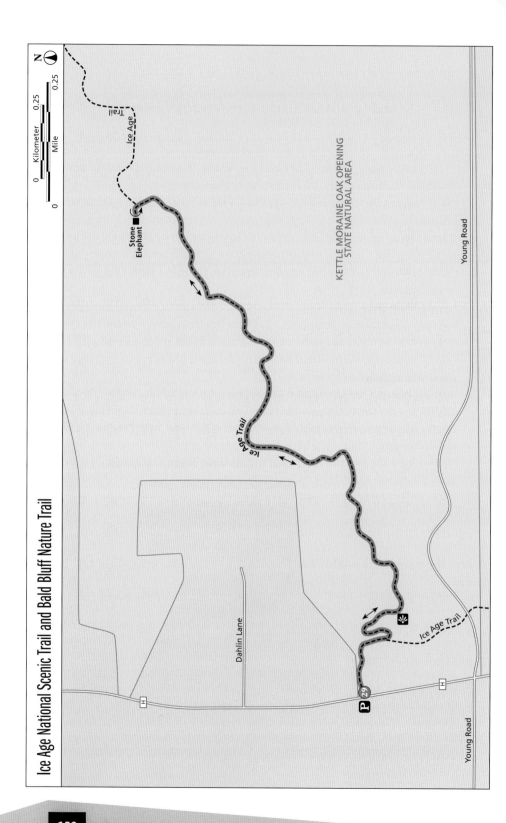

Stone Elephant

Ice Age Trail

Ice Age Trail

Ice Age Trail

KETTLE MORAINE OAK OPENING
STATE NATURAL AREA

Dahlin Lane

Young Road

Young Road

N

Kilometer   0.25

Mile   0.25

MILES AND DIRECTIONS

0.0 Start from the trailhead; head east and go left on the Ice Age Trail at its juncture.

0.3 Reach the viewpoint from the top of the bluff.

1.1 Cross a snowmobile trail; stay straight.

1.7 Take the spur trail left to the Stone Elephant. Return the way you came.

3.4 Arrive back at the trailhead.

HIKE INFORMATION

Local Information
Palmyra Area Chamber of Commerce, PO Box 139, Palmyra, WI 53156; (262) 495-8316; www.palmyrawi.com.

Local Attractions
Rushing Waters Fisheries, N301 CR H, Palmyra, WI 53156; (262) 495-2089; www.rushingwaters.net. Catch your own rainbow trout either from the pond or from the freezer in the store, or dine at the fishery's own restaurant, The Trout House. Try the smoked trout.

🌱 Green Tip:
Observe wildlife from a distance. Don't interfere in their lives—both of you will be better for it.

30

Kettle Moraine State Forest—Southern Unit: John Muir Trails

Some of the best mountain biking trails in southeastern Wisconsin, this trail system is also a rugged hiking destination through a lot of kettle moraine terrain. The long outside loop follows footpaths through some pine plantation and forest, as well as along narrow moraine ridges and past water-filled kettles. A hiker's-only spur trail ventures to an old lime kiln.

Start: From the hiking trailhead (counterclockwise) on the blue loop
Distance: 12-mile loop
Hiking time: 5 hours
Difficulty: Moderate with some strenuous climbs
Trail surface: Dirt
Best season: Spring through fall
Other trail users: Mountain bikers
Canine compatibility: Leashed dogs permitted
Land status: State park
Fees and permits: Vehicle admission sticker required; available for purchase at park entrance, self-pay station, or state forest headquarters
Schedule: Daily, 6 a.m. to 11 p.m.

Maps: USGS Little Prairie; at state park office, on map boards and website
Trail contact: Kettle Moraine State Forest—Southern Unit, S91 W39091 Hwy. 59, Eagle, WI 53119; (262) 594-6200; http://dnr.wi.gov
Special considerations: Hikers must walk the trail loop in a counterclockwise direction, opposite the one-way traffic of mountain bikers, at all times. Trails can be quite busy with bikers on weekends, so it may be best to avoid hiking here during those times. The map is constantly evolving due to trail erosion, maintenance, and re-routing. Think of it as an approximation.

Finding the trailhead: From Milwaukee head south on I-43 about 33 miles and take exit 38 for WI 20. Go right on WI 20 for 9.4 miles, then take a slight right onto US 12. Drive 2 miles and turn right onto CR H. Go 1.5 miles; the park entrance is on the left. The trailhead is at the parking lot. **GPS:** N42 49.206' / W88 36.202'

THE HIKE

Kettle Moraine is the name of the state forest, and kettle moraines are some of the defining characteristics of this hike. The rough terrain made it ideal for laying out singletrack for mountain bikers, but it is also a joy for hikers. Give way to bikers and be sure to hike opposite the direction of bike traffic—they can come quickly. Take note of the map irregularities. Even online the distances for the Blue Trail range from 9.5 to 12 miles, and yet the trail as it is drawn on those maps is almost identical. A series of extra switchbacks might appear on the actual trail and isn't apparent on the map, and thus don't count on mileage readings too much. Here the distance is figured to be about 12 miles. The trees, switchbacks, and terrain also make GPS use tricky. Look for the most recent park maps at the trailhead and on the state forest's website.

That said, lace up your hiking boots. After you leave the trailhead, take the trail to the right, heading north, against bike traffic. At the first trail juncture, stay straight on the Blue/Red/Green Trails. The Rainy Dew, Kids, and brown loops intersect from the left. You could cut roughly 3 miles off by taking the Orange, or Rainy Dew, across to the Blue Trail on the west side of the loop.

The trail is still rather tame, showing some loose rock as you make your way north to a connector trail to the Emma Carlin Trail system, about 15 miles away. Keep following the trail to the left; on a switchback to the south, the trail heads through pine plantation. At the end of a long straight run, cross an old fire lane and continue to follow the Blue Trail for almost 0.2 mile east before turning south.

At about the 5.0-mile mark, a trail to the left leads to a historical lime kiln area. Continue straight as the trail angles to the southwest a bit, passing between two kettle bogs, one very close on the left. The next juncture is at 5.5 miles, but

John Muir in Wisconsin

The famous naturalist may often be associated with California and other points west, but much of his American childhood was spent in Wisconsin. Immigrating from Scotland, he arrived first with his father, Daniel, and two siblings, David and Sarah, settling on land in Fountain Lake, Wisconsin. His mother and four remaining siblings would join them once the farm was established. Right away he fell in love with "that glorious Wisconsin wilderness." The work was hard as was his father, a Calvinist, and both forged in him a strength that supported him in his travels. He attended the University of Wisconsin, but left without a degree, choosing to study what the wilderness had to teach him. His passion for those wild places would lead him to found the Sierra Club and become a preeminent conservationist, pushing for the creation of national parks, first in California. He had the ear of President Theodore Roosevelt, from whose presidency the national park system arose. But the very first piece of land John Muir sought to preserve was a meadow on his childhood farm. His brother-in-law didn't sell it to him, but over a century and a half later, his fans and followers succeeded in creating John Muir Memorial Park in Marquette County, which includes the land he grew up on.

where the Orange Trail splits to the left, you must stay straight in order to continue facing bike traffic.

The trail starts gaining elevation and getting rougher. Some of the views off the edge of the trail are down steep, rocky slopes. At about 6.0 miles, first the Rainy Way Trail departs to the left and soon after the Orange Trail as well. By 6.3 miles the Green Trail splits off to the left—an optional cutoff to take off about 3 miles. Taking the trail to the right leaves you on a Blue-only route through the southwestern corner of the system—the most rugged segment of all. The trail tangles on itself like spaghetti, and the paths are steeper, descend faster, and overlook open kettles and narrow ridges. It's quite breathtaking in all respects.

At 9.2 miles the Green Trail joins again from the left; when you come to the White Trail juncture, take the Blue/Green Trail to the right, passing another much larger wet kettle. At the next juncture, at 9.5 miles, the Orange Trail splits to the left, a potential cutoff of almost 1.5 miles from your hike. Take the Blue/Green Trail to the right. A long loop—still a bit rough but not like that last Blue-only route—heads south, descending through pine initially, then making the turn east and back to the north mostly through brush and prairie. When you return to the Orange Trail on the left, you have 1 mile left to go. The trail never ceases switching back and forth, but it's a relatively easy return to the trailhead.

While much of the trail is over rolling glacial terrain, there is also a section of pine plantation.

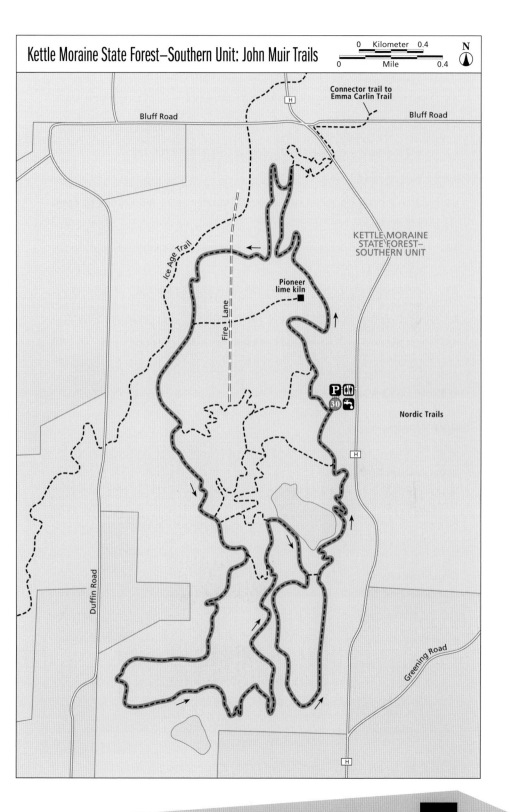

Kettle Moraine State Forest–Southern Unit: John Muir Trails

0 Kilometer 0.4
0 Mile 0.4

N

Connector trail to
Emma Carlin Trail

Bluff Road

Bluff Road

KETTLE MORAINE
STATE FOREST–
SOUTHERN UNIT

Ice Age Trail

Fire Lane

Pioneer
lime kiln

Nordic Trails

Duffin Road

Greening Road

MILES AND DIRECTIONS

0.0 Start from the trailhead and take the trail to the right against bike traffic.

0.3 Stay left at the first juncture with the Kids, Brown, and Rainy Dew Trails.

3.7 Pass the connector trails to the Emma Carlin Trails; stay left.

4.2 Cross an old fire lane.

5.0 Go straight at the juncture with a 0.6-mile trail to the left leading to a pioneer lime kiln.

5.5 The trail passes between two kettle bogs and the Orange Trail splits to the left; keep right on the Blue.

6.3 The Green Trail splits to the left; stay right on the Blue Trail.

9.2 The Blue Trail reconnects to the Green coming in on your left; stay right.

9.5 Pass the Orange Trail on your left; take the trail to the right.

11.0 The Orange Trail connects from the left; take the Blue Trail to the right.

12.0 Arrive back at the trailhead.

HIKE INFORMATION

Local Information

Backyard Bikes and Ski/LaGrange General Store, W6098 US 12, Whitewater, WI 53190; (262) 495-8600; www.backyardbikes.com. This corner stores combines a cafe and convenience store with a bike repair and sales shop. Rent bikes, skis, and snowshoes here for use on the nearby trails.

Organizations

Kettle Moraine Hiking Club, www.kmhikingclub.webs.com

Kettle Moraine State Forest—Southern Unit: Nordic Ski Trails

If you are looking for a long trek with a bit of a workout, this may be it. The loop listed as most difficult surely earns its label. The terrain of Kettle Moraine is frequently marked by repeated steep ascents and declines—short distances, to be fair, but at times coming like waves. But the forest, the bluff-top views, old oaks, pine plantation and sections of prairie are fantastic, and options for shorter routes or bypasses for the hardest sections are numerous.

Start: From the trailhead of the Blue Trail near the parking lot
Distance: 9.1-mile loop
Hiking time: 4 hours
Difficulty: Moderately strenuous
Trail surface: Dirt, grass
Best season: Spring through fall, with great fall colors
Other trail users: None
Canine compatibility: Leashed dogs permitted
Land status: State park
Fees and permits: Vehicle admission sticker required; available for purchase at park entrance, self-pay station, or state forest headquarters

Schedule: Daily, 6 a.m. to 11 p.m.
Maps: USGS Little Prairie; at state park office, on map boards and website
Trail contact: Kettle Moraine State Forest—Southern Unit, S91 W39091 Hwy. 59, Eagle, WI 53119; (262) 594-6200; http://dnr.wi.gov
Special considerations: When trails are groomed for skiers, hiking is not allowed. This is a good option when the John Muir Trails across the road have too many mountain bikers for comfortable hiking. Bikes are not allowed here.

Finding the trailhead: From Milwaukee head south on I-43 about 33 miles and take exit 38 for WI 20. Go right on WI 20 for 9.4 miles, then take a slight right onto US 12. Drive 2 miles and turn right onto CR H. Go 1.5 miles; the park entrance is on the right. The trailhead is at the parking lot, behind the shelter house. **GPS:** N42 49.318' / W88 36.012'

THE HIKE

While you are not likely to encounter a lot of people, those here are often runners since the distances are long and you can pick and choose when it comes to the challenge of the terrain. The described hike takes the longest of the routes, the Blue Trail, but throughout the system, other colored trails are embedded within the larger loops and offer places to either shave off a couple of miles, skip a series of steep hills, or just give you a different part of the park to look at from the last time you were here. Blue is longest and hardest. The Green Trail is no slouch either, but only covers 3.9 miles and skips the final stretch of Blue Trail, which is some of the steepest. Orange at 2.7 miles and Red at 2.1 miles are just moderate and rather short. Easy trails are the White (3.2 miles), Purple (1.7 miles), and Brown (0.7 mile).

The trails are considered one-way for the sake of skiers, a rule hikers need not be concerned about except when following maps. Two trailheads lie at the parking area, but don't mistake the return trails with these. From left to right (if your back is to the parking lot), the Blue/Green/Orange/Red trailhead—the harder trails—begins at the far left. The return trails of Red/Orange/Green/Brown

Two-track through pine plantation along the Nordic Trails. Preamtip Satasuk

are at the next opening in the woods. To the right of that at an angle into the trees is the trailhead of the Brown/Purple trails. Finally, the Purple, White, and Blue come across from the far right.

From the trailhead take the Blue through an unshaded, often prairie-lined corridor through the woods. At 0.6 mile is the first juncture. Blue descends on the trail to the left, passing through a lot of pine plantation, and comes back on the other side of this intersection for a total of 1.8 miles. From this juncture it joins the other trails again for just 0.1 mile, then takes the trail to the left up onto grassy bluffs for the best overlooks in the park. At 3.4 miles green joins it again from the right; take the trail left through some nice old, gnarly oak trees. At 3.8 miles the Green Trail goes to the right, while Blue covers more hilly forest until they meet again at 4.7 miles. Drop 0.8 mile from your hike if you sneak across on the Green.

The Blue and Green Trails remain together until green splits off to the right at the next juncture at 5.6 miles. Here's the "difficult" part: The next 3.2 miles, except for a brief 0.1-mile share with the Purple Trail at 6.6 miles, are on the Blue and White Trails, and the frequency of the ramps up and down the kettles is more than in the rest of the park. Good exercise, to be sure! At 8.8 miles the Purple Trail joins from the right, and it's easy hiking back to the parking lot.

MILES AND DIRECTIONS

0.0 Start from the Blue trailhead and head straight into the woods.

0.6 Take the Blue Trail on the left and follow it around a long loop back to this same intersection.

2.4 Take the Blue/Green/Red/Orange Trails to the left.

2.5 Take the Blue Trail left up onto the bluffs.

3.4 At the next juncture, take the Blue/Green Trails left.

3.8 Take the Blue Trail on the left; green cuts off to the right.

4.7 Stay straight as the Green Trail joins from the right and both Blue and Green continue forward.

5.6 Stay left when the Green Trail splits to the right.

6.6 The Purple Trail joins from the right for 500 feet; stay left through here.

8.8 The Purple Trail joins from the right again; keep straight on the Blue Trail.

9.1 Arrive back at the picnic and parking area.

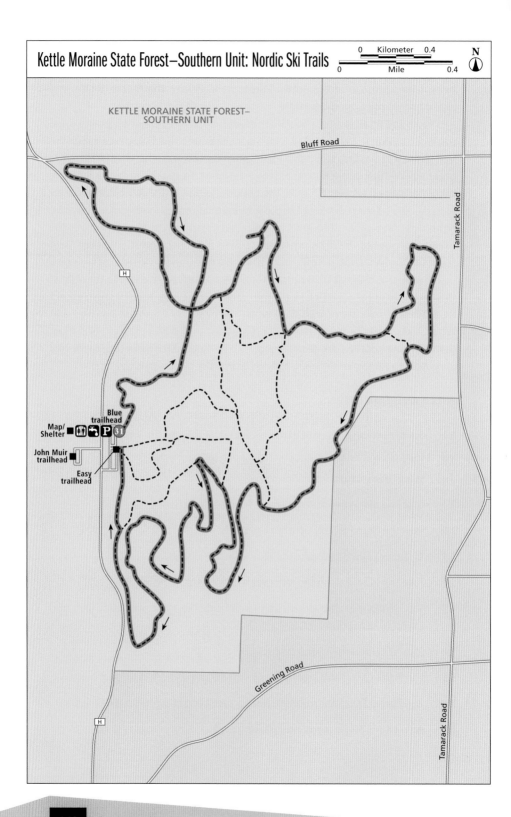

Kettle Moraine State Forest–Southern Unit: Nordic Ski Trails

0   Kilometer   0.4
0   Mile   0.4

N

KETTLE MORAINE STATE FOREST–
SOUTHERN UNIT

Bluff Road

Tamarack Road

Blue
trailhead

Map/
Shelter

John Muir
trailhead

Easy
trailhead

Greening Road

Tamarack Road

Local Information

Backyard Bikes and Ski/LaGrange General Store, W6098 US 12, Whitewater, WI 53190; (262) 495-8600; www.backyardbikes.com. This corner stores combines a cafe and convenience store with a bike repair and sales shop. Rent bikes, skis, and snowshoes here for use on the nearby trails.

Organizations

Kettle Moraine Hiking Club, www.kmhikingclub.webs.com

Green Tip:
Never feed wild animals under any circumstances. You may damage their health and expose yourself (and them) to danger.

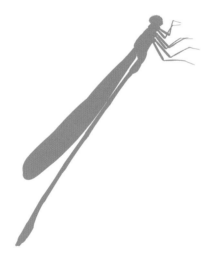

Ice Age National Scenic Trail: Whitewater Lake Segment

While the hike ends at Whitewater Lake, the dominating features are the abundant kettles along the way. Hike it in either direction, one-way or round-trip; fans speak highly of it in any season, even winter. Old oak forest, pine plantation, overlooks, and a footpath along the backs of glacial hills—this is classic Ice Age Trail terrain. At the lake end is a recreation area for camping and more hiking.

Start: From the trailhead across US 12 from the Ice Age Trail parking lot

Distance: 8.9 miles out-and-back with a small loop

Hiking time: 3.5 to 4 hours

Difficulty: Moderate to strenuous due to distance, trail surface, and strenuous climbs

Trail surface: Uneven packed dirt, with tree roots and stones

Best season: Spring through fall, with great fall colors

Other trail users: None

Canine compatibility: Leashed dogs permitted

Land status: State park

Fees and permits: Vehicle admission sticker required for the Ice Age Trail parking lot or the Whitewater Lake Recreation Area; available for purchase at self-pay stations, the recreation area, or state forest headquarters

Schedule: Daily, 6 a.m. to 11 p.m. within the state park; otherwise no restrictions

Maps: USGS Whitewater; *Ice Age Trail Atlas*

Trail contacts: Ice Age Trail Alliance, 2110 Main St., Cross Plains, WI 53528; (800) 227-0046; www .iceagetrail.org; Whitewater Lake Visitor Center and Campground, W7796 Kettle Moraine Dr., Whitewater, WI 53190; (262) 473-7501 (Memorial Day to Labor Day); http://dnr.wi.gov

Special considerations: You can also hike this trail in reverse from the Whitewater Lake Recreation Area. From mid-May to mid-October the recreation area offers 63 rustic campsites with no showers and only pit toilets. Reserve at (888) 947-2757 or www .reserveamerica.com.

Finding the trailhead: From downtown Milwaukee take I-43 south toward Beloit for 33 miles. Turn right onto WI 20 and go 9.4 miles. Take a slight right onto US 12 and continue 4.7 miles. The parking lot for the Ice Age Trail is on the right side of the highway. The trailhead for this segment is on the opposite side of the highway. **GPS:** N42 48.240' / W88 39.158'

THE HIKE

The trailhead is marked clearly with an Ice Age Trail mammoth emblem and begins straight through a gate. The wider path going straight and another going left are part of the Moraine Ridge Trail, a state horse and snowmobile trail. You take the rustic footpath that angles away on the right. The Ice Age Trail is marked with yellow blazes on posts and trees. Climb the ridge on broken rock and packed dirt; the path starts to turn to the southwest. In a clearing stop at a bench and enjoy the scenic overlook. What lies before you is a glacial outwash plain. Much of the tree cover is aspen here but oaks soon take over.

The trail follows along the top of the moraine and then crosses to another one. At 1.1 miles you pass under power lines. Much of the hike is under the trees, but as you wind around the next ridge you come into pine plantation. The trail descends a bit and crosses Esterly Road. At 2.5 miles the Ice Age Trail intersects

Whitewater Creek near the turnaround point of the hike.

with the bridle trail again. Follow the IAT gently to the right; signage prohibits horses and snowmobiles. The trail heads downhill, switching back on wood-beam and earth steps in a forest of mixed hardwoods and pine, and then you come to CR P. The trail goes straight across and shortly is climbing again on wood-beam steps after passing through a small clearing.

Now it's back to moraine climbing, but with the occasional wood-beam steps here and there. You know you are just about at the campground in White-water Lake Recreation Area when you come to a bench with a nice view of the lake at 3.6 miles. About 300 feet of steps take you down off the ridge, and there is a trail into the campsites on your right. Keep on the main trail; it crosses Hi Lo Road, heads into the woods, and comes to another trail juncture. Take the trail to the right, cross the bridle path once more, and arrive at Whitewater Creek. A bridge crosses the creek, and the trail heads left on the other side. Just beyond this is Clover Valley Road, heading left down to the lake, *Rice* Lake to be precise. At Kettle Moraine Drive, go left again and follow the road back to Hi Lo Road, where you pick up the Ice Age Trail for your return to the trailhead.

MILES AND DIRECTIONS

0.0 Start from the trailhead and take the narrow footpath to the right, ascending the ridge.

1.2 Cross a clearing under power lines and head back into the woods.

1.8 The trail crosses Esterly Road and picks up on the other side.

2.5 Cross the bridle trail.

2.7 Cross CR P.

3.6 Pass a bench with a scenic overlook of the lake; take the stairs down to the campground.

3.9 Cross Hi Lo Road and at the trail juncture in the woods on the other side, take the trail to the right.

4.4 Take the bridge across Whitewater Creek and turn left onto Clover Valley Road.

4.7 Take a left onto Kettle Moraine Drive.

5.0 Turn left onto Hi Lo Road and backtrack along the Ice Age Trail back to US 12.

6.2 Cross CR P.

8.9 Arrive back at the trailhead.

Ice Age National Scenic Trail: Whitewater Lake Segment

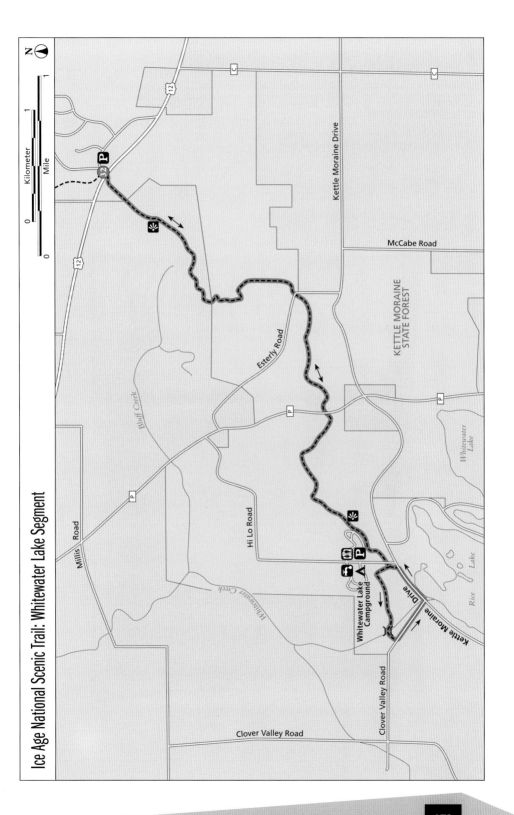

Local Information

Whitewater Tourism Council, 150 W. Main St., Whitewater, WI 53190; (866) 499-8687; www.discoverwhitewater.org

Lodging

Hamilton House Bed & Breakfast, 328 W. Main St., Whitewater, WI 53190; (262) 473-1900; www.bandbhamiltonhouse.com

A glimpse of Whitewater Lake from the top of a moraine.

South of Milwaukee

Petrifying Springs County Park Trail. **Preamtip Satasuk**

33

Geneva Lake Shorepath

It's difficult to imagine but this 21-mile lakeshore path along one of southeastern Wisconsin's most beautiful and touristy lakes remains a public-access trail despite being primarily through the backyards of some rather well-to-do properties. This 7-mile segment shows off some of the best of the homes and, in most places, follows a nicely paved pathway with no shortage of flowers and gardens.

Start: From the trailhead behind the Lake Geneva Public Library
Distance: 7.0 miles point-to-point
Hiking time: 2.5 hours
Difficulty: Easy
Trail surface: Paved, dirt, some steps
Best season: Spring through fall
Other trail users: None
Canine compatibility: Leashed dogs permitted
Land status: Public easement
Fees and permits: None
Schedule: Daily, sunrise to sunset
Maps: USGS Lake Geneva and Walworth; available for purchase in gift shops and bookstores
Trail contact: Lake Geneva Area Convention & Visitors Bureau, 201 Wrigley Dr., Lake Geneva, WI

53147; (800) 345-1020; www.lakegenevawi.com
Special considerations: During winter and the shoulder seasons, homeowners may pull up their docks and these may obstruct the path. The route is almost entirely through private property so be sure to stay on the trail. Facilities are limited to those found at the library and the adjacent park, and then there is nothing public until you reach Williams Bay. Parking is metered near the Lake Geneva Public Library, but a block into the residential area is free. Lake Geneva Cruises offers pickup and drop-off service for hikers by appointment.

Finding the trailhead: From downtown Milwaukee drive 34 miles south on I-43 and take WI 120 south 11.8 miles to Lake Geneva. Continue as it becomes Interchange N and then East Sheridan Springs Road. Turn left onto Williams Street, which becomes Broad Street, and after 0.9 mile turn right onto Main Street. The library is on the left. The hike starts on the paved walk behind the library. Parking is on the street. **GPS:** N42 35.459' / W88 26.226'

THE HIKE

Lake Geneva is on Geneva Lake and no matter which you mention, most Wisconsinites think of it as a popular tourist destination, particularly for the Chicago crowd. To be fair, the arrival of the railroad in 1871 did make the area an easy target for lumber barons and other wealthy residents to the south for their large mansions and summer homes. The lake and its three communities—Lake Geneva, Williams Bay, and Fontana—are resort areas. With all that private lakefront property you'd imagine lake access would be limited. However, back in the day the workers at the various properties beat a path along the edge of the water on the way to their respective jobs. The first European settlers declared that the first 20 feet of shoreline would remain public, and when property owners tried to reverse that claim, they were unsuccessful. The result is that you can walk freely across this narrow 21-mile trail through the backyards of some gorgeous mansions. The shoreline path, however, goes back much farther than the nineteenth century. Chief Big Foot and his people of the Potawatomi tribe had worn it between villages, and archaeologists suggest the area was already occupied as far back as 2500 BCE.

Begin behind the public library in Lake Geneva, where the trail is a proper sidewalk starting near the beach and marina. Head north (with the lake on your left) along Elm Park, and at the end of the park look for a gate on your left and a

Some property owners put up decorative fences along their section of the path. Preamtip Satasuk

> *Some families who survived the Chicago Fire on October 8, 1871, took the train bound for Geneva Lake and stayed there while their homes were rebuilt.*

sign marking it as the trail. To your right are the last public restrooms and water until Williams Bay.

The trail begins on crushed rock but will vary throughout the hike, from nice decorative bricks to packed dirt and tree roots through strips of woods between properties. At 0.5 mile the trail actually turns to the right and goes around a fenced property, across its driveway, and back to the lakeshore between fences on both sides. Pass a private beach on your left at 0.6 mile; Covenant Harbor Bible Camp has the lakefront at 0.9 mile. The path is quite level, but you get your first bit of a climb at 1.4 miles: just a few steps up and then the trail crosses 100 feet of trees and brush.

Undeveloped paths where the surface is packed dirt can be a little muddy in rainy periods. Cross the old tracks of a boathouse at 2.1 miles and soon after see a wooden rainbow bridge to a small island; keep off, this is private. At 2.7 miles the landscaper has created a bit of an arboretum, and there are signs identifying the trees and plants. Climb a short, steep ramp at 3.0 miles; you are now 50 feet above the waterline. Down the other side an asphalt path switches back, moderately steeply, to bring you back to the lake. The Alta Vista estate, built in 1919 by Colonel William N. Pelouze, the founder of Pelouze Scale and Balance Company, stands at 3.4 miles and is clearly marked.

Black Point Estate

Sure it's lovely to see the manicured grounds and admire the architecture of the many mansions along the lakeshore, but how about a tour of one of the finest? You are in luck, as Black Point Estate is open to the public. A German immigrant beer baron from Chicago, Conrad Seipp, had this twenty-room summer home built in the Queen Anne style in 1888. This may make you envious, but consider the fact that for thirteen bedrooms there was only one bathroom. The family donated the mansion to the State of Wisconsin in 2005, and it is managed by the Wisconsin Historical Society. Original fixtures and furnishings, along with a fantastic collection of Victorian furniture, make this mansion a time capsule from a bygone era when boats were the only method of travel to these lakeside homes. In fact, one still arrives by water. Lake Geneva Cruise Line handles ticket bookings and picks up from Riviera Docks in Lake Geneva for a 3-hour tour.

Frank Lloyd Wright fans may admire the copy of Fallingwaters at 5.2 miles. At 6.0 miles the path comes to a point along the shore and rounds it to the right past a pebbled beach. Stairs ascend near Walnut Grove Park and offer an overlook of the lake as the trail makes the turn into Williams Bay. At 7.0 miles cross a footbridge near the marina and come to Geneva Street and Harris Road and the parking lot.

Option: Extend the Hike

Of course, ambitious power hikers might attempt to complete the entire 21 miles, and the trail along the south shore heads into Big Foot Beach State Park. But also check out Kishwauketoe Nature Conservancy across the road from the end of this trail segment. There are five hiking loops, the longest being 3.4 miles and starting right at the parking lot.

Geneva Lake Shorepath. **Preamtip Satasuk**

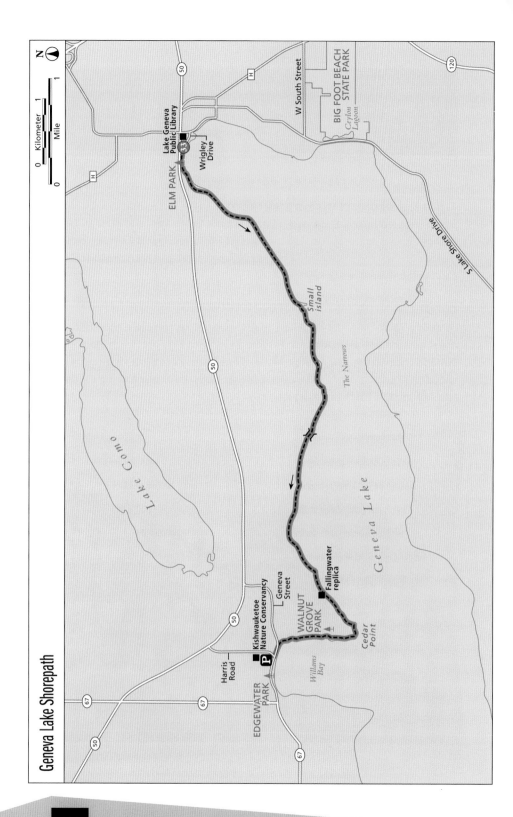

Geneva Lake Shorepath

MILES AND DIRECTIONS

0.0   Start from behind the library and head north with the lake on your left.

0.3   Pass the last restrooms and enter a narrow gate and pathway.

0.9   Cross the property of Covenant Harbor Bible Camp.

2.2   Pass a small private island on the left.

3.7   Cross a decorative wrought-iron bridge.

4.7   Enter the Knollwood property.

5.2   Pass behind the replica of Fallingwaters.

6.0   Round Cedar Point.

7.0   Arrive at Edgewater Park in Williams Bay.

HIKE INFORMATION

Local Information
Lake Geneva Area Convention & Visitors Bureau, 201 Wrigley Dr., Lake Geneva, WI 53147; (800) 345-1020; www.lakegenevawi.com

Local Events/Attractions
Big Foot Beach State Park, 1452 S. Wells St., Lake Geneva, WI 53147; (262) 248-2528; http://dnr.wi.gov
Black Point Estate, http://blackpointestate.wisconsinhistory.org
Events Calender, www.lakegenevawi.com/Events. August is especially notable for the annual Art in the Park and the five-day Venetian Festival.
Kishwauketoe Nature Conservancy, WI 67, Williams Bay, WI 53191; (262) 903-3601; www.kishwauketoe.org

Hike Tours
Lake Geneva Cruise Line, 812 Wrigley Dr., Lake Geneva, WI 53147; (800) 558-5911; www.cruiselakegeneva.com. Offers pickup or drop-off service to hikers by appointment.

Other Resources
Geneva Lake Shore Path Guide, Nei-Turner Media Group, Inc., 93 W. Geneva St., P.O. Box 1080, Williams Bay, WI 53191; (262) 245-1000; www.ntmediagroup.com
Walk, Talk & Gawk by Chris Hawver and Pat Groh, P.O. Box 413, Lake Geneva , WI 53147; www.walktalkgawk.com. Available at bookstores and gift shops.

Richard Bong State Recreation Area Trails

Take a long stroll through one of the area's most popular state park retreats. Trails pass through the largest managed grassland in this corner of the state—and it's just burgeoning with wildflowers.

Start: From the trailhead at the hiking trails parking lot
Distance: 4.2-mile loop
Hiking time: 2 hours
Difficulty: Easy to moderate due to some steepness
Trail surface: Grass, packed dirt; may be quite muddy in spring
Best season: Spring through fall
Other trail users: None
Canine compatibility: Leashed dogs permitted
Land status: State park
Fees and permits: Vehicle admission sticker required; available for purchase at park entrance

Schedule: Daily, 6 a.m. to 11 p.m.
Maps: USGS Rochester, Union Grove, Silver Lake, Paddock Lake; at park office and on website
Trail contact: Richard Bong State Recreation Area, 26313 Burlington Rd., Kansasville, WI 53139; (262) 878-5600; http://dnr.wi.gov
Special consideration: Hunting pheasant and hunting waterfowl from lake blinds are permitted on the Blue Trail in the fall from 9 a.m. to 2 p.m. The Green Trail is in a non-hunting area.

Finding the trailhead: From downtown Milwaukee take I-94 south 27.8 miles and take exit 339 for 12th Street/Somers Road. Turn right and go 3.3 miles to turn left on 172nd Avenue. Continue 0.8 mile, and turn right on WI 142. Drive 5.7 miles and enter the park on the left. From the entrance station take the next road to the left; the trailhead parking lot is on your left. The trailhead for the Blue and Green Trails is at the far end of the parking lot. **GPS:** N42 38.05' / W88 7.44'

THE HIKE

This 4,515-acre state park is named for Wisconsin native and World War II flying ace, Major Richard I. Bong. Activities range from hiking and swimming to model airplane flying and hunting. The trail system collectively totals over 41 miles, and hiking trails are color coded. The park is the largest managed grassland in southeastern Wisconsin, and if you enjoy wildflowers, this is a hotspot for them. Benches are spread intermittently throughout.

The difference between the Green and Blue Trails, other than length (1.8 and 4.2 miles, respectively), is that the Blue has more moderate to strenuous steep sections, although these are short stretches of never more than about 75 feet. Additionally the Blue Trail gets its extra length by going all the way around Wolf Lake. The bridle trail crosses at several points, and there are some spur trails, which are clearly marked as such. The hiking trails are marked with color-coded posts.

From the parking lot the trail begins on a boardwalk through cattails with a couple of observation points. On the other side the grass trail begins, crossing the park road to arrive at the first trail juncture. Take the left path, following the arrows, and shortly pass a sledding hill and some forested portions. The Blue Trail leaves the Green at 0.9 mile and goes south around the lake. At 2.0 miles is a shaded bench with a shoreline scenic view of the lake.

The trail crosses the roads to the beach and fishing pier areas before rejoining the Green Trail for the short distance back to the trailhead. There are also two self-guided nature trails within the park (dogs not allowed), one of which intersects with the Blue Trail. The Orange, Red, and Gray Trails are north of WI 142.

The boardwalk through the wetlands is a great place for bird watching. Preamtip Satasuk

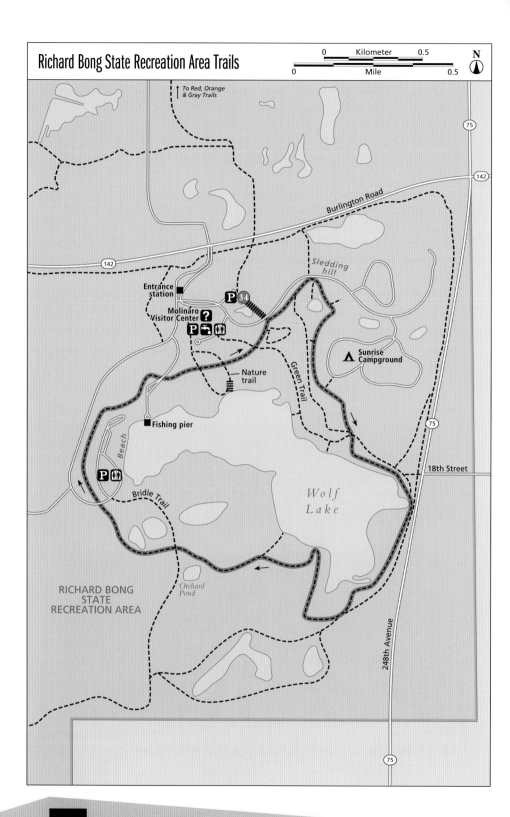

Richard Bong State Recreation Area Trails

Kilometer
0 — 0.5

Mile
0 — 0.5

N

To Red, Orange & Gray Trails

75

142

Burlington Road

142

Sledding hill

Entrance station

P 34

Molinaro Visitor Center

P

Sunrise Campground

Nature trail

Green Trail

Beach

Fishing pier

75

P

18th Street

Wolf Lake

Bridle Trail

RICHARD BONG STATE RECREATION AREA

Orchard Pond

248th Avenue

75

MILES AND DIRECTIONS

0.0 Start from the trailhead.

0.3 Pass the sledding hill.

0.9 Stay left at the juncture with the Green Trail.

2.0 Pass the lakeview bench.

2.5 See Orchard Pond on the left.

2.8 Cross the road leading to the beach area.

3.5 Cross the road leading to the fishing pier.

4.2 Arrive back at the trailhead.

HIKE INFORMATION

Local Information

City of Burlington, 300 N. Pine St., Burlington, WI 53105; (262) 342-1161; www
.burlington-wi.gov

Local Events/Attractions

Chocolate Experience Museum, 113 E. Chestnut St., Burlington, WI 53105; (262)
763-6044; www.chocolateexperiencemuseum.com
Chocolate Fest, www.chocolatefest.com. Held in Burlington every Memorial Day
weekend

Richard I. Bong

The Richard Bong State Recreation Area is infamous for having its highway signs
stolen, no doubt by pranksters who get a giggle out of the marijuana reference,
but Dick Bong meant serious business. As a fighter pilot in World War II, he shot
down over forty Japanese planes, earning the Medal of Honor and the record
for the great American ace. He grew up in Poplar, Wisconsin, near Superior,
where the Richard I. Bong Veterans Historical Center is today. There you can find
more information about his life and see a P-38 Lightning, a double-tailed fighter
he flew in the South Pacific on more than 200 missions. Ironically he survived
the war but died in August 1945, as a test pilot flying something completely
new: a jet-powered plane.

Petrifying Springs County Park Trail

Take the pleasant, easy path around this nicely wooded park offering views of the Pike River and then stop for a picnic in the center of the park or even a round of golf on the park's eighteen-hole course.

Start: From the trailhead near the first parking lot off County Road A
Distance: 2.7-mile loop
Hiking time: 1 hour
Difficulty: Easy to moderate due to some steepness
Trail surface: Packed dirt, some cedar chips
Best season: Spring, summer, and especially fall for colors
Other trail users: None
Canine compatibility: Leashed dogs permitted; Carlisle Family Dog Park also lies within the park and exacts a use fee

Land status: County park
Fees and permits: None
Schedule: Daily, 7 a.m. to 10 p.m.
Maps: USGS Racine South; on park website
Trail contact: Petrifying Springs County Park, 761 Green Bay Rd., Kenosha, WI 53144; (262) 857-1869; www.co.kenosha.wi.us

Finding the trailhead: From downtown Milwaukee follow I-94 south 25.8 miles to exit 337 for CR KR. Turn left and go 4.2 miles. Turn right onto WI 31, go 1.1 miles, and turn left onto CR A/7th Street. Continue 0.1 mile; the park entrance is on the right. **GPS:** N42 39.25' / W87 52.45'

THE HIKE

Sounds terrifying, but the 360-acre park with a golf course, commonly referred to as "Pets," actually takes its name from springs rich with minerals. The amount of limestone in the water was so great that even acorns or leaves that fell in would get coated with a hard mineral shell, as if they were being petrified. Those springs now lie in a ravine along the southern edge of the property. The Pike River flows through the park, which is the oldest in the county's park system. Facilities are many, including volleyball and ball diamonds, picnic areas, and even some chessboards (but no pieces), making this a great family destination. The abundance of hardwoods makes this an ideal destination for fall color viewing.

The main loop trail, the Yellow Trail, passes through hardwood forest, open areas of the park, and along a golf course. Begin at the parking lot at the park entrance on CR A. Cross the county road where the park road enters the woods to the north. Go to the right side of the road and look for a map board and a cedar-chip trail leading up at an angle to the right. At 0.2 mile you come to a three-way juncture with the Green Trail to the right and the Red Trail straight ahead. Either of these will take you across the upper half of the park and shorten your hike a bit. Instead, go left, cross the park road, and go right, following its edge to where you find a trail splitting like a V into the woods. Take the right branch of this, and again at the next juncture, and this trail curves east across the top of the park, eventually curving to the south where it meets up with the Red and Green Trails on your right just before CR A near the entrance of the golf course. Cross the county road and seek the trail to the left of the entry. It passes along the edge of the course and through woods, joins the park road for a short stretch, and then follows along the Pike River into the picnic areas. Cross the park road with a bridge at your left, and at the next playground go left and cross the river on a footbridge. The trail climbs a bit as it heads north. Descend into a parking area, pass another playground, and follow the park road over the bridge and to the parking lot where you began.

One of the best stretches of the trail is along the Pike River. Preamtip Satasuk

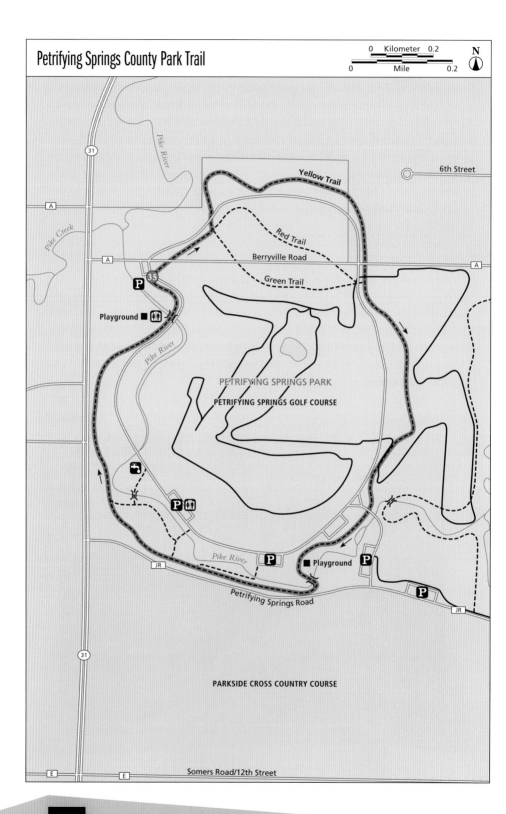

Petrifying Springs County Park Trail

0 Kilometer 0.2

0 Mile 0.2

N

31

Pike River

6th Street

A

Yellow Trail

Pike Creek

A

Red Trail

Berryville Road

A

35

Green Trail

P

Playground

Pike River

PETRIFYING SPRINGS PARK

PETRIFYING SPRINGS GOLF COURSE

P

JR

Pike River

P

Playground

P

Petrifying Springs Road

P

JR

PARKSIDE CROSS COUNTRY COURSE

31

E

E

Somers Road/12th Street

MILES AND DIRECTIONS

0.0   Start from the trailhead.

0.2   Cross the park road.

0.8   Cross CR A, then pass the entrance to the golf course.

1.4   Pass a park bridge on the left.

1.6   Cross the Pike River on a footbridge.

2.7   Arrive back at the trailhead and parking lot.

HIKE INFORMATION

Local Information
Visit Kenosha, 812 56th St., Kenosha, WI 53140; (800) 654-7309; www.visit kenosha.com

Local Attractions
Civil War Museum, 5400 First Ave., Kenosha, WI 53140; (262) 653-4141; www .kenosha.org/wp-civilwar. An outstanding modern museum from the perspective of the upper Midwest.

🍂 Green Tip:
Stay on the trail. Cutting through from one part of a switchback to another can destroy fragile plant life.

Bristol Woods County Park Trails

Explore the 197 acres of this heavily wooded county park, which encompass four different habitats: upland forest, bottomland forest, oak savanna, and wetlands. The trail network allows you to extend the hike, crisscrossing throughout. Birds and other wildlife are plentiful. Pay a visit to the Pringle Nature Center and learn to identify the many species of trees and other plants along the route.

Start: From the trailhead behind the nature center (or the playground)

Distance: 2.5-mile loop

Hiking time: 1.5 hours

Difficulty: Easy

Trail surface: Dirt, mowed grass

Best season: Year-round

Other trail users: Skiers in winter

Canine compatibility: Leashed dogs permitted

Land status: State park

Fees and permits: None

Schedule: Daily 7 a.m. to 10 p.m.

Maps: USGS Paddock Lake; at nature center, trail junctures, and on county parks website

Trail contacts: Pringle Nature Center, 9800 160th Ave., Bristol, WI 53104; (262) 857-8008; www.pringlenc.org; Kenosha County Parks, 1010 56th St., Kenosha, WI 53140; (262) 857-1869; http://www.co.kenosha.wi.us

Special considerations: Mosquitoes and mud can be nuisances during rainy periods. Numbered posts in the forest correspond to nature center booklets: dark for orienteering and white for a nature guide. Check the Pringle Nature Center website for upcoming events or hikes guided by the naturalist. Explorer packs are available for families, and the center rents GPS devices and snowshoes or loans guidebooks and binoculars if you leave an ID.

Finding the trailhead: From downtown Milwaukee take I-94 south 34.5 miles to exit 345. Turn right onto Wilmot Road and go 2.5 miles. At the traffic circle take the third exit onto 160th Avenue/CR MB. Go 0.5 mile and turn right at the park entrance. Drive through the lower lot and on to the nature center lot. The trailhead is behind the center; there is an alternate trailhead behind the playground in the lower lot. **GPS:** N42 31.952' / W88 0.430'

THE HIKE

Like many places in Wisconsin, Bristol Woods was once part of a farm. That's hard to imagine now with the towering trees and thick brush, but several other families joined the Pringle family in putting together these nearly 200 acres that are some of the wildest in Kenosha County. Combined with the resources of the nature center, a hike here can be quite educational.

The park has a color-coded trail map, and this loop combines several trails. The trail begins behind the nature center on the Yellow Trail. At the first juncture the alternate trail from the lower lot joins from the left. Go right and soon come to the Red Trail; go left. The woods are dominated by white, black, and red oak trees, and the understory shows a lot of intervening brush. At 0.5 mile turn left onto the Orange Trail. This is a short sort of lollipop loop into an area characterized by the plants of a wetland marsh, such as arrowhead, cattails, and sedges, and the trail may get soggy at times. Follow the path and it is soon joined by your return trail angling back on your right; the small lollipop extends from this point. Go left around the short loop at the end and back to this point, then head back

Stop in at the Pringle Nature Center and borrow a field guide to help you identify the many species of trees here in the woods. **Preamtip Satasuk**

toward the Red Trail, but on the left branch of the Orange Trail. Go left onto the Red Trail and pass through larger, older oaks.

At 1.1 miles you encounter a connector trail to the Green Trail on your left. Following the Red Trail deeper into the woods and then back out on the Green can extend the hike. For this hike cross on the connector trail and go left onto the Green at the next juncture. The trail follows the edge of the park, and the trees give way from oaks to other species such as ash, basswood, elm, and box elder.

At 1.6 miles pass the juncture with the White Trail on your right, pass over a small hill, and arrive at the Blue Trail. Just off on the right, the Green continues up into the forest. Blue goes either left or right, left taking you out of the park past the Old Town Hall. Go right on the Blue; it follows a sort of land bridge straight through a marshy area in the forest. At the next juncture you stay the course on this land bridge. The Blue Trail departs to the right, up toward the center of the forest, ending at the Red Trail there. From behind you on the right, the Green Trail joins. You are following the Green Trail now without having taken any turns. At 2 miles the Green Trail ascends and at the top of a short hill meets the Red Trail. Take this left, and at 2.3 miles the trail touches on the mowed yard of the nature center, but then takes a right turn back into the woods for the last 0.1 mile back to the Yellow Trail. Turn left onto the Yellow and take the next trail left again to the center's back door.

MILES AND DIRECTIONS

0.0 Start from the trailhead and go right at the first juncture, then left soon after on the Red Trail.

0.5 Take a left onto the Orange Trail.

0.8 Return to the Red Trail and turn left.

1.1 Take the connector trail to the Green Trail on your left.

1.6 Stay on the Green Trail past the White Trail juncture.

1.8 Reach the Blue Trail and turn right onto a land bridge.

1.9 Take the Green Trail left.

2.0 Turn left onto the Red Trail.

2.4 Arrive back at the Yellow Trail, take it left, and then another quick left to arrive back at the nature center.

2.5 Arrive back at the trailhead.

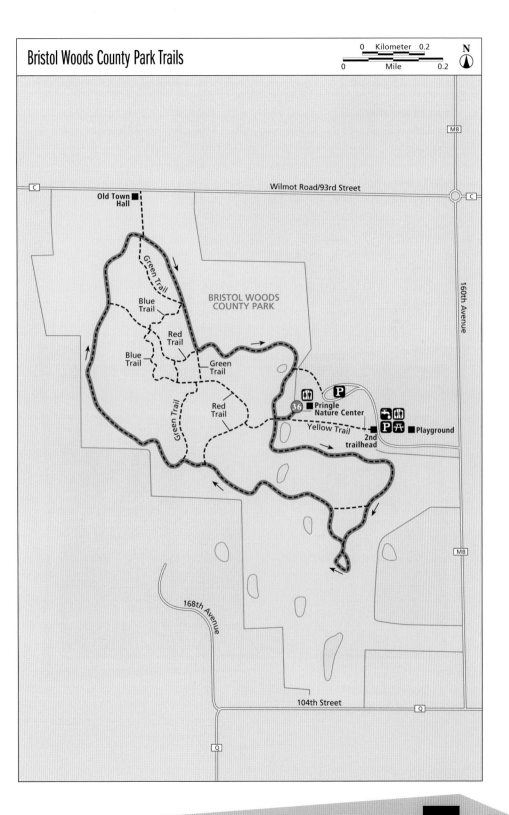

Bristol Woods County Park Trails

Old Town Hall

Wilmot Road/93rd Street

BRISTOL WOODS
COUNTY PARK

Green Trail

Blue Trail

Red Trail

Blue Trail

Green Trail

Green Trail

Red Trail

Pringle Nature Center

Yellow Trail

2nd trailhead

Playground

160th Avenue

168th Avenue

104th Street

0   Kilometer   0.2
0   Mile   0.2

N

Local Information

Visit Kenosha, 812 56th St., Kenosha, WI 53140; (800) 654-7309; www.visit kenosha.com

Local Events

Bristol Renaissance Faire, 12550 120th Ave., Kenosha, WI 53142; (847) 395-7773; www.renfair.com/Bristol. The popular themed fair runs on weekends from July through Labor Day.

Restaurants

Bristol 45 Diner, 8321 200th Ave., Bristol, WI 53104; (262) 857-4545; www.bristol 45diner.com

Bristol Woods. Preamtip Satasuk

Chain O'Lakes State Park Trails

The Fox River flows along the edge of the park, and the first of the three loops in this hike passes right along its banks before crossing through wetlands and prairie to a higher path along prairie grass and savanna bluffs with nice views out over the park. The third loop takes a turn through the woods and brings you back across those hills again.

Start: From the trailhead at the office parking lot
Distance: 4.6-mile series of loops
Hiking time: 2 hours
Difficulty: Easy
Trail surface: Crushed stone, some paved, dirt
Best season: Spring through fall
Other trail users: Bicyclists; skiers in winter
Canine compatibility: Leashed dogs permitted
Land status: State park
Fees and permits: None
Schedule: Daily, 6 a.m. to 9 p.m. Apr 1 through the last weekend of Oct; 8 a.m. to sunset winter.

The park is closed for all activities, except hunting, from the end of Oct until late Dec. Check the website for specific dates.
Maps: USGS Fox Lake; at park office and trail junctures
Trail contact: Chain O'Lakes State Park, 8916 Wilmot Rd., Spring Grove, IL 60081; (847) 587-5512; http://dnr.state.il.us
Special considerations: The state park also has several miles of horse trails you can hike, as well as 238 campsites, which can be reserved at (888) 947-2757 or www.reserveamerica.com.

Finding the trailhead: From downtown Milwaukee take I-94 south 38 miles and stay left to use exit 1B to merge onto US 41. At the next intersection, go right onto IL 173 for 13.8 miles. Turn left onto Johnsburg Wilmot Road and drive 1.6 miles to the state park entrance on the left. Follow the park road for 1.4 miles and turn left onto James Road toward the visitor center. After 0.3 mile turn right to the visitor center; the trailhead is in the parking lot to the left of the sidewalk to the visitor center. **GPS:** N42 28.027' / W88 11.418'

THE HIKE

The trail starts downhill from the parking lot on a wide asphalt path through thick woods and brush. After 300 feet you arrive at the first loop, the Gold Finch Trail, and the trail becomes a nicely maintained crushed-rock surface. Take the trail to the left at this first juncture; the path curls around a flower-filled section of prairie grass before heading into mixed hardwood forest, primarily oaks and some hickory. By 0.9 mile you are walking along the Fox River. Jacques Marquette and Louis Joliet paddled through here in 1673, but now you are likely to find herons and waterfowl and the occasional angler in a boat.

The trail doesn't linger long by the river, and after 1 mile is already heading away from it, albeit with open water and cattails on your left. At 1.4 miles you pass a map board and picnic table on the right, and soon the brush opens up as you enter a pine plantation. As you come around the pines, take a left at the next trail juncture. This connects you to the next loop, the Badger Trail. Take the Badger Trail to the left when you reach it; the trail runs right along the forest on your left but with open prairie to your right. It feels like a good old country road. Around the next bend to the left, you can see open water in the distance as you head across open prairie to the next bit of forest.

The trail rises between two low ridges, and at 2.3 miles you exit the woods with a rock wall on your right. The trail makes a right turn through prairie, climbing a grassy bluff to the next trail juncture. Benches here offer a nice spot to enjoy the view to the east and west from the hilltop. Take the trail to the left; it descends into the woods to a juncture with the Sunset Trail. Take this to the left as well; it rises and falls just a bit as it passes through what may have once been savanna but is now mostly forest overtaken by brush. At 2.9 miles enter the Hickory Grove Picnic Area with pit toilets and tables on your left. At 3.1 miles you

Wetlands near the Fox River are good for bird watching. Preamtip Satasuk

pass through a metal gate and the trail becomes asphalt as you approach the Pike Marsh North Picnic Area. Your path is across the road to your right, but it's a good idea to go straight a short distance to the bridge overlooking the marsh if you want to spot some birds or other wildlife. This trail actually continues all the way into the southern half of the park where there are concessions, camping, and a boat landing.

Backtrack to the metal gate and cross the park road to continue the hike through mixed forest and then into an open area with scattered cattails. Beyond this, as you reenter the trees, is a trail juncture. To the left is the Cattail Trail, which leads all the way to the park entrance station and can connect you to the horse trails if you want to make a much longer hike. Continue straight across this juncture and into the Deer Path Picnic Area. Follow the trail as it crosses the park road once again, and at the next juncture turn left. This takes you back up that grassy hill with the great view. At the trail juncture at the top near the benches, take the trail to the left. This is the second half of the Badger Trail, which is mostly exposed from here on out. Cross a bike path at 3.9 miles and climb the next grassy hill with a scattering of large old trees. Odds are good you will spot bluebirds here.

At 4.3 miles pass a bench with a scenic overlook to the right, and a map board and gate to an alternate parking area on the left. Continue straight; the trail descends behind the visitor center and to the connecting trail back to the Gold Finch Trail. Take the connector to the left, then turn left again onto the Gold Finch Trail. After another 200 feet take the trail on the left up to the trailhead and parking lot.

Chain O'Lakes

When the glaciers of the last ice age melted, they left behind a line of lakes. Native American tribes occupied the area for many years before the first Europeans arrived, mostly French traders and explorers, including the famed pair Jacques Marquette, a Jesuit missionary, and Louis Joliet, a fur trader. The railroad arrived in the area in 1901 and with it followed tourism. Today the Chain comprises fifteen lakes, including ten that are strung together by the Fox River and five others connected by channels. Visitors come to the area in droves to fish and go boating. Chain O'Lakes State Park is located at the point where the Fox River enters Grass Lake, about midway down the Chain.

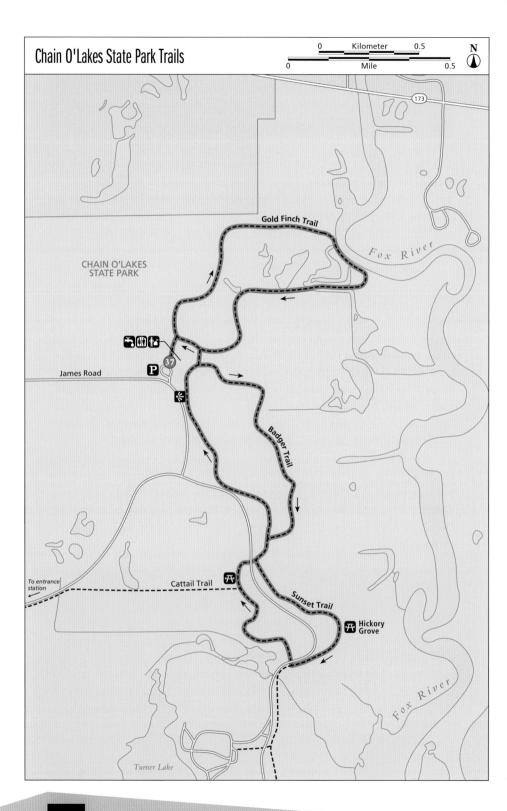

Chain O'Lakes State Park Trails

Kilometer 0 — 0.5

Mile 0 — 0.5

N

173

CHAIN O'LAKES STATE PARK

Fox River

Gold Finch Trail

James Road

37

P

Badger Trail

To entrance station

Cattail Trail

Sunset Trail

Hickory Grove

Turner Lake

Fox River

MILES AND DIRECTIONS

0.0   Start from the trailhead.

0.1   Take the Gold Finch trail left at the first juncture.

1.7   At the trail juncture turn left, hike 500 feet, and turn left again to start on the Badger Trail.

2.5   At the top of a hill come to a trail juncture, benches, and map board. Take the trail to the left into the woods.

2.6   At the trail juncture with the Sunset Trail, turn left.

2.9   Pass through the Hickory Grove Picnic Area.

3.2   At the juncture just before Pike Marsh North Picnic Area, cross the road to the right to continue on the Sunset Trail return path.

3.7   At a juncture the Cattail Trail goes to your left; stay straight and pass through Deer Path Picnic Area.

3.8   Cross the park road, and at the next trail juncture take the left trail up the hill on the Badger Trail. Continue straight (the left trail) at the next juncture.

4.4   Come to the end of the Badger Trail and take the connector trail on the left the short distance to the Gold Finch Trail. Take this left as well.

4.5   At the trail juncture turn left and return to the parking lot near the visitor center.

4.6   Arrive back at the trailhead.

HIKE INFORMATION

Local Information
Lake County Convention & Visitor's Bureau, 5465 Grand Ave., #100, Gurnee, IL 60031; (847) 662-2700; www.visitlakecounty.org

Local Attractions
Stade's Farm and Market, 3709 W. Miller Rd., McHenry, IL ; (815) 675-6396; www .stadesfarmandmarket.com. Farm-fresh produce and U-pick-it opportunities, plus other agri-tourism-related entertainment. Watch for the pumpkin cannon in fall.

Lodging
Chain O'Lakes State Park Campground has 238 sites; make reservations at (800) 246-5082 or www.reserveamerica.com.

Glacial Park Trails

This 3,410-acre preserve and its visitor center are a true treasure for nature lovers: Within the park are glacial formations, varied habitats, a canoe trail, and over 8 miles of trails. In a short distance this hike passes through bog, marsh, prairie, sedge meadow, and oak savanna and across the backs of a couple of glacial kames, offering nice views and great wildlife spotting along an interpretive trail.

Start: From the trailhead next to the visitor center
Distance: 2.6-mile loop
Hiking time: 1.5 hours
Difficulty: Easy, with one short, steep climb for the kame
Trail surface: Dirt, grass
Best season: Spring through fall
Other trail users: None
Canine compatibility: Leashed dogs permitted
Land status: County park
Fees and permits: None
Schedule: Daily, sunrise to sunset

Maps: USGS Richmond; at trailheads and visitor center
Trail contact: Lost Valley Visitor Center, 6316 Harts Rd, Ringwood, IL 60072; (815) 678-4532; www.mccdistrict.org
Special considerations: Stop at the visitor center to pick up free guides covering history, geology, plant communities, and wildlife for the interpretive trail, which is marked with numbered signposts corresponding to text in each booklet.

Finding the trailhead: From downtown Milwaukee take I-94 south about 39 miles and get off on IL 173 west. Go right for 19 miles and turn left onto US 12/Main Street. Drive 2 miles and continue straight on IL 31/Richmond Road for another 2 miles. Turn right onto Harts Road, drive 0.9 mile, and turn right following the signs to the visitor center. Park and walk up the sidewalk to the visitor center; the trailhead is on the left just before you reach the building. **GPS:** N42 25.545' / W88 19.566'

THE HIKE

The trail starts off crossing a prairie full of wildflowers, but in only 0.1 mile arrives at the first trail juncture. The trail to the left is a 0.2 mile trek out to Wiedrich Barn and an alternate trailhead, but you go right on Deerpath Trail, entering oak savanna. The trail shows some cedar chips but is mostly packed dirt and grass. At 0.4 mile pass a bench and head over a short rise in the trail. At 0.5 mile a footpath on the right offers you a closer look at the cemetery there. The Thomas family, pioneers who arrived here in the 1860s, buried five of their children here under an oak tree that is now over 300 years old. The path comes back out on the trail.

You'll come to another trail juncture at 0.6 mile. Deerpath Trail goes to the left here; just to the right is a bench with a view. A mowed trail there presents another option for long-hikers, descending the hill toward a bridge over Nippersink Creek and out to the equestrian trails. But this hike continues up a steep, narrow footpath on the hill to your left (south).

These are the Camelback Kames, a double-humped formation composed of deposits from the last advance of glaciers. It's only a short climb, but if you prefer, you can bypass it on the Deerpath Trail. At the top of the kames your view extends in all directions. The trail follows the back of the two kames and descends at the southern end through a couple patches of loose sand and stones. At the bottom the Deerpath Trail joins from the left, and a park service road goes west behind you to the right. Stay straight here, passing through some trees and out into another prairie.

On your left is a bog, a wetland area that became filled in by spongy, floating sphagnum moss. At the next juncture stay right; the trail heads back into oak and hickory, taking a long curve east and then north again until the trail comes out in a picnic area at Kettle Lot. Follow the path left before the parking lot; an arrow guides you through some trees and across the park road. On the other side the Marsh Loop Trail goes right, but you take the trail straight ahead across the southern edge of the marsh. Before you do, however, a very short distance down the trail to the right is an observation deck overlooking the water and cattails.

Camelback Kames are one of the several highlights at Glacial Park. Preamtip Satasuk

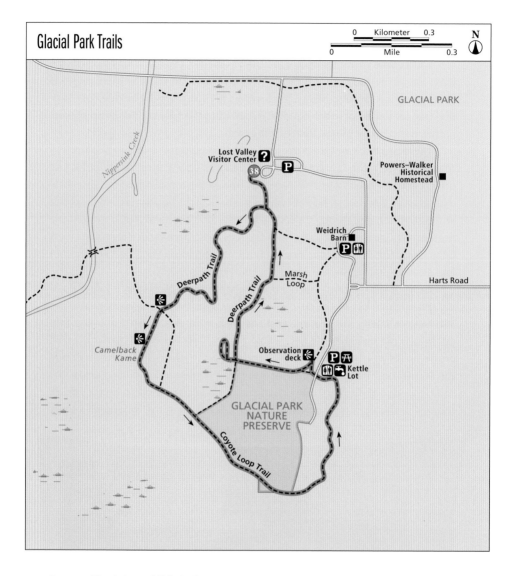

Glacial Park Trails

0   Kilometer   0.3
0   Mile   0.3
N

GLACIAL PARK

Nippersink Creek

Lost Valley Visitor Center
38
P
Powers–Walker Historical Homestead

Weidrich Barn
P

Deerpath Trail

Deerpath Trail

Marsh Loop

Harts Road

Camelback Kame

Observation deck
P
Kettle Lot

GLACIAL PARK NATURE PRESERVE

Coyote Loop Trail

Stop and look for wildlife before crossing the marsh. This area is a kettle marsh, formed when ice chunks from the last glacier melted beneath glacial till and left a water-filled depression.

Backtrack a bit and cross the marsh to the next juncture, just inside the woods again and with a couple of benches. Go straight ahead to a boardwalk extending into the bog. It bobs a bit with the springy terrain underneath, sometimes even allowing a bit of water to rise up between the planks. The loop is short and brings you back to terra firma minutes later. Come back to the intersection with the two benches and go left (north), continuing on the Deerpath Trail.

You've got about 2.1 miles under your boots now. Pass through more oaks on a low ridge; through the trees and brush on either side are the bog on the left and the marsh on the right. At 2.2 miles the trail descends to about marsh level, curving right. At 2.4 miles is another juncture. Straight ahead the Marsh Loop Trail heads back to the observation deck and also connects to the alternate trailhead by Wiedrich Barn. Go left and head up the prairie hill, passing another trail to the barn on the right and then at the juncture to the right, crossing the short distance back to the visitor center.

MILES AND DIRECTIONS

0.0   Start from the visitor center.

0.1   Take the trail to the right into the woods.

0.6   Go right to see the view and then follow the trail up the kame.

0.9   Go straight at the trail juncture and into prairie.

1.0   Go right to follow Coyote Loop Trail.

1.7   Pass Kettle Lot and cross the park road.

2.0   Take the short bog boardwalk loop.

2.1   From the boardwalk go left (north).

2.4   Take the trail to the left up the hill.

2.5   Turn right to return to the visitor center.

2.6   Arrive back at the trailhead.

HIKE INFORMATION

Local Information

McHenry County Conservation District, 18410 US Hwy. 14, Woodstock, IL 60098; (815) 338-6223; www.mccdistrict.org

Lost Valley Visitor Center, 6316 Harts Rd., Ringwood, IL 60072; (815) 678-4532; open 8 a.m. to 4:30 p.m. weekdays, 9 a.m. to 4 p.m. weekends

Volo Bog State Natural Area Trails

A short boardwalk loop offers an up-close look at the unusual quaking bog. Then the hike takes a turn around the largest of three trail loops in this state natural area. The terrain isn't very hilly and offers some stretches of forest, prairie, and wetlands as well as three designated observation points, including a marsh blind. Near the end of the loop is a trail across Brandenberg Road to 2 more miles of trail: a woodlands loop and a prairie loop.

Start: From the trailhead to the Tamarack View Trail past the visitor center

Distance: 5.1-mile series of loops (5.5 miles with bog boardwalk)

Hiking time: 2.5–3 hours

Difficulty: Easy

Trail surface: Dirt, grass, crushed rock, some boardwalk

Best season: Year-round

Other trail users: None

Canine compatibility: Leashed dogs permitted except on Bog Interpretive Trail

Land status: State natural area

Fees and permits: None

Schedule: Daily from 8 a.m.; closing at 8 p.m. Memorial Day through Labor Day weekends, at 7 p.m. in Apr, May, and Sept, at 6 p.m. in Oct, at 5 p.m. in Feb and Mar, and at 4 p.m. Nov through Jan. Closing times may vary seasonally but are posted at the entrance.

Maps: USGS Wauconda; at visitor center

Trail contact: Volo Bog State Natural Area, 28478 W. Brandenburg Rd., Ingleside, IL 60041; (815) 344-1294; http://dnr.state.il.us

Special considerations: Be sure to acquire a brochure for the interpretive trail.

Finding the trailhead: From downtown Milwaukee take I-94 south 38 miles and stay left to use exit 1B to merge onto US 41. At the next intersection, go right onto IL 173 for 5.9 miles. Turn left onto Deep Lake Road, go 1.7 miles, and turn right onto Grass Lake Road. Drive 2.5 miles, then turn left onto IL 59 and go 7.8 miles. Turn right onto Brandenberg Road and go 1.3 miles; the park entrance is on the left. From the parking lot, follow the sidewalk past the visitor center to the trailhead marked by a sign reading Tamarack View Trail. **GPS:** N42 21.057' / W88 11.276'

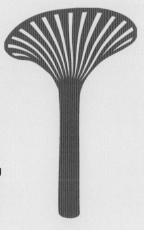

THE HIKE

The bog boardwalk is shorter than posted, only 0.35 mile rather than 0.5 mile. Hike it either before or after the bigger hike, but be sure not to miss it. Parts of the boardwalk are free-floating so you can experience the "quaking" bog. Then begin your hike at the trailhead. Only 100 feet in on the right is an area behind wood fences labeled as Chipmunk Woods. This is a nice space for children for "unstructured play," as the signage indicates. The trail continues through a mix of trees, brush, and remnants of prairie, then comes to an observation platform overlooking a bit of open water.

The trail heads into the woods for 0.5 mile, coming out and crossing a marshy area on a boardwalk. Follow the trail around the edge of the park land, with the road noise a bit closer than you might like, but soon the path curves left and leaves it all behind. At 1.5 miles you come to a wide view of prairie and a trail juncture. Take the trail to the left; this spur trail crosses the prairie to an observation tower overlooking the park. After enjoying the view, backtrack to this juncture. The trek to the tower is 0.7 mile round-trip.

Continue on the main, mostly exposed trail. At 2.6 miles the trail angles northwest and starts to circle the wetlands at the heart of the park. In fact, at 2.8 miles a short spur trail on the left leads to a blind where you can watch for waterfowl and other critters right from the water's edge. Continue on the trail with more views over some open water before entering the woods once again.

A bench with a nice view of the wetlands. Preamtip Satasuk

Volo Bog State Natural Area Trails

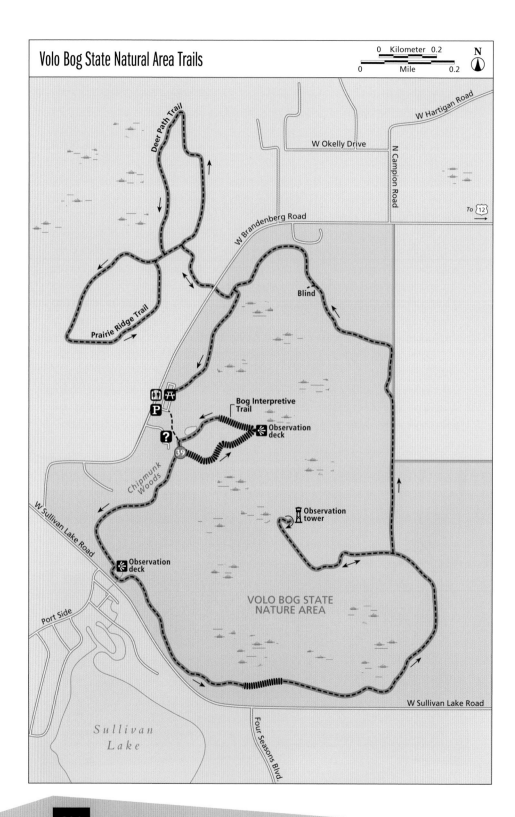

At 3.1 miles is a trail juncture presenting you with an option. Go left back to the parking lot, or for this hike take the trail to the right for another two loops totaling 2 more miles. Cross Brandenburg Road and enter the brush on a grassy path. It splits again; take Deer Path Trail to the right. Parts of this trail can get a bit muddy in low spots, and the entire length is through the woods. At the end of the loop, the trail comes to another juncture. Take the trail to the right (left heads back to the road) to connect to the Prairie Ridge Loop, which is exactly what the name indicates: a grassy path that crosses over a prairie-covered ridge, circling back with a view to wetlands and finally returning to the starting point. From there take the trail to the right, back into the woods, and stay right, passing the return trail of the Deer Path, then its starting point, and finally arriving back at the roadside.

Cross back over the road to the trail into the woods again, stay right at the next trail juncture, and complete the last 0.3 mile of trail back to the parking lot. The trail comes out behind the toilets, and a sidewalk leads to the lot.

MILES AND DIRECTIONS

0.0 Start with a 0.35-mile turn around the bog boardwalk, then begin at the Tamarack View trailhead.

0.4 Stop at an observation deck on the left, then continue into the forest.

0.9 Cross a boardwalk over a marshy area.

1.5 At a trail juncture take the left trail out to a prairie observation tower, then backtrack to this juncture again to continue on the trail.

2.8 Check out a blind overlooking the marsh down a short spur trail on the left.

3.1 At a trail juncture in the woods, take the trail to the right across the park road to the forest and prairie loop trails.

3.3 At the next juncture go right onto the Deer Path Trail.

4.0 Take a right at the next trail juncture and meet the Prairie Ridge Trail; take the trail to the right.

4.5 Complete the prairie loop, then take the trail to the right at the next two junctures to get back across the road.

4.8 Turn right and follow the last bit of Tamarack View Trail back to the parking lot.

5.1 Arrive back at the trailhead.

HIKE INFORMATION

Local Information
Lake County Convention & Visitor's Bureau, 5465 Grand Ave., #100, Gurnee, IL 60031; (847) 662-2700; www.visitlakecounty.org

Local Attractions
Lake County Discovery Museum—Lakewood Forest Preserve, 27277 Forest Preserve Dr., Wauconda, IL 60084; (847) 968-3400; www.lcfpd.org/discovery_museum

The Quaking Bog

Sounds ominous, no? Volo Bog is the only bog of this sort in the state of Illinois. First off, a bog is an acidic-water wetland that accumulates dead plant material called peat. Typically, the primary plant life is sphagnum moss, which builds upon itself, pushing the moss of the past deeper below. But a quaking bog occurs when large, thick mats of moss and sedges are actually floating over a layer of water or really loose peat, so that they quake when disturbed or even send ripples of a sort along the surface.

Adeline Jay Geo-Karis Illinois Beach State Park Trails

This hike takes you to the dunes and swales along Lake Michigan. Spend a bit of time on the beach, if you like, but then follow the trail amid the grassy dunes heading south toward the appropriately named Dead River, which is cut off from the lake periodically by sandbars. On its return the trail follows along the edge of this wetlands area, offering a completely different environment such a short distance from the lake and the dunes. The loop doesn't take long, and inside the loop are other trail segments straddling the line between the two ecosystems. Expect good bird watching along the river and lakeshore, and great views of the bright blue waters.

Start: From the trailhead marked Beach Access in the nature preserve parking lot
Distance: 2.0-mile loop
Hiking time: 1 hour
Difficulty: Easy
Trail surface: Crushed stone, dirt, sand, cedar chips
Best season: Spring through fall
Other trail users: None
Canine compatibility: Dogs not permitted within the nature preserve area
Land status: State park

Fees and permits: None
Schedule: Daily, sunrise to sunset Apr through Memorial Day weekend; sunrise to 8 p.m. Memorial Day through Labor Day weekends; sunrise to sunset Labor Day through Oct; 8 a.m. to sunset Nov through Mar
Maps: USGS Zion; at park office, trailhead, and on website
Trail contact: Adeline Jay Geo-Karis Illinois Beach State Park, 1 Lake Front Dr., Zion, IL 60099; (847) 662-4811; http://dnr.state.il.us

Finding the trailhead: From downtown Milwaukee take I-94 south toward Chicago for 38 miles and use exit 1B on the left to merge onto US 41 for 0.6 mile. Turn left onto IL 173 and go 6.4 miles. Turn right onto IL 137 and go 1.9 miles. Turn left onto Wadsworth Road following the park signs. This runs right into the park, so from this turn onto Wadsworth, continue 1.6 miles and turn right into the parking lot of the nature preserve. The trailhead is at the parking lot and marked as Beach Access. **GPS:** N42 25.283' / W87 48.476'

THE HIKE

Views of Lake Michigan are sometimes surprising whenever dunes are involved. All that light-colored sand reflects penetrating sunlight, and the blues sometimes rival those of tropical seas. The trail itself only offers glimpses of the water from behind the long ridges of grass-covered sand dunes, but spur trails access the beach officially at two places on the trail.

40

Despite suggestions of signage for the Dune Trail and Dead River Trail, this hike starts at the trail that says Beach Access. The return of the Dune Trail follows a park road access at the end of the lot, and the return of the Dead River Trail is opposite the lake side of the lot under some trees. Start down the Beach Access trail; it crosses over a nice boardwalk above a grassy, low area of sensitive plant life. In fact, even the woods here have grown in over the dunes, which is remarkable, and you should never wander from the designated trail to disrupt that process.

Just after the boardwalk is a trail juncture. The trail to the left connects to the beach resort to the north. The trail straight ahead goes up over the dunes a short distance to the beach. Take the trail to the right, the Dune Trail, and begin heading south along the backs of the dunes. At first the hike is through mostly brush and some rather small oak trees, but soon the view opens up to the roll of dunes. On your left you can see glimpses of the deep blue lake in contrast to the bright sand and green grasses waving in the breeze. Any wind off the lake will cool this experience, and that's not a bad thing on hot summer days when this area can take a beating from the sun.

At the next juncture at 0.9 mile, another spur trail leads left to the beach. Be aware that the dunes south of here are not accessible without a permit and that a natural danger occurs from time to time (see the sidebar). Take the trail

Access points along the trail bring hikers to the beach along Lake Michigan. Preamtip Satasuk

to the right (west from the lake toward the trees). Pass a bench as you enter the trees. The terrain has changed so it could almost be a country road. At 1.1 miles is the next trail juncture. The trail to the right heads back to the parking lot with another alternate trail splitting off and rejoining it. This is more area to explore, but from the juncture here take the trail to the left, the path to the Dead River.

Oaks get larger, and the trail comes to the edge of open water. This interdunal wetlands is referred to as a *panne*, created when wind-formed depressions amid the dunes gather water, thus giving wetland plants a chance to grow and take over the dunes. You can expect to find good birdlife through here. The trail is more rustic, with packed dirt and tree roots to contend with. The trees are getting more water and are thus larger and able to offer at least partial shade. As you continue north, the open water begins to give way to wetland plants. At 1.8 miles you come to an observation platform for a nice view. Past here is more sedge meadow and gradually more grasses accustomed to dry land. The trail ends at the parking lot, where you can visit the nature center or perhaps hike the two segments you missed by taking the loop.

MILES AND DIRECTIONS

0.0   Start from the Beach Access trailhead.

0.1   At a three-way trail juncture, take the trail to the right.

0.9   At a beach access trail, take the trail to the right. (Check out the beach a short distance to the left, if desired.)

1.1   From the next juncture, take the trail to the left toward the Dead River.

1.8   Pass an observation deck on the left.

2.0   Arrive back at the parking lot.

Dead River Danger

Forces of nature come in many shapes and potencies, but here's one you aren't likely to find very often. Lake Michigan wind and waves have formed and reformed these dunes since the end of the last ice age. The Dead River accumulates water that at times is able to flow into the lake. When the big lake pushes up sandbars and dunes, the amount of that water increases and the pressure builds. You don't want to be standing in front of it when the levy breaks. The outrush of water is dangerous and can last 10 to 15 minutes. A warning sign on the beach tells visitors not to go south of the Dead River for this reason.

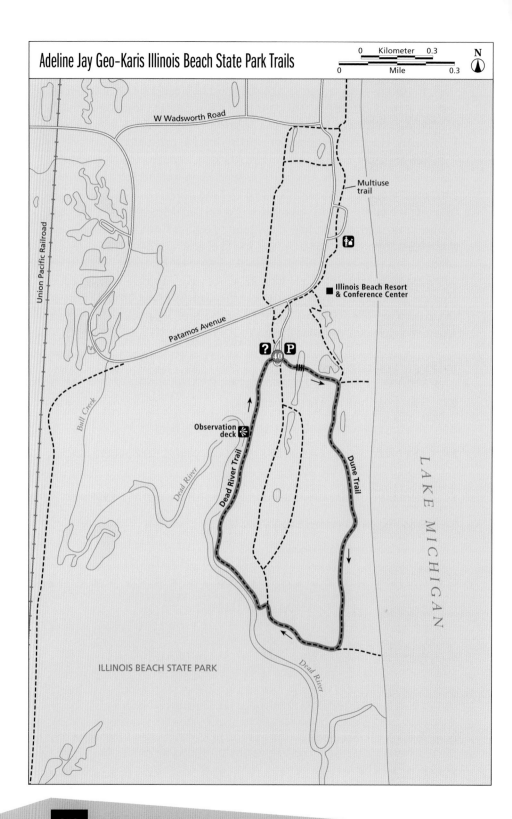

Adeline Jay Geo-Karis Illinois Beach State Park Trails

W Wadsworth Road

Multiuse trail

Union Pacific Railroad

Illinois Beach Resort & Conference Center

Patamos Avenue

Bull Creek

Observation deck

Dead River Trail

Dead River

Dune Trail

LAKE MICHIGAN

ILLINOIS BEACH STATE PARK

Dead River

The Dune Trail. Preamtip Satasuk

HIKE INFORMATION

Local Information
Lake County Convention & Visitor's Bureau, 5465 Grand Ave. #100, Gurnee, IL 60031; (847) 662-2700; www.visitlakecounty.org

Lodging
Illinois Beach Resort & Conference Center, 1 Lake Front Dr., Zion, IL 60099; (847) 625-7300; www.ilresorts.com
Illinois Beach State Park Campground has 241 sites; make reservations at (800) 246-5082 or www.reserveamerica.com.

Honorable Mentions

Thru-Hikes on the Ice Age National Scenic Trail— Kettle Moraine

As mentioned before, the Ice Age Trail is a work in progress. Of the 1,000 miles planned for the rustic trail through Wisconsin's most scenic, glacially carved lands, just over 600 miles are completed. The various segments, marked by signs and yellow blazes along the trail, sometimes are contiguous, but in other instances connecting routes or even the trail itself follows country roads and city streets to get to the next stretch of the off-road footpath. The trail is designed for thru-hiking, so with the exception of the occasional loop formed by alternate white-blazed trails, it's an out-and-back trek. Two excellent long sections lie within an hour of Milwaukee, both through the Kettle Moraine State Forest.

A. Kettle Moraine State Forest—Northern Unit

This stretch of rugged footpath only leaves the woods to cross the road less than a couple dozen times in 31 miles, and when it does it is often the Kettle Moraine Scenic Drive. This is the heart of the state forest, and the terrain rises and falls over moraines and eskers and around kettles. The Ice Age Trail passes through or nearby the New Fane Trails, Mauthe Lake's Tamarack Circle Trail, Butler Lake Trail, Parnell Tower Trail, and the Greenbush Trails, all of which are included in greater detail within this book. Unlike the Southern Unit, the Northern Unit offers water pumps a reasonable distance from each of the trail's camping shelters. The five backcountry shelters are accessible year-round and offer a roofed structure, fire ring, and a pit toilet. No more than ten campers are allowed and only for one night. Get the required permit by calling (888) 947-2757 or stopping in at the state forest headquarters, Ice Age Visitor Center, or Mauthe or Long Lake entrance stations. The campground at Mauthe Lake Recreation Area is also just off the trail. The trailheads, along CR H in the south and CR P in the north, have parking lots, and a number of lots along the length of this segment offer shorter alternatives for your thru-hike. A general map and a chart showing point-to-point mileage from either trailhead are available on the state forest's website or in the *Ice Age Trail Atlas & Guidebook 2014*.

GPS: N43 29.881' / W88 11.583' (CR H); N43 47.786' / W88 2.102' (CR P)
Kettle Moraine State Forest—Northern Unit, Forest Headquarters, N1765 Hwy.

G, Campbellsport WI 53010; (262) 626-2116; http://dnr.wi.gov/topic/parks/name/kmn

Ice Age Visitor Center, N2875 WI 67, Campbellsport, WI 53010; (920) 533-8322; http://dnr.wi.gov/topic/parks/name/kmn/naturecenter.html

B. Kettle Moraine State Forest—Southern Unit

Starting in the Whitewater Lake Recreation Area, the Ice Age Trail meanders north and northeast 30 miles to Pinewoods Campground. In addition to the camping available at the parks at the start and end points, there are three shelters—numbered from 3 to 1 if you are coming from the south—located at the 8.2-, 18.7-, and 26.2-mile marks. Much of the route is through hardwood forest and scattered pine plantation, but there are a few prairie areas as well. The southern section is characterized by a lot of moraine hiking as you follow the ridges through the Whitewater Lake Segment and past the mountain biking areas of the John Muir and Emma Carlin Trails. The first shelter is after rounding La Grange Lake and crossing Duffin Road, just before the John Muir Trails. Beyond that lies Bald Bluff with its scenic overlook and the Emma Carlin Trails before you come to Shelter #2 not far from the state forest headquarters on WI 59, a good place to get more water. The last stretch crosses a couple of streams and passes spur trails to notable natural features before heading through the Scuppernong Trails system to arrive at Pinewoods Campground. While the two campgrounds are open from mid-May to mid-October, the three backcountry shelters are accessible year-round and offer a roofed structure, a fire ring, and a pit toilet. No more than ten campers are allowed and only for one night. Get the required permit by calling (888) 947-2757. A number of parking lots for the Ice Age Trail lie along the length of this segment, offering a number of ways to shorten a thru-hike. A general map and mileage chart are available on the state forest's website or in the *Ice Age Trail Atlas & Guidebook 2014*.

GPS: N42 46.860' / W88 41.708' (Whitewater Lake); N42 57.635' / W88 27.266' (Pinewoods Campground)

Kettle Moraine State Forest—Southern Unit, S91 W39091 Hwy. 59, Eagle, WI 53119; (262) 594-6200; http://dnr.wi.gov/topic/parks/name/kms

C. Bender Park Trails

Just south of Milwaukee in Oak Creek, Bender Park along Lake Michigan is oddly often overlooked, and when visitors come here it is most often for the beach or the boat launch. The trails, totaling just about 4 miles, cross easy bluffs overlooking the lake, and loops through trees and prairie present a surprising amount of wildlife and natural beauty. The routes are not laid out in loops, and you may end up doing some out-and-back segments, but it is dog-friendly and offers some real respite from the city. Come in spring when the apple trees are in blossom.

This park is part of the Forked Aster Hiking Trail System, a collection of short nature trails throughout Milwaukee County.

GPS: N42 52.031' / W87 50.414'

Bender Park, 4503 E. Ryan Rd., Oak Creek, WI 53154; (414) 762-1550; www.county parks.com

Forked Aster Hiking Trail System, www.county.milwaukee.gov/ForkedAsterTrail

D. Emma Carlin Trails

Much like the John Muir Trails, this trail network of color-coded singletrack routes is popular with mountain bikers and hikers alike. Set in the Southern Unit of the Kettle Moraine State Forest, these trails are primarily wooded and run over more hills and narrow bits than the John Muir. An easy Brown loop runs 3.5 miles, but the two longer trails, the Green and the Orange, measure 8 and 6 miles, respectively, and visit some scenic overlooks lacking on the Brown Trail. The two trails overlap almost the entire route except where the Green Trail follows an erratic extra 2 miles of sharp turns and switchbacks and a lot of steep inclines and declines before rejoining the Orange Trail less than 0.25 mile from the trailhead. A connecting trail from about the halfway point, the farthest point west, runs 15 miles to the John Muir Trails. As with other popular mountain biking trails, hikers should hike against bike traffic. The trailhead is on CR Z just 1.7 miles west of the state forest headquarters.

GPS: N42 52.220' / W88 32.634'

Kettle Moraine State Forest—Southern Unit, S91 W39091 Hwy. 59, Eagle, WI 53119; (262) 594-6200; http://dnr.wi.gov/topic/parks/name/kms/trails.html

E. Moraine Hills State Park Trails

Repeating a common theme in this book, this state park showcases more work of the last glaciers. Four trails—three of crushed limestone, one paved—explore 2,200 acres of scenic terrain. But the hills are just half of it; wetlands make up the rest. The glacially formed Lake Defiance at the center is practically undeveloped, and the wetlands include a rare fen and pitcher plants. Wildlife is abundant, and birders have counted more than 200 species. The 1.7-mile River Road Trail is wheelchair accessible. The longest trail is the 3.7-mile Lake Defiance Trail, which has multiple access points and combines nicely with the 3.2-mile Leatherleaf Bog Trail for a longer hike. The 2-mile Fox River Trail is a lollipop add-on as well, and a portion of it runs along the river.

GPS: N42 18.456' / W88 13.708'

Moraine Hills State Park, 1510 S. River Rd., McHenry, IL 60051; (815) 385-1624; http://dnr.state.il.us/lands/landmgt/parks/r2/morhills.htm

F. Glacial Drumlin State Trail

This 52-mile rails-to-trails path runs from Waukesha to Cottage Grove, just outside Madison. Only 1.5 miles—just outside of Jefferson actually—are routed on public roads. Don't expect a lot of hills; the terrain is rather flat, originally to accommodate the trains of yesteryear. The surface is crushed limestone, although from Waukesha to Dousman it runs asphalt for the 13 miles. Dogs are allowed on leashes. State trail passes are required for bicyclists, but not hikers. The easternmost trailhead is near the Fox River Sanctuary in Waukesha at College and Prairie Avenues. The section between WI 26 and Lake Mills crosses the Crawfish and Rock Rivers. Maps on the state trail's website can help you plan what portion of the trail you want to explore and where you can park.

GPS: N43 00.175′ / W88 14.736′

Friends of the Glacial Drumlin Trail, www.glacialdrumlin.com

Glacial Drumlin Trail—East, W329 N846 County Highway C, Delafield WI 53018; (262) 646-3025; http://dnr.wi.gov/topic/parks/name/glacialdrumlin

Glacial Drumlin Trail—West, 1213 S. Main St., Lake Mills WI 53551; (920) 648-8774

G. Riveredge Nature Center Trails

Since 1968 the center has been educating the public and working on a variety of ecological projects, including returning the sturgeon to the Milwaukee River. The 380 acres include a nice stretch of that river as well as a variety of other ecosystems. A collection of eight trails totaling 10 miles, ranging from an easy 0.75-mile prairie loop to a more strenuous 3.5-mile loop that circumnavigates much of the park, offers something for everyone. Families with kids will appreciate the nature center's family-specific activities and event calendar as well as the natural play area and a children's tree-top library. In winter many of the trails are groomed for skiers. Snowshoers have their own designated paths, but can also use the ski trails provided they do not step on the ski tracks. Watch on the website for frequently scheduled events. Visitors can expect a lot of wildlife—birders have recorded over 180 species—and plant varieties approach 600. The center is open daily with standard business hours, but the trails are open from dawn to dusk daily.

GPS: N43 26.384′ / W88 01.462′

Riveredge Nature Center, 4458 County Hwy. Y, Saukville, WI 53080; (262) 375-2715; www.riveredgenaturecenter.org

Glossary

The follow terms, often relating to glaciers and the landforms they created in the Milwaukee area, appear frequently throughout the trail descriptions.

bog—A form of wetlands containing peat, often formed by decomposing sphagnum moss, and characterized by acidic waters; similar to but distinct from a fen. The water source is primarily precipitation, and the bog forms in a depression with no surface outflows.

drumlin—A hill carved into the shape of an egg on its side by the passing of a glacier. The shape reveals the direction the ice was moving.

erratics—Any rocks, but especially large boulders, that have been carried by glaciers far from their points of origin to be deposited when the ice melts.

esker—A long, snake-like ridge of gravel and sand left by streams that flow through tunnels under a glacier.

fen—A form of wetland that accumulates decomposing plant life to make peat. Unlike a bog, a fen accumulates water primarily from ground sources and the surrounding watershed, and also releases water via outflows on the surface. Watershed terrain affects the chemistry of a fen, resulting in alkaline or acidic water, but when it happens to be acidic, it is not as acidic as a bog.

glacial lake—A lake that forms when a glacier is melting or "retreating." These can be held back by ice dams that eventually melt away or break open and release a violent flood.

ice sheet—More than an ordinary glacier, this continental glacier is massive and is not limited by the land, such as is the case with glaciers descending between mountain peaks, for example.

interlobate moraine—A long ridge of glacial deposits formed when two lobes of an ice sheet come together.

kame—A hill of glacial deposits, generally in a cone-like shape, left by water flowing down shafts in a glacier.

kettle—A depression formed when a large chunk of ice is trapped under glacial deposits of sand and gravel and then later melts, leaving the "kettle."

kettle moraine—The interlobate moraine formed by the Green Bay and Lake Michigan lobes of the Laurentide ice sheet. The moraine is approximately 120 miles long but very narrow, and its name comes from the abundance of kettles along its length.

Drumlins in the distance as seen from Parnell Tower.

lobe—Large extensions of an ice sheet as it spreads across the earth. During the last advance of the Laurentide ice sheet in North America, there were six such lobes. Two of them covered territory described in this book: the Green Bay and Lake Michigan lobes.

moraine—A hill or ridge created by glacial deposits at the edge of the glacier's advance. A terminal moraine is such a ridge formed at the glacier's farthest advance before it melts away.

outwash plain—A wide plain of sand created by streams from melting glacial ice in front of a glacier.

swale—A depression or lowland area, typically of wetlands, often wet or marshy.

Wisconsin glaciation—The most recent advance of glaciers over North America, which occurred from 85,000 to just over 10,000 years ago. The ice sheets reached their farthest extent during the period between 21,000 and 25,000 years ago.

Clubs and Trail Groups

Badger Trails, Inc.
P.O. Box 44135
West Allis, WI 53214
(414) 777-3920
www.badgertrails.org
Badger Trails is a nonprofit organization promoting hiking in Wisconsin. They sponsor three events each year.

Ice Age Trail Alliance
2110 Main St.
Cross Plains, WI 53528
(800) 227-0046
www.iceagetrail.org
Though many segments of this national scenic trail have been created, some are still on the way and the rest are always being maintained. Local chapters organize hikes and trail maintenance events. This is a great bunch of people and a fantastic hiking trail. Check their website to find local chapters of the Ice Age Trail Alliance nearest the Milwaukee area.

MeetUp.com
This social networking group helps you hook up with like-minded locals. Several Milwaukee-area groups have outdoor interests including hiking.

Wisconsin Go Hiking Club
(414) 299-9285
wisconsingohiking.homestead.com
Since its inception in 1924, this club has been promoting outdoor activity. Often there are several hikes scheduled each week, in destinations both near and far. Member dues are nominal, and event costs are shared by participants.

Further Reading

Ali, Barbara. *101 Things to Do in Milwaukee Parks*. Milwaukee: Barbara Ali, 2013.

Dott, Robert H., and John W. Attig. *Roadside Geology of Wisconsin*. Missoula: Mountain Press Publishing Co., 2004.

Ice Age Trail Atlas & Guidebook 2014. Cross Plains: Ice Age Trail Alliance, 2014.

Mickelson, David M., Louis J. Maher Jr., and Susan L. Simpson. *Geology of the Ice Age National Scenic Trail*. Madison: The University of Wisconsin Press, 2011.

Revolinski, Kevin. *Backroads and Byways of Wisconsin*. Countryman Press, 2009.

Sherman, Eric, and Andrew Hanson III. *Along Wisconsin's Ice Age Trail*. Madison: The University of Wisconsin Press, 2008.

Parnell Tower Hiking Trail. Preamtip Satasuk

About the Author

Kevin Revolinski is a freelance writer and photographer. He is the author of several books, and his work has appeared in the *New York Times*, *Chicago Tribune*, and *Sydney Morning Herald*. He maintains a website and blog called The Mad Traveler (www.TheMadTravelerOnline .com, Revtravel.com) and is an avid outdoorsman. He has lived abroad in several places including Italy, Guatemala, Turkey, Panama, and Thailand, but currently lives in Madison, Wisconsin.

Other Globe Pequot Press titles by Kevin Revolinski

Best Easy Day Hikes Grand Rapids (FalconGuides)
Best Easy Day Hikes Milwaukee (FalconGuides)
Best Rail Trails Wisconsin (FalconGuides)
Camping Michigan (FalconGuides)
Insiders' Guide® to Madison, WI (FalconGuides)
Paddling Wisconsin (FalconGuides)

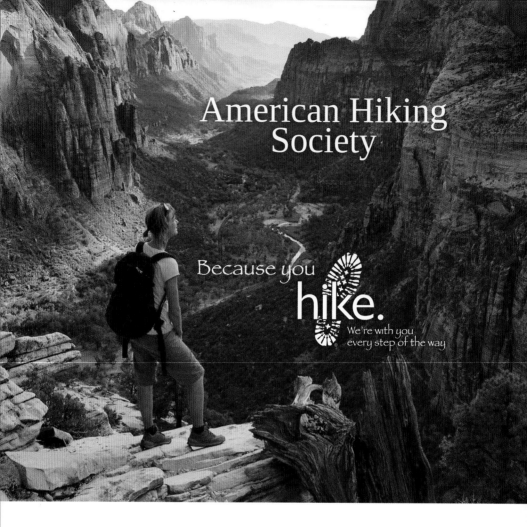

American Hiking Society

Because you **hike.**
We're with you every step of the way

As a national voice for hikers, **American Hiking Society** works every day:

- Building and maintaining hiking trails
- Educating and supporting hikers by providing information and resources
- Supporting hiking and trail organizations nationwide
- Speaking for hikers in the halls of Congress and with federal land managers

Whether you're a casual hiker or a seasoned backpacker, become a member of American Hiking Society and join the national hiking community! You'll enjoy great member benefits and help preserve the nation's hiking trails, so tomorrow's hike is even better than today's. We invite you to join us now!

American Hiking Society